LET'S COOK

italian & pasta

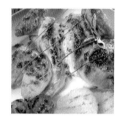

This is a Starfire book
First published in 2001

02 04 05 03

1 3 5 7 9 10 8 6 4 2

Starfire is part of
The Foundry Creative Media Company Limited
Crabtree Hall, Crabtree Lane, Fulham, London, SW6 6TY

Visit the Foundry website: www.foundry.co.uk/recipes

ISBN: 1-903817-08-0

The CIP record for this book is available from the British Library.

Printed in China

ACKNOWLEDGEMENTS

Authors: Catherine Atkinson, Juliet Barker, Liz Martin, Gina
Steer, Carol Tennant, Mari Mererid Williams and Elizabeth Wolf-Cohen
Photography: Colin Bowling, Paul Forrester and Stephen Brayne
Home Economists and Stylists: Jacqueline Bellefontaine,
Mandy Phipps, Vicki Smallwood and Penny Stephens

All props supplied by Barbara Stewart at Surfaces

NOTE
Recipes using uncooked eggs should be avoided by infants,
the elderly, pregnant women and anyone suffering from an illness.

LET'S COOK

italian & pasta

STAR
FIRE

Contents

FISH & SHELLFISH

MEATS

POULTRY & GAME

VEGETABLES & SALADS

ENTERTAINING & DESERTS

HYGIENE IN THE KITCHEN

It is well worth remembering that many foods can carry some form of bacteria. In most cases, the worst it will lead to is a bout of food poisoning or gastroenteritis, although for certain groups this can be more serious – the risk can be reduced or eliminated by good food hygiene and proper cooking.

Do not buy food that is past its sell-by date and do not consume any food that is past its use-by date. When buying food, use the eyes and nose. If the food looks tired, limp or a bad colour or it has a rank, acrid or simply bad smell, do not buy or eat it under any circumstances.

Do take special care when preparing raw meat and fish. A separate chopping board should be used for each; wash the knife, board and the hands thoroughly before handling or preparing any other food.

Regularly clean, defrost and clear out the refrigerator or freezer – it is worth checking the packaging to see exactly how long each product is safe to freeze.

Avoid handling food if suffering from an upset stomach as bacteria can be passed through food preparation.

Dish cloths and tea towels must be washed and changed regularly. Ideally use disposable cloths which should be replaced on a daily basis. More durable cloths should be left to soak in bleach, then washed in the washing machine on a boil wash.

Keep the hands, cooking utensils and food preparation surfaces clean and do not allow pets to climb on to any work surfaces.

BUYING

Avoid bulk buying where possible, especially fresh produce such as meat, poultry, fish, fruit and vegetables unless buying for the freezer. Fresh foods lose their nutritional value rapidly so buying a little at a time minimises loss of nutrients. It also eliminates a packed refrigerator which reduces the effectiveness of the refrigeration process.

When buying prepackaged goods such as cans or pots of cream and yogurts, check that the packaging is intact and not damaged or pierced at all. Cans should not be dented, pierced or rusty. Check the sell-by dates even for cans and packets of dry ingredients such as flour and rice. Store fresh foods in the refrigerator as soon as possible – not in the car or the office. When buying frozen foods, ensure that they are not heavily iced on the outside and the contents feel completely frozen. Ensure that the frozen foods have been stored in the cabinet at the correct storage level and the temperature is below 18°C/-0.4°F. Pack in cool bags to transport home and place in the freezer as soon as possible after purchase.

PREPARATION

Make sure that all work surfaces and utensils are clean and dry. Hygiene should be given priority at all times. Separate chopping boards should be used for raw and cooked meats, fish and vegetables. Currently, a variety of good-quality plastic boards come in various designs and colours. This makes

differentiating easier and the plastic has the added hygienic advantage of being washable at high temperatures in the dishwasher. (NB: If using the board for fish, first wash in cold water, then in hot to prevent odour!) Also, remember that knives and utensils should always be thoroughly cleaned after use.

When cooking, be particularly careful to keep cooked and raw food separate to avoid any contamination. It is worth washing all fruits and vegetables regardless of whether they are going to be eaten raw or lightly cooked. This rule should apply even to prewashed herbs and salads.

Do not reheat food more than once. If using a microwave, always check that the food is piping hot all the way through. (In theory, the food should reach 70°C/158°F and needs to be cooked at that temperature for at least three minutes to ensure that all bacteria are killed.)

All poultry must be thoroughly thawed before using, including chicken and poussin. Remove the food to be thawed from the freezer and place in a shallow dish to contain the juices. Leave the food in the refrigerator until it is completely thawed. A 1.4 kg/3 lb whole chicken will take about 26–30 hours to thaw. To speed up the process immerse the chicken in cold water. However, make sure that the water is changed regularly. When the joints can move freely and no ice crystals remain in the cavity, the bird is completely thawed.

Once thawed, remove the wrapper and pat the chicken dry. Place the chicken in a shallow dish, cover lightly and store as close to the base of the refrigerator as possible. The chicken should be cooked as soon as possible.

Some foods can be cooked from frozen including many prepacked foods such as soups, sauces, casseroles and breads. Where applicable follow the manufacturers' instructions.

Vegetables and fruits can also be cooked from frozen, but meats and fish should be thawed first. The only time food can be refrozen is when the food has been thoroughly thawed then cooked. Once the food has cooled then it can be frozen again. On such occasions the food can only be stored for one month.

All poultry and game (except for duck) must be cooked thoroughly. When cooked the juices will run clear from the thickest part of the bird – the best area to try is usually the thigh. Other meats, like minced meat and pork should be cooked right the way through. Fish should turn opaque, be firm in texture and break easily into large flakes.

When cooking leftovers, make sure they are reheated until piping hot and that any sauce or soup reaches boiling point first.

STORING, REFRIGERATING AND FREEZING

Meat, poultry, fish, seafood and dairy products should all be refrigerated. The temperature of the refrigerator should be between 1–5°C/34–41°F while the freezer temperature should not rise above -18°C/-0.4°F.

To ensure the optimum refrigerator and freezer temperature, avoid leaving the door open for a long time. Try not to overstock the refrigerator as this reduces the airflow inside and affects the effectiveness in cooling the food within.

When refrigerating cooked food, allow it to cool down quickly and completely before refrigerating. Hot food will raise the temperature of the refrigerator and possibly affect or spoil other food stored in it.

Food within the refrigerator and freezer should always be covered. Raw and cooked food should be stored in separate parts of the refrigerator. Cooked food should be kept on the top shelves of the refrigerator, while raw meat, poultry and fish should be placed on bottom shelves to avoid drips and cross-contamination. It is recommended that eggs should be refrigerated in order to maintain their freshness and shelf life.

Take care that frozen foods are not stored in the freezer for too long. Blanched vegetables can be stored for one month; beef, lamb, poultry and pork for six months and unblanched vegetables and fruits in syrup for a year. Oily fish and sausages should be stored for three months. Dairy products can last four to six months while cakes and pastries should be kept in the freezer for three to six months.

HIGH-RISK FOODS

Certain foods may carry risks to people who are considered vulnerable such as the elderly, the ill, pregnant women, babies, young infants and those suffering from a recurring illness.

It is advisable to avoid those foods listed below which belong to a higher-risk category.

There is a slight chance that some eggs carry the bacteria salmonella. Cook the eggs until both the yolk and the white are firm to eliminate this risk. Pay particular attention to dishes and products incorporating lightly cooked or raw eggs which should be eliminated from the diet. Sauces including Hollandaise, mayonnaise, mousses, soufflés and meringues all use raw or lightly cooked eggs, as do custard-based dishes, ice creams and sorbets. These are all considered high-risk foods to the vulnerable groups mentioned above.

Certain meats and poultry also carry the potential risk of salmonella and so should be cooked thoroughly until the juices run clear and there is no pinkness left. Unpasteurised products such as milk, cheese (especially soft cheese), pâté, meat (both raw and cooked) all have the potential risk of listeria and should be avoided.

When buying seafood, buy from a reputable source which has a high turnover to ensure freshness. Fish should have bright clear eyes, shiny skin and bright pink or red gills. The fish should feel stiff to the touch, with a slight smell of sea air and iodine. The flesh of fish steaks and fillets should be translucent with no signs of discolouration.

Molluscs such as scallops, clams and mussels are sold fresh and are still alive. Avoid any that are open or do not close when tapped lightly. In the same way, univalves such as cockles or winkles should withdraw back into their shells when lightly prodded. When choosing cephalopods such as squid and octopus they should have a firm flesh and pleasant sea smell.

As with all fish, whether it is shellfish or seafish, care is required when freezing it. It is imperative to check whether the fish has been frozen before. If it has been frozen, then it should not be frozen again under any circumstances.

ESSENTIAL INGREDIENTS

Italian cuisine is popular all over the world and basic Italian storecupboard ingredients are commonplace items on supermarket shelves. Even fresh ingredients that used to be difficult to find are available all year round, often in parts of the world where previously they were unheard of. For those who enjoy Italian food and cooking this is good news – delicious, authentic Italian cuisine can now be enjoyed anywhere and at any time.

CHEESES

Dolcelatte This cheese, which translates as 'sweet milk', comes from the Lombardy region. Dolcelatte is a creamy, blue cheese and has a luscious, sweet taste. It is very soft and melts in the mouth, often appealing to those who find more traditional blue cheeses, like Roquefort and Gorgonzola, too strongly flavoured.

Fontina This is a dense, smooth and slightly elastic cheese with a straw-coloured interior. Fontina is made in the Valle d'Aosta region and has a delicate nutty flavour with a hint of mild honey. It is often served melted in which case the flavour becomes very earthy.

Gorgonzola This is a traditional blue cheese from the Lombardy region. Made from cow's milk, the cheese has a sharp, spicy flavour as well as being rich and creamy.

Mascarpone Technically, mascarpone is not a cheese but a by-product obtained from making Parmesan. A culture is added to the cream that has been skimmed off the milk that was used to make the cheese. This is then gently heated and allowed to mature and thicken. Mascarpone is most famous as the main ingredient in Tiramisu, but it is a very versatile ingredient and is used in all sorts of sweet and savoury recipes.

Mozzarella di Bufala Mozzarella is a fresh cheese, prized more for its texture than its flavour which is really quite bland. Mozzarella cheese melts beautifully, however, on pizzas and in pasta dishes, and is also good served cold in salads. It is usually sold in tubs along with its whey and should have a floppy rather than a rubbery texture. The fresher it is when eaten, the better.

Parmigiano-Reggiano One of the world's finest cheeses, Parmigiano-Reggiano is also one of the most versatile cooking cheeses. Its production is very carefully regulated to guarantee a consistent high-quality result. The trademark is branded all over the rind, so that even a small piece is easily identified. Buy it in pieces, rather than ready-grated.

Pecorino This is the generic term for cheeses made purely from sheep's milk. All Pecorino cheeses are excellent for grating or shaving on to both hot and cold dishes. Each type of Pecorino is characteristic of a particular region and a particular breed of sheep. Pecorino Romano is made in the countryside around Rome between November and late June. Pecorino Sardo is made in Sardinia and Pecorino Toscano comes from Tuscany and tends to mature younger than other Pecorino cheeses.

Ricotta When cheese is made, the solids in the milk are separated from the liquid by coagulation, however, some solids are always lost to the whey. To retrieve these solids, the milk is heated until they come to the surface. They then are skimmed off and drained in woven baskets until the curd is solid enough to stick together. The resulting cheese is ricotta (literally meaning 'recooked'). Good-quality ricotta should be firm but not solid and consist of fine, delicate grains. Ricotta is used in both savoury and sweet dishes.

CURED MEATS

Coppa This boned shoulder of pork is rolled and cured with salt, pepper and nutmeg and then aged for about three months. It has a flavour not unlike prosciutto but contains equal amounts of fat and lean. It is excellent for larding the breasts of game birds, adding both fat and flavour, or for wrapping leaner types of meats.

Pancetta Essentially, pancetta is Italian streaky bacon but its depth of flavour is unrivalled by ordinary bacon. It is often flavoured with herbs, cloves, nutmeg, garlic, salt and pepper and sometimes fennel seeds – it is then often air-dried. It is also available smoked. Use it in slices or cut into lardons.

Prosciutto There are many types of cured ham available, but the two best types are Prosciutto di San Daniele and Prosciutto di Parma. The first comes from the Friuli region where the pigs feed in the fields and oak woods, accounting for the leanness of the meat. The second type, also known as Parma ham or prosciutto crudo, is made from pigs that have been fed on local grain as well as the whey left over from the making of Parmigiano-Reggiano. This meat is usually fattier.

Salami Italy produces a huge range of salamis, each with its own local character. The one most commonly available in Britain is probably Milano salami which comes sliced in packets or in one piece from major supermarkets.

VEGETABLES AND HERBS

Artichokes Very popular in Italian cooking, artichokes are available in many different varieties and forms: from tiny, young artichokes cooked and eaten whole to enormous globe artichokes, prized for their meaty hearts which can be sliced, stuffed or grilled. Artichokes are often cooked and preserved and served as an antipasto, on pizzas or in pasta dishes.

Aubergines These vegetables are popular all over the Mediterranean, probably because of their affinity with olive oil and garlic. In Britain, aubergines tend to be fatter and somewhat juicier than the Mediterranean varieties which are often elongated and marked with bright purple streaks.

Broad Beans Fresh broad beans are a prized early-summer speciality and in Italy are eaten raw with pecorino cheese. As the season progresses, they are best cooked and peeled as they tend to become coarse and grainy.

Cavallo Nero A member of the cabbage family, cavallo nero has long, slender, very ridged leaves which are dark green in colour. It has a strong but rather sweet cabbage flavour. Large supermarkets stock it in season, but if it is unavailable, use Savoy cabbage instead.

Garlic Garlic is one of the most important flavours in Italian cooking. When buying garlic, check it carefully – the heads should be firm without soft spots. Look for fresh, green garlic in spring.

Herbs A number of fresh herbs are used in Italian cooking but the most important ones are basil, parsley, rosemary, sage, marjoram and oregano. These are all widely used herbs and are available from most supermarkets but are also very easy to grow, even on a windowsill.

Lemons Italian lemons tend to be a little sweeter than the ones available in Britain. They are an essential flavour in many Italian dishes, especially seafood and sweet dishes.

Pumpkins and Squashes Often overlooked in Britain, pumpkins and the many varieties of squash are widely used in Italian cooking. They are excellent for enriching stews – some varieties have flesh which breaks down during cooking. They are also used for risottos and pasta fillings. Pumpkins and squashes and have an affinity with prosciutto, sage, pine nuts, Parmesan cheese and mostardo di cremona (see the Dry Ingredients section).

Rocket This peppery salad leaf has become popular in recent years and is now very easy to find. It is known by many other names including rucola, rughetta, arugula and roquette. It does not keep well.

Tomatoes Tomatoes are another essential flavour in Italian recipes. Unfortunately, British tomatoes tend not to be as good as their Italian counterparts. It is best to use tomatoes only in season and, at other times, to use good-quality, tinned Italian tomatoes.

Wild Mushrooms Mushroom hunting is a very popular and lucrative business in Italy, so much so that there are strict regulations regarding the minimum size for picking mushrooms. Many excellent edible varieties of wild mushrooms grow in Britain, but it is vital to seek expert advice before picking them on your own as some varieties are poisonous.

Many large supermarkets now sell varieties of wild mushrooms in season but they tend to be expensive.

BREAD

Italian breads tend to be coarser and more open-textured than British breads. They are made with unbleached flours and are left to prove for longer so that the flavour develops fully. Italian breads also tend to have a crustier exterior. Look out for Pugliese and ciabatta breads. Foccacia, a soft-crusted bread, is also popular and can be flavoured with herbs, sun-dried tomatoes or garlic.

SEAFOOD

Italy has a large coastline relative to its size and, as a result, seafood is a very popular choice. A huge variety of fish and shellfish are available, and large meals such as those served at weddings or other special celebrations will always include a fish course.

MEAT, POULTRY AND GAME

Italians are amongst the world's greatest meat eaters. Most meals will be based on meat of some kind. Popular choices include beef, chicken, pork and lamb but duck, guinea fowl, pheasant, pigeon, rabbit, veal and many kinds of offal are also used.

DRY INGREDIENTS

As with fresh ingredients, many items previously unavailable have, in recent years, appeared on supermarket and delicatessen shelves. Many dry ingredients keep well and are worth stocking up on.

Amaretti Biscuits These delicious, little crisp biscuits are made from almonds and most closely resemble macaroons. They come individually wrapped in beautiful paper and are good to eat on their own or with a sweet dessert wine. They are also useful as ingredients in desserts as they add crunch and flavour.

Anchovies These come in several forms and are an essential Italian ingredient. Anchovies can be treated almost as a seasoning in many recipes. Salted anchovies are sold in bottles and must be rinsed thoroughly to remove the excess salt. If the anchovies are whole, remove the heads and bones before using. If they are preserved in oil, remove them from the oil and drain them on absorbent kitchen paper. Some recipes require that anchovies are soaked in milk for 10–15 minutes (this makes the fillets less salty and less oily). By doing so the anchovies will simply melt on cooking. Do not soak the anchovies in milk if the fillets are to be used uncooked as in salads, for example.

Bottarga This is the salted and sun-dried roe of either grey mullet or tuna. It is available from Italian delicatessens or speciality shops (tuna bottarga is less delicately flavoured). Spaghetti with mullet bottarga, olive oil and chilli flakes is listed on every restaurant menu in Sardinia. Bottarga can also be finely shaved into a salad of raw fennel, lemon juice and olive oil.

Candied Peel Citrus fruit plays an important part in Italian cooking. Candied peel is found in all sorts of desserts. Buy it whole and chop it finely for the best flavour.

Canned Tomatoes As the British climate does not produce an abundance of outdoor grown, sun-ripened tomatoes, good-quality, tinned Italian plum tomatoes are the next best thing for making sauces. The fruit should be deep red and the liquid should be thick and not watery. Buy them whole or chopped.

Capers The flower buds of a bush native to the Mediterranean, capers are available both salted and preserved in vinegar. Small capers generally have a better flavour than larger ones. When using salted capers, it is important to soak and rinse them to remove the excess salt. Those preserved in vinegar should be drained and rinsed before use.

Coffee Italians prefer dark, roasted coffee and they pioneered the drinking of cappuccino and espresso. It is best to buy whole beans, as freshly roasted as possible, and grind them yourself as needed.

Dried Herbs These days, most recipes call for fresh herbs but dried herbs still have their place. Oregano dries particularly well and has a much less astringent flavour when dried; it is essential in tomato sauces. Other herbs that dry well are rosemary, sage and thyme. Dried basil, however, is no substitute for fresh.

Dried Mushrooms The most commonly available – and most affordable – type of dried mushroom is porcini. They are usually sold in 10 g packets which is generally plenty for one or two recipes and should be soaked in almost boiling water or stock

for 20–30 minutes, until tender. Carefully squeeze out any excess liquid – it will still be hot – and then chop as needed. Reserve the liquor as it contains a great deal of flavour. It is wise, however, to strain it before use as it can contain grit.

Dried Pulses Pulses are an excellent source of carbohydrate and also contain protein, making them particularly useful to vegetarians. Dried pulses should all be treated in the same way – soak them overnight in plenty of water (2 to 3 times their volume), then drain and cover with fresh water. Bring to the boil and boil hard for 10 minutes, reduce the temperature and simmer gently, until tender (check packet instructions for full cooking times). Do not add salt to dried pulses until they are cooked as salt will make the skins tough.

Italians make use of a large number of different types of pulses and lentils.

Cannellini Beans These beans are long and slender with a creamy texture. Cannellini beans take up other flavours very well, especially garlic, herbs and olive oil.

Borlotti Beans These are large, rounded beans which cook to a uniform brown colour. They also have a creamy texture and are very good in soups and stews.

Broad Beans These are available dried; either whole, with skins or split. The whole ones are excellent in soups. The split beans are popular in Eastern European countries, as well as Greece and Turkey where they are used in dishes such as falafel.

Chickpeas *Ceci* in Italian, chickpeas were introduced from the Middle East. Look out for big ones when buying them dry. They are excellent in soups and also in vegetable dishes. Chickpeas need a long cooking time.

Lentils Look for Lentilles de Puy. Although not Italian, these lentils are possibly the best flavoured of the lentil family. They are small and beautifully coloured from green-brown to blue. They also hold their shape well when cooked, making them easy to serve as a side dish – simply dress with olive oil. Similar lentils named Castelluccio are also grown in Umbria. They are also small but paler green in colour. Lentils are traditionally served with Bollito Misto, a famous New Year's Eve dish consisting of various meats, lentils and mostarda di cremona (see below).

Flour In most Italian recipes where flour is required, plain flour can easily be substituted. However, when making pizza or pasta dough, look for Tipo '00' flour which is very fine and very strong, making it ideal for these two dishes. If you cannot find it, use strong bread flour instead.

Mostarda di cremona Also known as mostarda di frutta, it is made of candied fruits such as peaches, apricots, pears, figs and cherries which are preserved in a honey, white wine and mustard syrup. It is available from large supermarkets and specialist shops.

Nuts Almonds, hazelnuts, walnuts and pistachios are all popular in Italian cooking, particularly in dessert recipes. Buy from a supplier with a quick turnover to guarantee that the nuts are fresh.

Olives Olives grow all over Italy and are synonymous with Italian cooking. Olives are available in most supermarkets, although it is worth looking for them in specialist shops that might preserve them with more interesting flavours. If you are lucky enough to find fresh olives, soak them in a very strong brine for a couple of weeks, then rinse them and preserve in oil and flavourings of your choice.

Panettone Generally available around Christmas, panettone is a sweet bread enriched with egg and butter, similar to French brioche. It is usually flavoured with candied citrus fruits although it can be plain. It keeps very well and is delicious toasted and spread with butter or used in bread and butter pudding.

Pine Nuts An essential ingredient in pesto sauce, pine nuts are found in all sorts of Italian recipes, both savoury and sweet. They are widely available and are delicious toasted and tossed in with pasta. They burn very easily, however, and are relatively expensive, so take care when toasting.

Raisins Italy is a large grape-producing nation so, not surprisingly, raisins feature alongside citrus fruits in many recipes. Look for plump, juicy looking fruit and try to buy only what you need as raisins can become sugary if kept for too long.

Semolina Not to be confused with the semolina used in puddings, semola di grano duro is flour from Italian durum wheat. This produces a granular-textured flour as opposed to finer-textured flour

used in breadmaking. Large supermarkets and Italian delicatessens sell semola di grano duro, but if it is unavailable, use strong bread flour instead.

Sun-dried Tomatoes Although they seem ubiquitous now, sun-dried tomatoes were unavailable outside Italy until the end of the 1980s. Sun-dried tomatoes are ripe plum tomatoes which have been dried in the sun. Often they have been rehydrated by being soaked in water and then preserved in oil. To use them, simply drain them on absorbent kitchen paper and chop as necessary. Also available now are semi-dried tomatoes, which have a sweeter, fresher flavour and a softer, less leathery texture. If you find sun-dried tomatoes which are not in oil, put them into a bowl and cover with boiling water. Leave for about 30 minutes, or until softened, before using.

Sun-dried Tomato Purée As the name suggests, this a paste made from sun-dried tomatoes. Use it in the same way as you would tomato purée. Sometimes it has other flavours added, such as garlic or herbs, in which case it can be used in salad dressings or mixed with pesto to dress pasta.

HOW TO MAKE PASTA

Home-made pasta has a light, almost silky texture and is very different from the fresh pasta that you can buy vacuum packed in supermarkets. It is also surprisingly easy to make and little equipment is needed; just a rolling pin and a sharp knife, although if you make pasta regularly it is worth investing in a pasta machine.

MAKING BASIC EGG PASTA DOUGH

Ingredients

225 g/8 oz type 001 pasta flour,
*   plus extra for dusting*
1 tsp salt
2 eggs, plus 1 egg yolk
1 tbsp olive oil
1–3 tsp cold water

1 Sift the flour and salt into a mound on a clean work surface and make a well in the middle, keeping the sides quite high, so that the egg mixture will not trickle out when added.
2 Beat together the eggs, yolk, oil and 1 teaspoon of water. Add to the well, then gradually work in the flour, adding extra water if needed, to make a soft but not sticky dough.
3 Knead on a lightly floured surface for 5 minutes, or until the dough is smooth and elastic. Wrap in clingfilm and leave to rest for 20 minutes at room temperature.

USING A FOOD PROCESSOR

Sift the flour and salt into the bowl of a food processor fitted with a metal blade. Add the eggs, yolk, oil and water and pulse-blend until the ingredients are mixed and until the dough begins to come together, adding the extra water if needed. Knead for 1–2 minutes, then wrap and rest as before.

ROLLING PASTA BY HAND

1 Unwrap the pasta dough and cut in half. Work with just half at a time and keep the other half wrapped in clingfilm.
2 Place the dough on a large, clean work surface lightly dusted with flour, then flatten with your hand and start to roll out. Always roll away from you, starting from the centre and giving the dough a quarter turn after each rolling. Sprinkle a little more flour over the dough if it starts to get sticky.
3 Continue rolling and turning until the dough is as thin as possible; ideally about 3 mm/$\frac{1}{8}$ inch. Make sure that you roll it evenly, or some shapes will cook faster than others.

ROLLING PASTA BY MACHINE

A machine makes smoother, thinner, more-even pasta than that made by hand-rolling. Most pasta machines work in the same way but you should refer to the manufacturers' instructions before using.

1 Clamp the machine securely and attach the handle. Set the rollers at their widest setting and sprinkle lightly with flour. Cut the pasta into four pieces. Wrap 3 of them in clingfilm and reserve.
2 Flatten the unwrapped pasta dough slightly, then feed it through the rollers. Fold the strip of dough in 3, rotate and feed through the rollers a second time. Continue to roll the pasta this way, narrowing the roller setting by one notch every second time and flouring the rollers if the pasta starts to get sticky. Only fold the dough the first time it goes through each roller width. The dough will get longer and thinner with every rolling – if it gets too difficult to handle, cut the strip in half and work with 1 piece at a time.

3 If making spaghetti or noodles such as tagliatelle, the second last setting is generally used. For pasta shapes and filled pastas, the dough should be rolled to the finest setting.

4 Fresh pasta should be dried slightly before cutting. Either drape over a narrow wooden pole for 5 minutes or place on a clean tea towel sprinkled with a little flour for 10 minutes.

You can also buy electric pasta machines that carry out the whole pasta-making process, from dough mixing and kneading, to extruding it through cutters into the required shapes – all you have to do is weigh out and add the individual ingredients. They can make over 900 g/2 lb of pasta at a time, but are expensive to buy and take up a lot of space.

SHAPING UP

When cutting and shaping freshly made pasta, have 2 or 3 lightly floured tea-towels ready. Arrange the pasta in a single layer, spaced slightly apart, or you may find that they stick together. When they are dry, you can freeze them successfully for up to 6 weeks, by layering in suitable freezer containers between sheets of baking parchment. Spread them out on baking parchment for about 20 minutes, or slightly longer if stuffed, before cooking. When making pasta, do not throw away the trimmings. They can be cut into tiny shapes or thin slivers and used in soups.

Farfalle Use a fluted pasta wheel to cut the pasta sheets into rectangles about 2.5 x 5 cm/1 x 12 inches. Pinch the long sides of each rectangle in the middle to make a bow. Spread out on a floured tea towel and leave to dry for at least 15 minutes.

Lasagne This is one of the easiest to make. Simply trim the pasta sheets until neat and cut into lengths the same size as your lasagne dish. Spread the cut sheets on tea towels sprinkled with flour.

Macaroni This is the generic name for hollow pasta. Cut the rolled-out pasta dough into squares, then wrap each around a chopstick, thick skewer or similar, starting from one of the corners. Slip the pasta off, curve slightly if liked and leave to dry for at least 15 minutes.

Noodles If using a pasta machine, use the cutter attachment to produce tagliatelle or fettucine, or use a narrower one for tagliarini or spaghetti. To make by hand, sprinkle the rolled-out pasta with flour, then roll up like a Swiss roll and cut into thin slices. The thickness of these depends on the noodles required. For linguine, cut into 5 mm/¼ inch slices and for tagliatelle cut into 8 mm/⅓ inch slices. Unravel them immediately after cutting. To make thicker ribbon pasta such as pappardelle, use a serrated pastry wheel to cut into wide strips. Leave over a wooden pole for up to 5 minutes to dry out.

Ravioli Cut the rolled-out sheet of dough in half widthways. Cover one half with clingfilm to stop it drying out too quickly. Brush the other sheet of dough with beaten egg. Pipe or spoon small mounds – using about 1 teaspoon of filling in even rows, spacing them at 4 cm/1½ inch intervals. Remove the clingfilm from the reserved pasta sheet and using a rolling pin carefully lift over the dough with the filling. Press down firmly between the pockets of filling to push out any air. Finally, cut into squares with a pastry cutter or sharp knife. Leave on a floured tea towel for 45 minutes before cooking.

You can also use a ravioli tray (*raviolatore*) to produce perfect even-sized ravioli. A sheet of rolled-out dough is laid over the tray, then pressed into the individual compartments. The filling can then be spooned or piped into the indentations and the second sheet of dough placed on top. To create the individual ravioli squares, a rolling pin is gently rolled over the serrated top. These tins are excellent for making small ravioli containing a little filling.

Three or four simple ingredients combined together make the best fillings. Always season generously with salt and freshly ground black pepper and where the filling is soft, stir in a little beaten egg. Why not try chopped cooked spinach, ricotta and freshly grated nutmeg; finely ground turkey, curd cheese, tarragon and Parmesan cheese; white crabmeat with mascarpone, finely grated lemon rind and dill; or ricotta, roasted garlic and fresh herbs.

Silhouette Pasta If rolled out very thinly, fresh herb leaves can be sandwiched between 2 layers of pasta for a stunning silhouette effect. Put the pasta through a machine set on the very last setting, so that it is paper-thin. Cut in half and lightly brush 1 piece with water. Arrange individual fresh herb leaves at regular intervals over the moistened pasta (you will need soft herbs for this – flat-leaf parsley, basil and sage are all ideal). Place the second sheet of dry pasta on top and gently press with a rolling pin to seal them together. Sprinkle the pasta with a little flour, then put it through the machine on the second to finest setting. Use a pastry wheel, dipped in flour, to cut around the herb leaves to make squares, or use a round or oval cutter to stamp out the pasta if preferred. Leave to dry on a floured tea towel for 20 minutes before cooking.

Tortellini Use a plain biscuit cutter to stamp out rounds of pasta about 5 cm/2 inches in diameter. Lightly brush each with beaten egg, then spoon or pipe about 1 teaspoon of filling into the middle of each round. Fold in half to make a half-moon shape, gently pressing the edges together to seal. Bend the 2 corners round and press together to seal. Allow to dry on a floured tea towel for 30 minutes before cooking. To make tortelloni, use a slightly larger cutter; about 6.5 cm/2½ inches.

VARIATIONS

Flavoured pastas are simple and there are dozens of delicious ways that you can change the flavour and colour of pasta. You will find that you get a more-even colour when using a machine, but the speckled appearance of flavoured hand-rolled pasta can be equally attractive.

Chilli Add 2 teaspoons of crushed, dried red chillies to the egg mixture before you mix with the flour.

Herb Stir 3 tablespoons of chopped fresh herbs such as basil, parsley, marjoram or sage or 2 tablespoons of finely chopped, strongly-flavoured herbs like thyme or rosemary into the flour.

Olive Blend 2 tablespoons of black olive paste with the egg mixture, leaving out the water.

Porcini Soak 15 g/½ oz dried porcini mushrooms in boiling water for 20 minutes. Drain and squeeze out as much water as possible, then chop very finely. Add to the egg mixture. (Reserve the soaking liquor, strain and use to flavour the pasta sauce.)

Saffron Sift 1 teaspoon of powdered saffron with the flour.

Spinach Cook 75 g/3 oz prepared spinach in a covered pan with just the water clinging to the leaves, until wilted. Drain and squeeze dry, then chop finely. Add to the egg mixture.

Sun-dried Tomato Blend 2 tablespoons of sun-dried tomato paste into the egg mixture, leaving out the water.

Wholemeal Pasta Substitute half the wholemeal flour for half of the white flour and add an extra 1–2 teaspoons water to the mixture.

PASTA VARIETIES

Pasta has been twisted and curled into an unimaginable number of shapes. There is a vast range of both fresh and dried pasta; short and long, tiny varieties for soup, larger ones for stuffing and more unusual designer shapes and flavours.

DRIED PASTAS

Buckwheat Pasta Darker in colour than wholewheat pasta, this is made from buck wheat flour. It is gluten-free so is suitable for people who are intolerant to wheat products. Pizzoccheri are thin, flat noodles twisted into nests and are the most common type of buckwheat pasta.

Corn Pasta Now found on most supermarket shelves, corn pasta is made with maize flour and the plain variety is a bright yellow colour. Like buckwheat pasta, it is gluten-free. When cooking, make sure you use a large saucepan as it tends to cause the water to foam more than ordinary wheat pasta.

Coloured and Flavoured Pasta The varieties of these types of pasta are endless. The most popular and easily obtainable are spinach and tomato. Often three colours (white, red and green) are packed together and labelled 'tricolore'. Others available in larger food stores and delicatessens include beetroot, saffron, herb, poppy seed, garlic, chilli, mushroom, smoked saffron and black ink.

More unusual types such as blue curaco liqueur pasta, which has a bright turquoise colour, have also been created.

Durum Wheat Pasta This is the most readily available and may be made with or without eggs. Generally plain wheat pasta is used for long, straight shapes such as spaghetti, whereas pasta containing eggs is slightly more fragile, so is packed into nests or waves. Look for the words 'Durum wheat' or '*pasta di semola di grano duro*' on the packet when buying, as pastas made from soft wheat tend to become soggy when cooked.

Wholewheat Pasta Made with wholemeal flour, this has a higher fibre content than ordinary pasta which gives it a slightly chewy texture, nutty flavour and rich brown colour. Whole-wheat pasta takes longer to cook, however, than the refined version. We tend to think of it as a modern product associated with the growth in interest of health foods, but it has been made in north-eastern Italy for hundreds of years, where it is known as *bigoli* and is like a thick spaghetti.

PASTA SHAPES
long pasta
Spaghetti Probably the best known type of pasta, spaghetti derives its name from the word *spago* meaning string, which describes its round, thin shape perfectly. Spaghettini is a thinner variety and spaghettoni is thicker. Vermicelli is a very fine type of spaghetti.

Tagliatelle Tagliatelle is the most common type of ribbon-noodle pasta and each ribbon of pasta is usually slightly less than 1 cm/½ inch wide. It is traditionally from Bologna where it always accompanies bolognaise sauce (rather than spaghetti). It is sold coiled into nests that unravel when cooked. Thinner varieties of tagliarini or tagliolini are also available.

A mixture of white and spinach-flavoured tagliatelle is known as *paglia e fieno* which translates as straw and hay. Fettucine is the Roman version of tagliatelle and is cut slightly thinner.

Ziti Long, thick and hollow, ziti may be ridged but is usually smooth. It takes its name from *zita*, meaning fiancee, as it was once traditional to serve it at weddings in southern Italy. Zitoni is a similar larger pasta; mezza zita is thinner.

Short pasta
There are basically two types of short pasta: *secca* is factory-made from durum wheat and water, which is pressed into assorted shapes and sizes, and *pasta all'uovo* is made with eggs, which is particularly popular in northern Italy, where it is served with meat or creamy sauces. *Pasta all'uovo* is slightly more expensive than plain pasta, but cooks in less time and is less likely to go soggy if overcooked. It is also much more nutritious and has an attractive golden colour. There are hundreds of different shapes and some of the most popular ones are listed below.

Conchiglie As the name implies, these pasta shapes resemble conch shells and are ideal for serving with thinner sauces which will get trapped in the shells. Sizes vary from very tiny ones to large ones which are suitable for stuffing. They may be smooth or ridged conchiglie rigate.

Eliche and Fusilli These are twisted into the shape of a screw, which is where their name comes from. Eliche is often wrongly labelled as fusilli as the two are similar, but fusilli is more tightly coiled and opens out slightly during cooking.

Farfalle A popular pasta shape, these are bow or butterfly shaped, often with crinkled edges.

Gnocchi Sardi These come from Sardinia and are named after the little gnocchi potato dumplings. Often served with rich meat sauces, they have a somewhat chewy texture.

Macaroni This is known as maccheroni in Italy. You may find it labelled as 'elbow macaroni' which describes its shape (although it is sometimes almost straight). This was once the most popular imported pasta and is particularly good in baked dishes, notably macaroni cheese. A thin, quick-cook variety is also available.

Penne Slightly larger, hollow tubes than macaroni, the ends are cut diagonally and are pointed like quills. There are also less well-known varieties including the thinner pennette and even thinner pennini. They are often made with egg or flavoured with tomato or spinach.

Pipe This is curved, hollow pasta and is often sold ridged as pipe rigate. The smaller type is known as pipette.

Rigatoni This is substantial, chunky, tubular pasta and is often used for baking. Because the pasta is thick, it tends to be slightly chewier than other short pastas. Rigatoni goes well with meat and strongly flavoured sauces.

Rotelle This is thin, wheel-shaped pasta, also known as ruote and trulli and often sold in packets of two or three colours.

FLAT PASTA

There are many types of long, flat ribbon pastas, but there is only one flat pasta – lasagne – which is usually used for baking in the oven (al forno). These thin sheets are layered up with a sauce or may be curled into large tubes about 10 cm/4 inches long to make cannelloni. In Italy, they are usually made from fresh sheets of lasagne rolled around the filling, however, dried tubes are easily available and simple to use. Three flavours of lasagne are available: plain,

spinach or wholewheat. Most sheets are flat, but some have curled edges which help trap the sauce during cooking and stop it running to the bottom of the dish. Lasagnette are long, narrow strips of flat pasta and are crimped on one or both long edges. Like lasagne, they are designed to be layered up with a sauce and baked.

STUFFED PASTA

Tortellini are the most common of dried pasta shapes and consist of tiny, stuffed pieces of pasta which are folded, and then the ends are joined to make a ring. A speciality of Bologna, larger ones are made from rounds or squares and are joined without leaving a hole in the middle. They are called tortelloni and generally are made with a meat (*alla carne*) or cheese (*ai formaggi*) filling and will keep for up to a year (but always check the sell-by date). Cappelletti, ravioli and agnalotti are sometimes sold dried, but more often fresh.

SOUP PASTA

Tiny pasta shapes known as *pastina* in Italy come in hundreds of different shapes and are often added to soups. Risi is the smallest type of pasta and looks like grains of rice, whereas orzi, another soup pasta, resembles barley. Slightly larger ones include, stellette (stars), and rotelli (wheels). Many are miniature shapes of larger pasta; farfallette (little bows) and conchigliette (little shells).

FRESH PASTA

Fresh pasta has become increasingly popular over the past decade and can be found in the chilled cabinets of supermarkets, as well as being sold loose in specialist shops. Ideally, you should buy fresh pasta on the day you are going to cook it, or use within a day or two. It must be stored in the refrigerator until you are ready to use it, as it contains eggs, which shorten its keeping

time. It is generally available in the same shapes as dried pasta, but has a much greater range of stuffed fillings. Ravioli is one of the most common. It is shaped into large squares with fluted edges and is made with many different pasta doughs including saffron and fresh herbs. The fillings may be anything, for example, spinach and ricotta, mushroom, fish and shellfish, meat, but especially chicken. They may also be shaped into long rectangles, circles or ovals.

ORIENTAL NOODLES

Pasta originated in China and not in Italy, so it is hardly surprising that there is a vast range of oriental noodles.

Buckwheat Noodles Soba are the most common and are a dark, greyish-brown colour. They feature in Japanese cooking in soups and stir-fries.

Cellophane Noodles Made from mung beans, these are translucent, flavourless noodles and are only available dried. They are never boiled and simply need soaking in very hot water.

Egg Noodles Commonly used in Chinese cooking, they come in several thicknesses; thin and medium being the most popular.

Rice Noodles These are fine, delicate, opaque noodles which are made from rice and are often used in Thai and Malaysian cooking.

Urdon Noodles These are thick Japanese noodles which can be round or flat and are available both fresh, dried or precooked.

White Bean Soup with Parmesan Croûtons

1 Preheat oven to 200°C/400°F/Gas Mark 6. Place the cubes of bread in a bowl and pour over the groundnut oil. Stir to coat the bread, then sprinkle over the Parmesan cheese. Place on a lightly oiled baking tray and bake in the preheated oven for 10 minutes, or until crisp and golden.

2 Heat the olive oil in a large saucepan and cook the onion for 4–5 minutes until softened. Add the bacon and thyme and cook for a further 3 minutes. Stir in the beans, stock and black pepper and simmer gently for 5 minutes.

3 Place half the bean mixture and liquid into a food processor and blend until smooth.

4 Return the purée to the saucepan. Stir in the pesto sauce, pepperoni sausage and lemon juice and season to taste with salt and pepper.

5 Return the soup to the heat and cook for a further 2–3 minutes, or until piping hot. Place some of the beans in each serving bowl and add a ladleful of soup. Garnish with shredded basil and serve immediately with the croûtons scattered over the top.

INGREDIENTS
Serves 4

3 thick slices of white bread, cut into 1 cm/½ inch cubes

3 tbsp groundnut oil

2 tbsp Parmesan cheese, finely grated

1 tbsp light olive oil

1 large onion, peeled and finely chopped

50 g/2 oz unsmoked bacon lardons (or thick slices of bacon, diced)

1 tbsp fresh thyme leaves

2 x 400 g cannellini beans, drained

900 ml/1½ pints chicken stock

salt and freshly ground black pepper

1 tbsp prepared pesto sauce

50 g/2 oz piece of pepperoni sausage, diced

1 tbsp fresh lemon juice

1 tbsp fresh basil, roughly shredded

Tasty Tip

Make your own pesto: in a food processor, finely chop a large handful of fresh basil leaves with 2 peeled garlic cloves, 1 tablespoon pine nuts and seasoning. Gradually add 6–8 tablespoons good-quality olive oil. Scrape into a bowl and stir in 2–3 tablespoons freshly grated Parmesan cheese. Add a little more olive oil if necessary and adjust the seasoning.

Rice Soup with Potato Sticks

1 Preheat oven to 190°C/ 375°F/Gas Mark 5. Heat 25 g/1 oz of the butter and the olive oil in a saucepan and cook the onion for 4–5 minutes until softened, then add the Parma ham and cook for about 1 minute. Stir in the rice, the stock and the peas. Season to taste with salt and pepper and simmer for 10–15 minutes, or until the rice is tender.

2 Beat the egg and 125 g/ 4 oz of the butter together until smooth, then beat in the flour, a pinch of salt and the potato. Work the ingredients together to form a soft, pliable dough, adding a little more flour if necessary.

3 Roll the dough out on a lightly floured surface into a rectangle 1 cm/½ inch thick and cut into 12 thin long sticks. Brush with milk and sprinkle on the poppy seeds. Place the sticks on a lightly oiled baking tray and bake in the preheated oven for 15 minutes, or until golden.

4 When the rice is cooked, stir the remaining butter and Parmesan cheese into the soup and sprinkle the chopped parsley over the top. Serve immediately with the warm potato sticks.

INGREDIENTS
Serves 4

175 g/6 oz butter
1 tsp olive oil
1 large onion, peeled and finely chopped
4 slices Parma ham, chopped
100 g/3½ oz Arborio rice
1.1 litres/2 pints chicken stock
350 g/12 oz frozen peas
salt and freshly ground black pepper
1 medium egg
125 g/4 oz self-raising flour
175 g/6 oz mashed potato
1 tbsp milk
1 tbsp poppy seeds
1 tbsp Parmesan cheese, finely grated
1 tbsp freshly chopped parsley

Food Fact

The Parma ham used in this recipe is a luxury Italian ham which originates from the northern Italian province of Parma – the same area famous for Parmesan cheese. Parma pigs enjoy a special diet of chestnuts and whey which produces an excellent quality of meat. Parma hams are not smoked but seasoned, salt cured and air dried.

Tasty Tip

These potato sticks also make a delicious snack with drinks. Try sprinkling them with sesame seeds or grated cheese and allow to cool before serving.

Rich Tomato Soup with Roasted Red Peppers

1 Preheat oven to 200°C/ 400°F/Gas Mark 6. Lightly oil a roasting tin with 1 teaspoon of the olive oil. Place the peppers and tomatoes cut side down in the roasting tin with the onion quarters and the garlic cloves. Spoon over the remaining oil.

2 Bake in the preheated oven for 30 minutes, or until the skins on the peppers have started to blacken and blister. Allow the vegetables to cool for about 10 minutes, then remove the skins, stalks and seeds from the peppers. Peel away the skins from the tomatoes and onions and squeeze out the garlic.

3 Place the cooked vegetables into a blender or food processor and blend until smooth. Add the stock and blend again to form a smooth purée. Pour the puréed soup through a sieve, if a smooth soup is preferred, then pour into a saucepan. Bring to the boil, simmer gently for 2–3 minutes, and season to taste with salt and pepper. Serve hot with a swirl of soured cream and a sprinkling of shredded basil on the top.

INGREDIENTS
Serves 4

2 tsp light olive oil
700 g/1½ lb red peppers, halved
   and deseeded
450 g/1 lb ripe plum tomatoes,
   halved
2 onions, unpeeled and quartered
4 garlic cloves, unpeeled
600 ml/1 pint chicken stock
salt and freshly ground black
   pepper
4 tbsp soured cream
1 tbsp freshly shredded basil

Helpful Hint

To help remove the skins of the peppers more easily, remove them from the oven and put immediately into a plastic bag or a bowl covered with clingfilm. Leave until cool enough to handle then skin carefully.

Bread & Tomato Soup

1 Make a small cross in the base of each tomato, then place in a bowl and cover with boiling water. Allow to stand for 2 minutes, or until the skins have started to peel away, then drain, remove the skins and seeds and chop into large pieces.

2 Heat 3 tablespoons of the olive oil in a saucepan and gently cook the onion until softened. Add the skinned tomatoes, chopped basil, garlic and chilli powder and season to taste with salt and pepper. Pour in the stock, cover the saucepan, bring to the boil and simmer gently for 15–20 minutes.

3 Remove the crusts from the bread and break into small pieces. Remove the tomato mixture from the heat and stir in the bread. Cover and leave to stand for 10 minutes, or until the bread has blended with the tomatoes. Season to taste. Serve warm or cold with a swirl of olive oil on the top, garnished with a spoonful of chopped cucumber and basil leaves.

INGREDIENTS
Serves 4

900 g/2 lb very ripe tomatoes
4 tbsp olive oil
1 onion, peeled and finely chopped
1 tbsp freshly chopped basil
3 garlic cloves, peeled and crushed
¼ tsp hot chilli powder
salt and freshly ground black pepper
600 ml/1 pint chicken stock
175 g/6 oz stale white bread
50 g/2 oz cucumber, cut into small dice
4 whole basil leaves

Tasty Tip

This soup is best made when fresh tomatoes are in season. If you want to make it at other times of the year, replace the fresh tomatoes with 2 x 400 g cans of peeled plum tomatoes – Italian, if possible. You may need to cook the soup for 5–10 minutes longer.

Rocket & Potato Soup
with Garlic Croûtons

1 Place the potatoes in a large saucepan, cover with the stock and simmer gently for 10 minutes. Add the rocket leaves and simmer for a further 5–10 minutes, or until the potatoes are soft and the rocket has wilted.

2 Meanwhile, make the croûtons. Cut the thick, white sliced bread into small cubes and reserve. Heat the butter and groundnut oil in a small frying pan and cook the garlic for 1 minute, stirring well. Remove the garlic. Add the bread cubes to the butter and oil mixture in the frying pan and

sauté, stirring continuously, until they are golden brown. Drain the croûtons on absorbent kitchen paper and reserve.

3 Cut the ciabatta bread into small dice and stir into the soup. Cover the saucepan and leave to stand for 10 minutes, or until the bread has absorbed a lot of the liquid.

4 Stir in the olive oil, season to taste with salt and pepper and serve at once with a few of the garlic croûtons scattered over the top and a little grated Parmesan cheese.

INGREDIENTS
Serves 4

700 g/1½ lb baby new potatoes
1.1 litres/2 pints chicken or
 vegetable stock
50 g/2 oz rocket leaves
125 g/4 oz thick white
 sliced bread
50 g/2 oz unsalted butter
1 tsp groundnut oil
2–4 garlic cloves, peeled and
 chopped
125 g/4 oz stale ciabatta bread,
 with the crusts removed
4 tbsp olive oil
salt and freshly ground black
 pepper
2 tbsp Parmesan cheese,
 finely grated

Helpful Hint

Rocket is now widely available in bags from most large supermarkets. If, however, you cannot get hold of it, replace it with
an equal quantity of watercress or baby spinach leaves.

Classic Minestrone

1 Heat the butter and olive oil together in a large saucepan. Chop the bacon and add to the saucepan. Cook for 3–4 minutes, then remove with a slotted spoon and reserve.

2 Finely chop the onion, garlic, celery and carrots and add to the saucepan, one ingredient at a time, stirring well after each addition. Cover and cook gently for 8–10 minutes, until the vegetables are softened.

3 Add the chopped tomatoes, with their juice and the stock, bring to the boil then

cover the saucepan with a lid, reduce the heat and simmer gently for about 20 minutes.

4 Stir in the cabbage, beans, peas and spaghetti pieces. Cover and simmer for a further 20 minutes, or until all the ingredients are tender. Season to taste with salt and pepper.

5 Return the cooked bacon to the saucepan and bring the soup to the boil. Serve the soup immediately with Parmesan cheese shavings sprinkled on the top and plenty of crusty bread to accompany it.

INGREDIENTS
Serves 6–8

25 g/1 oz butter
3 tbsp olive oil
3 rashers streaky bacon
1 large onion, peeled
1 garlic clove, peeled
1 celery stick, trimmed
2 carrots, peeled
400 g can chopped tomatoes
1.1 litre/2 pints chicken stock
175 g/6 oz green cabbage, finely shredded
50 g/2 oz French beans, trimmed and halved
3 tbsp frozen petits pois
50 g/2 oz spaghetti, broken into short pieces
salt and freshly ground black pepper
Parmesan cheese shavings, to garnish
crusty bread, to serve

Tasty Tip

There are many different variations of Minestrone. You can add drained canned cannellini beans either in place of or as well as the spaghetti, or use small soup pasta shells. For a vegetarian version, omit the bacon and use vegetable stock and a vegetarian cheese.

Cream of Pumpkin Soup

1 Cut the skinned and de-seeded pumpkin flesh into 2.5 cm/1 inch cubes. Heat the olive oil in a large saucepan and cook the pumpkin for 2–3 minutes, coating it completely with oil. Chop the onion and leek finely and cut the carrot and celery into small dice.

2 Add the vegetables to the saucepan with the garlic and cook, stirring for 5 minutes, or until they have begun to soften. Cover the vegetables with the water and bring to the boil. Season with plenty of salt and pepper and the nutmeg, cover and simmer for 15–20

minutes, or until all of the vegetables are tender.

3 When the vegetables are tender, remove from the heat, cool slightly then pour into a food processor or blender. Liquidise to form a smooth purée then pass through a sieve into a clean saucepan.

4 Adjust the seasoning to taste and add all but 2 tablespoons of the cream and enough water to obtain the correct consistency. Bring the soup to boiling point, add the cayenne pepper and serve immediately swirled with cream and warm herby bread.

INGREDIENTS
Serves 4

900 g/2 lb pumpkin flesh (after peeling and discarding the seeds)
4 tbsp olive oil
1 large onion, peeled
1 leek, trimmed
1 carrot, peeled
2 celery sticks
4 garlic cloves, peeled and crushed
1.7 litres/3 pints water
salt and freshly ground black pepper
¼ tsp freshly grated nutmeg
150 ml/¼ pint single cream
¼ tsp cayenne pepper
warm herby bread, to serve

Tasty Tip

If you cannot find pumpkin, try replacing it with squash. Butternut, acorn or turban squash would all make suitable substitutes. Avoid spaghetti squash which is not firm-fleshed when cooked.

Lettuce Soup

1 Bring a large saucepan of water to the boil and blanch the lettuce leaves for 3 minutes. Drain and dry thoroughly on absorbent kitchen paper. Then shred with a sharp knife.

2 Heat the oil and butter in a clean saucepan and add the lettuce, spring onions and parsley and cook together for 3–4 minutes, or until very soft.

3 Stir in the flour and cook for 1 minute, then gradually pour in the stock, stirring throughout. Bring to the boil and season to taste with salt and pepper. Reduce the heat, cover and simmer gently for 10–15 minutes, or until soft.

4 Allow the soup to cool slightly, then either sieve or purée in a blender. Alternatively, leave the soup chunky. Stir in the cream, add more seasoning, to taste, if liked, then add the cayenne pepper.

5 Arrange the slices of ciabatta bread in a large soup dish or in individual bowls and pour the soup over the bread. Garnish with sprigs of parsley and serve immediately.

INGREDIENTS
Serves 4

2 iceberg lettuces, quartered with hard core removed
1 tbsp olive oil
50 g/2 oz butter
125 g/4 oz spring onions, trimmed and chopped
1 tbsp freshly chopped parsley
1 tbsp plain flour
600 ml/1 pint chicken stock
salt and freshly ground black pepper
150 ml/¼ pint single cream
¼ tsp cayenne pepper, to taste
thick slices of stale ciabatta bread
sprig of parsley, to garnish

Helpful Hint

Do not prepare the lettuce too far in advance. Iceberg lettuce has a tendency to discolour when sliced, which may in turn discolour the soup.

Antipasti with Focaccia

1 Preheat oven to 220°C/425°F/Gas Mark 7, 15 minutes before baking. Arrange the fresh fruit, vegetables, prawns, sardines, olives, cheese and meat on a large serving platter. Drizzle over 1 tablespoon of the olive oil, then cover and chill in the refrigerator while making the bread.

2 Sift the flour, sugar, semolina and salt into a large mixing bowl then sprinkle in the dried yeast. Make a well in the centre and add the remaining 2 tablespoons of olive oil. Add the warm water, a little at a time, and mix together until a smooth, pliable dough is formed. If using fresh yeast, cream the yeast with the sugar, then gradually beat in half

the warm water. Leave in a warm place until frothy then proceed as for dried yeast.

3 Place on to a lightly floured board and knead until smooth and elastic. Place the dough in a lightly greased bowl, cover and leave in a warm place for 45 minutes.

4 Knead again and flatten the dough into a large, flat oval shape about 1 cm/½ inch thick. Place on a lightly oiled baking tray. Prick the surface with the end of a wooden spoon and brush with olive oil. Sprinkle on the coarse salt and bake in the pre-heated oven for 25 minutes, or until golden. Serve the bread with the prepared platter of food.

INGREDIENTS
Serves 4

3 fresh figs, quartered
125 g/4 oz green beans, cooked and halved
1 small head of radicchio, rinsed and shredded
125 g/4 oz large prawns, peeled and cooked
125 can sardines, drained
25 g/1 oz pitted black olives
25 g/1 oz stuffed green olives
125 g/4 oz mozzarella cheese, sliced
50 g/2 oz Italian salami sausage, thinly sliced
3 tbsp olive oil
275 g/10 oz strong white flour
pinch of sugar
3 tsp easy-blend quick-acting yeast or 15 g/½ oz fresh yeast
175 g/6 oz fine semolina
1 tsp salt
300 ml/½ pint warm water
a little extra olive oil for brushing
1 tbsp coarse salt crystals

Helpful Hint

Fresh yeast is available from health food shops as well as large supermarkets with in-store bakeries. Look for yeast that is moist and crumbly and has no dark patches. It will keep in the freezer up to six months.

Mozzarella Frittata
with Tomato & Basil Salad

1 To make the tomato and basil salad, slice the tomatoes very thinly, tear up the basil leaves and sprinkle over. Make the dressing by whisking the olive oil, lemon juice and sugar together well. Season with black pepper before drizzling the dressing over the salad.

2 To make the frittata, preheat the grill to a high heat, just before beginning to cook. Place the eggs in a large bowl with plenty of salt and whisk. Grate the mozzarella and stir into the egg with the finely chopped spring onions.

3 Heat the oil in a large, non-stick frying pan and pour in the egg mixture, stirring with a wooden spoon to spread the ingredients evenly over the pan.

4 Cook for 5–8 minutes, until the frittata is golden brown and firm on the under-side. Place the whole pan under the preheated grill and cook for about 4–5 minutes, or until the top is golden brown. Slide the frittata on to a serving plate, cut into 6 large wedges and serve immediately with the tomato and basil salad and plenty of warm crusty bread.

INGREDIENTS
Serves 6

FOR THE SALAD:

6 ripe but firm tomatoes
2 tbsp fresh basil leaves
2 tbsp olive oil
1 tbsp fresh lemon juice
1 tsp caster sugar
freshly ground black pepper

FOR THE FRITTATA:

7 medium eggs, beaten
salt
300 g / 11 oz mozzarella cheese
2 spring onions, trimmed and finely chopped
2 tbsp olive oil
warm crusty bread, to serve

Helpful Hint

Fresh mozzarella is sold in packets and is usually surrounded by a light brine. After grating the cheese, firmly press between layers of absorbent kitchen paper to remove any excess water which might leak out during cooking.

Fried Whitebait
with Rocket Salad

1 If the whitebait are frozen, thaw completely, then wipe dry with absorbent kitchen paper.

2 Start to heat the oil in a deep-fat fryer. Arrange the fish in a large, shallow dish and toss well in the flour, cayenne pepper and salt and pepper.

3 Deep fry the fish in batches for 2–3 minutes, or until crisp and golden. Keep the cooked fish warm while deep frying the remaining fish.

4 Meanwhile, to make the salad, arrange the rocket leaves, cherry tomatoes and cucumber on individual serving dishes. Whisk the olive oil and the remaining ingredients together and season lightly. Drizzle the dressing over the salad and serve with the whitebait.

INGREDIENTS
Serves 4

450 g/1 lb whitebait, fresh or frozen
oil, for frying
85 g/3 oz plain flour
½ tsp of cayenne pepper
salt and freshly ground black pepper

FOR THE SALAD:
125 g/4 oz rocket leaves
125 g/4 oz cherry tomatoes, halved
75 g/3 oz cucumber, cut into dice
3 tbsp olive oil
1 tbsp fresh lemon juice
½ tsp Dijon mustard
½ tsp caster sugar

Tasty Tip

Why not try a different salad. Mix together some cleaned baby spinach, cooled, cooked petits pois and chopped spring onions, then pour over 2 tablespoons of garlic olive oil. If serving with a chicken dish, top the salad with some feta cheese.

Bruschetta with Pecorino, Garlic & Tomatoes

1 Preheat grill and line the grill rack with tinfoil just before cooking. Make a small cross in the top of the tomatoes, then place in a small bowl and cover with boiling water. Leave to stand for 2 minutes, then drain and remove the skins. Cut into quarters, remove the seeds, and chop the flesh into small dice.

2 Mix the tomato flesh with the pecorino cheese and 2 teaspoons of the fresh oregano and season to taste with salt and pepper. Add 1 tablespoon of the olive oil and mix thoroughly.

3 Crush the garlic and spread evenly over the slices of bread. Heat 2 tablespoons of the olive oil in a large frying pan and sauté the bread slices until they are crisp and golden.

4 Place the fried bread on a lightly oiled baking tray and spoon on the tomato and cheese topping. Place a little mozzarella on top and place under the pre-heated grill for 3–4 minutes, until golden and bubbling. Garnish with the remaining oregano, then arrange the bruschettas on a serving plate and serve immediately with the olives.

INGREDIENTS
Serves 4

6 ripe but firm tomatoes
125 g/4 oz pecorino cheese, finely grated
1 tbsp oregano leaves
salt and freshly ground black pepper
3 tbsp olive oil
3 garlic cloves, peeled
8 slices of flat Italian bread, such as focaccia
50 g/2 oz mozzarella cheese
marinated black olives, to serve

Tasty Tip

Bitter leaves are excellent with these bruschettas because they help to offset the richness of the cheese and tomato topping. Try a mixture of frisée, radicchio and rocket. If these are unavailable, use a bag of mixed salad leaves.

Crostini with Chicken Livers

1 Heat 1 tablespoon of the olive oil and 1 tablespoon of the butter in a frying pan, add the shallot and garlic and cook gently for 2–3 minutes.

2 Trim and wash the chicken livers thoroughly and pat dry on absorbent kitchen paper as much as possible. Cut into slices, then toss in the flour. Add the livers to the frying pan with the shallot and garlic and continue to fry for a further 2 minutes, stirring continuously.

3 Pour in the white wine and brandy and bring to the boil. Boil rapidly for 1–2 minutes to allow the alcohol to evaporate, then stir in the sliced mushrooms and cook gently for about 5 minutes, or until the chicken livers are cooked, but just a little pink inside. Season to taste with salt and pepper.

4 Fry the slices of ciabatta or similar-style bread in the remaining oil and butter, then place on individual serving dishes. Spoon over the liver mixture and garnish with a few sage leaves and lemon wedges. Serve immediately.

INGREDIENTS
Serves 4

2 tbsp olive oil
2 tbsp butter
1 shallot, peeled and finely chopped
1 garlic clove, peeled and crushed
150 g/5 oz chicken livers
1 tbsp plain flour
2 tbsp dry white wine
1 tbsp brandy
50 g/2 oz mushrooms, sliced
salt and freshly ground black pepper
4 slices of ciabatta or similar bread

TO GARNISH:
fresh sage leaves
lemon wedges

Tasty Tip

If you prefer a lower fat alternative to the fried bread in this recipe, omit 1 tablespoon of the butter and brush the bread slices with the remaining 1 tablespoon of oil. Bake in a pre-heated oven 180°C/350°F/Gas Mark 4 for about 20 minutes, or until golden and crisp then serve as above.

Italian Baked Tomatoes with Curly Endive & Radicchio

1 Preheat oven to 190°C/ 375°F/Gas Mark 5. Lightly oil a baking tray with the teaspoon of oil. Slice the tops off the tomatoes and remove all the tomato flesh and sieve into a large bowl. Sprinkle a little salt inside the tomato shells and then place them upside down on a plate while the filling is prepared.

2 Mix the sieved tomato with the breadcrumbs, fresh herbs and mushrooms and season well with salt and pepper. Place the tomato shells on the prepared baking tray and fill with the tomato and mushroom mixture.

Sprinkle the cheese on the top and bake in the preheated oven for 15–20 minutes, until golden brown.

3 Meanwhile, prepare the salad. Arrange the endive and radicchio on individual serving plates and mix the remaining ingredients together in a small bowl to make the dressing. Season to taste.

4 When the tomatoes are cooked, allow to rest for 5 minutes, then place on the prepared plates and drizzle over a little dressing. Serve warm.

INGREDIENTS
Serves 4

1 tsp olive oil
4 beef tomatoes
salt
50 g/2 oz fresh white
 breadcrumbs
1 tbsp freshly snipped chives
1 tbsp freshly chopped parsley
125 g/4 oz button mushrooms,
 finely chopped
salt and freshly ground black
 pepper
25 g/1 oz fresh Parmesan
 cheese, grated

FOR THE SALAD:
½ curly endive lettuce
½ small piece of radicchio
2 tbsp olive oil
1 tsp balsamic vinegar
salt and freshly ground black
 pepper

Tasty Tip
As an alternative, try stirring in either 2 tablespoons of tapenade or ready-made pesto into the stuffing mixture. Alternatively, replace the chives with freshly chopped basil.

Spaghettini with Lemon Pesto & Cheese & Herb Bread

1 Preheat oven to 200°C/ 400°F/Gas Mark 6, 15 minutes before baking. Mix together the onion, oregano, parsley, butter and cheese. Spread the bread with the cheese mixture, place on a lightly oiled baking tray and cover with tinfoil. Bake in the preheated oven for 10–15 minutes, then keep warm.

2 Add the spaghettini with 1 tablespoon of olive oil to a large saucepan of fast-boiling, lightly salted water and cook for 3–4 minutes, or until 'al dente'. Drain, reserving 2 tablespoons of the cooking liquor.

3 Blend the basil, pine nuts, garlic, Parmesan cheese, lemon rind and juice and remaining olive oil in a food processor or blender until a purée is formed. Season to taste with salt and pepper, then place in a saucepan.

4 Heat the lemon pesto very gently until piping hot, then stir in the pasta together with the reserved cooking liquor. Add the butter and mix well together.

5 Add plenty of black pepper to the pasta and serve immediately with the warm cheese and herb bread.

INGREDIENTS
Serves 4

1 small onion, peeled and grated
2 tsp freshly chopped oregano
1 tbsp freshly chopped parsley
75 g/3 oz butter
125 g/4 oz pecorino cheese, grated
8 slices of Italian flat bread
275 g/10 oz dried spaghettini
4 tbsp olive oil
1 large bunch of basil, approximately 30 g/1 oz
75 g/3 oz pine nuts
1 garlic clove, peeled and crushed
75 g/3 oz Parmesan cheese, grated
finely grated rind and juice of 2 lemons
salt and freshly ground black pepper
4 tsp butter

Tasty Tip

It is important to use a good-quality, full-flavoured olive oil for this recipe. Look for an extra-virgin or cold-pressed oil and buy the best you can afford.

Mussels with Creamy Garlic & Saffron Sauce

1 Clean the mussels thoroughly in plenty of cold water and remove any beards and barnacles from the shells. Discard any mussels that are open or damaged. Place in a large bowl and cover with cold water and leave in the refrigerator until required, if prepared earlier.

2 Pour the wine into a large saucepan and bring to the boil. Tip the mussels into the pan, cover and cook, shaking the saucepan periodically for 6–8 minutes, or until the mussels have opened completely.

3 Discard any mussels with closed shells, then using a slotted spoon, carefully remove the remaining open mussels from the saucepan and keep them warm. Reserve the cooking liquor.

4 Heat the olive oil in a small frying pan and cook the shallot and garlic gently for 2–3 minutes, until softened. Add the reserved cooking liquid and chopped oregano and cook for a further 3–4 minutes. Stir in the saffron and the cream and heat through gently. Season to taste with salt and pepper. Place a few mussels in individual serving bowls and spoon over the saffron sauce. Serve immediately with plenty of fresh crusty bread.

INGREDIENTS
Serves 4

700 g / 1½ lb fresh live mussels
300 ml / ½ pint good-quality dry white wine
1 tbsp olive oil
1 shallot, peeled and finely chopped
2 garlic cloves, peeled and crushed
1 tbsp freshly chopped oregano
2 saffron strands
150 ml / ¼ pint single cream
salt and freshly ground black pepper
fresh crusty bread, to serve

Helpful Hint

Mussels are now farmed and are available most of the year. However, always try to buy mussels the day you intend to eat them. Place them in a bowl of cold water in the refrigerator as soon as possible, changing the water at least every 2 hours. If live mussels are unavailable, use prepacked, cooked mussels.

Peperonata
(Braised Mixed Peppers)

1 Remove the seeds from the peppers and cut into thin strips. Slice the onion into rings and chop the garlic cloves finely.

2 Heat the olive oil in a frying pan and fry the peppers, onions and garlic for 5–10 minutes, or until soft and lightly coloured. Stir continuously.

3 Make a cross on the top of the tomatoes then place in a bowl and cover with boiling water. Allow to stand for about 2 minutes. Drain, then remove the skins and seeds and chop the tomato flesh into cubes.

4 Add the tomatoes and oregano to the peppers and onion and season to taste with salt and pepper. Cover the pan and bring to the boil. Simmer gently for about 30 minutes, or until tender, adding the chicken or vegetable stock halfway through the cooking time.

5 Garnish with sprigs of oregano and serve hot with plenty of freshly baked focaccia bread or alternatively lightly toast slices of flat bread and pile a spoonful of peperonata on to each plate.

INGREDIENTS
Serves 4

2 green peppers
1 red pepper
1 yellow pepper
1 orange pepper
1 onion, peeled
2 garlic cloves, peeled
2 tbsp olive oil
4 very ripe tomatoes
1 tbsp freshly chopped oregano
salt and freshly ground black
  pepper
150 ml/¼ pint light chicken or
  vegetable stock
sprigs of fresh oregano, to garnish
focaccia (see recipe p. 46) or flat
  bread, to serve

Tasty Tip

Serve the peperonata cold as part of an antipasti platter.
Some good accompaniments would be marinated olives,
sun-dried or semi-dried marinated tomatoes, sliced salamis
and other cold meats, and plenty of Italian bread.

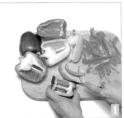

Wild Garlic Mushrooms with Pizza Breadsticks

1 Preheat oven to 240°C/ 475°F/Gas Mark 9, 15 minutes before baking. Place the dried yeast in the warm water for 10 minutes. Place the flour in a large bowl and gradually blend in the olive oil, salt and the dissolved yeast.

2 Knead on a lightly floured surface to form a smooth and pliable dough. Cover with clingfilm and leave in a warm place for 15 minutes to allow the dough to rise, then roll out again and cut into sticks of equal length. Cover and leave to rise again for 10 minutes. Brush with the olive oil, sprinkle with salt and bake in the preheated oven for 10 minutes.

3 Pour 3 tablespoons of the oil into a frying pan and add the crushed garlic. Cook over a very low heat, stirring well for 3–4 minutes to flavour the oil.

4 Cut the wild mushrooms into bite-sized slices if very large, then add to the pan. Season well with salt and pepper and cook very gently for 6–8 minutes, or until tender.

5 Whisk the fresh herbs, the remaining olive oil and lemon juice together. Pour over the mushrooms and heat through. Season to taste and place on individual serving dishes. Serve with the pizza breadsticks.

INGREDIENTS
Serves 6

FOR THE BREADSTICKS:
7 g/¼ oz dried yeast
250 ml/8 fl oz warm water
400 g/14 oz strong, plain flour
2 tbsp olive oil
1 tsp salt

9 tbsp olive oil
4 garlic cloves, peeled and crushed
450 g/1 lb mixed wild mushrooms, wiped and dried
salt and freshly ground black pepper
1 tbsp freshly chopped parsley
1 tbsp freshly chopped basil
1 tsp fresh oregano leaves
juice of 1 lemon

Helpful Hint

Never clean mushrooms under running water. Mushrooms absorb liquid very easily and then release it again during cooking, making the dish watery. When using wild mushrooms, wipe with a damp cloth or use a soft brush to remove any grit. Cut off the bases of stems to remove dirt.

Hot Tiger Prawns with Parma Ham

1 Preheat oven to 180°C/ 350°F/Gas Mark 4. Slice the cucumber and tomatoes thinly, then arrange on 4 large plates and reserve. Peel the prawns, leaving the tail shell intact and remove the thin black vein running down the back.

2 Whisk together 4 tablespoons of the olive oil, garlic and chopped parsley in a small bowl and season to taste with plenty of salt and pepper. Add the prawns to the mixture and stir until they are well coated. Remove the prawns, then wrap each one in a piece of Parma ham and secure with a cocktail stick.

3 Place the prepared prawns on a lightly oiled baking sheet or dish with the slices of bread and cook in the preheated oven for 5 minutes.

4 Remove the prawns from the oven and spoon the wine over the prawns and bread. Return to the oven and cook for a further 10 minutes until piping hot.

5 Carefully remove the cocktail sticks and arrange 3 prawn rolls on each slice of bread. Place on top of the sliced cucumber and tomatoes and serve immediately.

INGREDIENTS
Serves 4

½ cucumber, peeled if preferred
4 ripe tomatoes
12 raw tiger prawns
6 tbsp olive oil
4 garlic cloves, peeled and crushed
4 tbsp freshly chopped parsley
salt and freshly ground black
  pepper
6 slices of Parma ham, cut in half
4 slices flat Italian bread
4 tbsp dry white wine

Helpful Hint
The black intestinal vein needs to be removed from raw prawns because it can cause a bitter flavour. Remove the shell, then using a small, sharp knife, make a cut along the centre back of the prawn and open out the flesh. Using the tip of the knife, remove the thread that lies along the length of the prawn and discard.

Mozzarella Parcels with Cranberry Relish

1 Slice the mozzarella thinly, remove the crusts from the bread and make sandwiches with the bread and cheese. Cut into 5 cm/2 inch squares and squash them quite flat. Season the eggs with salt and pepper, then soak the bread in the seasoned egg for 1 minute on each side until well coated.

2 Heat the oil to 190°C/375°F and deep-fry the bread squares for 1–2 minutes, or until they are crisp and golden brown. Drain on absorbent kitchen paper

and keep warm while the cranberry relish is prepared.

3 Place the cranberries, orange juice, rind, sugar and port into a small saucepan and add 5 tablespoons of water. Bring to the boil, then simmer for 10 minutes, or until the cranberries have 'popped'. Sweeten with a little more sugar if necessary.

4 Arrange the mozzarella parcels on individual serving plates. Serve with a little of the cranberry relish.

INGREDIENTS
Serves 6

125 g/4 oz mozzarella cheese
8 slices of thin white bread
2 medium eggs, beaten
salt and freshly ground black pepper
300 ml/½ pint olive oil

FOR THE RELISH:

125 g/4 oz cranberries
2 tbsp fresh orange juice
grated rind of 1 small orange
50 g/2 oz soft light brown sugar
1 tbsp port

Helpful Hint

Frying in oil that is not hot enough causes food to absorb more oil than it would if fried at the correct temperature. To test the temperature of the oil without a thermometer, drop a cube of bread into the frying pan. If the bread browns in 30 seconds the oil is at the right temperature. If it does not, try again in a couple of minutes or increase the heat. If the bread goes very dark, reduce the temperature under the pan and add about 150 ml/¼ pint of cold oil and test again.

Fresh Tagliatelle with Courgettes

1 Sift the flour and salt into a large bowl, make a well in the centre and add the eggs and yolk, 1 tablespoon of oil with 1 teaspoon of water. Gradually mix to form a soft but not sticky dough, adding a little more flour or water as necessary. Turn out on to a lightly floured surface and knead for 5 minutes, or until smooth and elastic. Wrap in clingfilm and leave to rest at room temperature for about 30 minutes.

2 Divide the dough into 8 pieces. Feed a piece of dough through a pasta machine. Gradually decrease the settings on the rollers, feeding the pasta through each time, until the sheet is very long and thin. If the pasta seems sticky, dust the work surface and both sides of the pasta generously with flour. Cut in half crosswise and hang over a clean pole. Repeat with the remaining dough. Leave to dry for about 5 minutes. Feed each

sheet through the tagliatelle cutter, hanging the cut pasta over the pole. Leave to dry for a further 5 minutes. Wind a handful of pasta strands into nests and leave on a floured tea towel. Repeat with the remaining dough and leave to dry for 5 minutes.

3 Cook the pasta in plenty of salted boiling water for 2–3 minutes, or until 'al dente'.

4 Meanwhile, heat the remaining oil in a large frying pan and add the courgettes, garlic, chilli and lemon zest. Cook over a medium heat for 3–4 minutes, or until the courgettes are lightly golden and tender.

5 Drain the pasta thoroughly, reserving 2 tablespoons of the cooking water. Add the pasta to the courgettes with the basil and seasoning. Mix well, adding the reserved cooking water. Serve with the Parmesan cheese.

INGREDIENTS
Serves 4–6

225 g /8 oz strong plain bread flour or type 00 pasta flour, plus extra for rolling
1 tsp salt
2 medium eggs
1 medium egg yolk
3 tbsp extra virgin olive oil
2 small courgettes, halved lengthwise and thinly sliced
2 garlic cloves, peeled and thinly sliced
large pinch chilli flakes
zest of ½ lemon
1 tbsp freshly shredded basil
salt and freshly ground black pepper
freshly grated Parmesan cheese, to serve

Helpful Hint

Once made and shaped into nests, the pasta can be stored in an airtight container for 1–2 weeks.

Beetroot Ravioli
with Dill Cream Sauce

1 Make the pasta dough according to the recipe on page 70. Wrap in clingfilm and leave to rest for 30 minutes.

2 Heat the olive oil in a large frying pan, add the onion and caraway seeds and cook over a medium heat for 5 minutes, or until the onion is softened and lightly golden. Stir in the beetroot and cook for 5 minutes.

3 Blend the beetroot mixture in a food processor until smooth, then allow to cool. Stir in the ricotta cheese, breadcrumbs, egg yolk and Parmesan cheese. Season the filling to taste with salt and pepper and reserve.

4 Divide the pasta dough into 8 pieces. Roll out as for tagliatelle, but do not cut the sheets in half. Lay 1 sheet on a floured surface and place 5 heaped teaspoons of the filling 2.5 cm/1 inch apart.

5 Dampen around the heaps of filling and lay a second sheet of pasta over the top. Press around the heaps to seal.

6 Cut into squares using a pastry wheel or sharp knife. Put the filled pasta shapes on to a floured tea towel.

7 Bring a large pan of lightly salted water to a rolling boil. Drop the ravioli into the boiling water, return to the boil and cook for 3–4 minutes, until 'al dente'.

8 Meanwhile, heat the walnut oil in a small pan then add the chopped dill and green peppercorns. Remove from the heat, stir in the crème fraîche and season well. Drain the cooked pasta thoroughly and toss with the sauce. Tip into warmed serving dishes and serve immediately.

INGREDIENTS
Serves 4–6

fresh pasta (see Fresh Tagliatelle with Courgettes, page 70)
1 tbsp olive oil
1 small onion, peeled and finely chopped
½ tsp caraway seeds
175 g/6 oz cooked beetroot, chopped
175 g/6 oz ricotta cheese
25 g/1 oz fresh white breadcrumbs
1 medium egg yolk
2 tbsp grated Parmesan cheese
salt and freshly ground black pepper
4 tbsp walnut oil
4 tbsp freshly chopped dill
1 tbsp green peppercorns, drained and roughly chopped
6 tbsp crème fraîche

Gnocchi with Grilled Cherry Tomato Sauce

1 Preheat the grill just before required. Bring a large pan of salted water to the boil, add the potatoes and cook for 20–25 minutes until tender. Drain. Leave until cool enough to handle but still hot, then peel them and place in a large bowl. Mash until smooth then work in the egg, salt and enough of the flour to form a soft dough.

2 With floured hands, roll a spoonful of the dough into a small ball. Flatten the ball slightly on to the back of a large fork, then roll it off the fork to make a little ridged dumpling. Place each gnocchi on to a floured tea towel as you work.

3 Place the tomatoes in a flameproof shallow dish.

Add the garlic, lemon zest, herbs and olive oil. Season to taste with salt and pepper and sprinkle over the sugar. Cook under the pre-heated grill for 10 minutes, or until the tomatoes are charred and tender, stirring once or twice.

4 Meanwhile, bring a large pan of lightly salted water to the boil then reduce to a steady simmer. Dropping in 6–8 gnocchi at a time, cook in batches for 3–4 minutes, or until they begin bobbing up to the surface. Remove with a slotted spoon and drain well on absorbent kitchen paper before transferring to a warmed serving dish; cover with foil. Toss the cooked gnocchi with the tomato sauce. Serve immediately with a little grated Parmesan cheese.

INGREDIENTS
Serves 4

450 g / 1 lb floury potatoes, unpeeled
1 medium egg
1 tsp salt
75–90 g / 3–3½ oz plain flour
450 g / 1 lb mixed red and orange cherry tomatoes, halved lengthways
2 garlic cloves, peeled and finely sliced
zest of ½ lemon, finely grated
1 tbsp freshly chopped thyme
1 tbsp freshly chopped basil
2 tbsp extra virgin olive oil, plus extra for drizzling
salt and freshly ground black pepper
pinch of sugar
freshly grated Parmesan cheese, to serve

Helpful Hint

When cooking the gnocchi use a very large pan with at least 1.7 litres/3 pints of water to give them plenty of room so that they do not stick together.

Spinach & Ricotta Gnocchi with Butter & Parmesan

1 Squeeze the excess moisture from the spinach and chop finely. Blend in a food processor with the ricotta cheese, eggs, Parmesan cheese, seasoning and 1 tablespoon of the basil until smooth. Scrape into a bowl then add sufficient flour to form a soft, slightly sticky dough.

2 Bring a large pan of salted water to a rolling boil. Transfer the spinach mixture to a piping bag fitted with a large plain nozzle. As soon as the water is boiling, pipe 10–12 short lengths of the mixture into the water, using a sharp knife to cut the gnocchi as you go.

3 Bring the water back to the boil and cook the gnocchi for 3–4 minutes, or until they begin to rise to the surface. Remove with a slotted spoon, drain on absorbent kitchen paper and transfer to a warmed serving dish. Cook the gnocchi in batches if necessary.

4 Melt the butter in a small frying pan and when foaming add the garlic and remaining basil. Remove from the heat and immediately pour over the cooked gnocchi. Season well with salt and pepper and serve immediately with extra grated Parmesan cheese.

INGREDIENTS
Serves 2–4

125 g/4 oz frozen leaf spinach, thawed
225 g/8 oz ricotta cheese
2 small eggs, lightly beaten
50 g/2 oz freshly grated Parmesan cheese
salt and freshly ground black pepper
2 tbsp freshly chopped basil
50 g/2 oz plain flour
50 g/2 oz unsalted butter
2 garlic cloves, peeled and crushed
Parmesan cheese shavings, to serve

Food Fact

Ricotta is a crumbly, soft white cheese made from ewes' milk whey, a by-product from the manufacture of Pecorino Romano cheese. The curd is compacted so that the cheese can be cut with a knife. It can be eaten by itself, but normally it is used in dishes such as cheesecake.

Tagliatelle with Brown Butter, Asparagus & Parmesan

1 If using fresh pasta, prepare the dough according to the recipe on page 16. Cut into tagliatelle, wind into nests and reserve on a floured tea towel until ready to cook.

2 Bring a pan of lightly salted water to the boil. Add the asparagus and cook for 1 minute. Drain immediately, refresh under cold running water and drain again. Pat dry and reserve.

3 Melt the butter in a large frying pan, then add the garlic and hazelnuts and cook over a medium heat until the butter turns golden. Immediately remove from the heat and add the parsley, chives and asparagus. Leave for 2–3 minutes, until the asparagus is heated through.

4 Meanwhile, bring a large pan of lightly salted water to a rolling boil, then add the pasta nests. Cook until 'al dente': 2–3 minutes for fresh pasta and according to the packet instructions for dried pasta. Drain the pasta thoroughly and return to the pan. Add the asparagus mixture and toss together. Season to taste with salt and pepper and tip into a warmed serving dish. Serve immediately with grated Parmesan cheese.

INGREDIENTS
Serves 6

fresh pasta (see Fresh Tagliatelle
   with Courgettes, page 70) or
   450 g/1 lb dried tagliatelle, such
   as the white and green variety
350 g/12 oz asparagus, trimmed
   and cut into short lengths
75 g/3 oz unsalted butter
1 garlic clove, peeled and sliced
25 g/1 oz flaked hazelnuts or
   whole hazelnuts, roughly
   chopped
1 tbsp freshly chopped parsley
1 tbsp freshly snipped chives
salt and freshly ground black
   pepper
50 g/2 oz freshly grated
   Parmesan cheese, to serve

Food Fact

Asparagus is available all year round, but is at its best during May and June. If you buy loose asparagus, rather than pre-packed, choose stems of similar thickness so they will all cook in the same time. It is best to buy them no more than a day before using, but if you need to, you can keep stems fresh by standing them in a little water.

Pasta with Raw Fennel, Tomato & Red Onions

1 Trim the fennel and slice thinly. Stack the slices and cut into sticks, then cut crosswise again into fine dice. Deseed the tomatoes and chop them finely. Peel and finely chop or crush the garlic. Peel and finely chop or grate the onion.

2 Stack the basil leaves then roll up tightly. Slice crosswise into fine shreds. Finely chop the mint.

3 Place the chopped vegetables and herbs in a medium bowl. Add the olive oil and lemon juice and mix together. Season well with salt and pepper then leave for 30 minutes to allow the flavours to develop.

4 Bring a large pan of salted water to a rolling boil. Add the pasta and cook according to the packet instructions, or until 'al dente'.

5 Drain the cooked pasta thoroughly. Transfer to a warmed serving dish, pour over the vegetable mixture and toss. Serve with the grated Parmesan cheese and extra olive oil to drizzle over.

INGREDIENTS
Serves 6

1 fennel bulb
700 g / 1½ lb tomatoes
1 garlic clove
¼ small red onion
small handful fresh basil
small handful fresh mint
100 ml / 3½ fl oz extra virgin
  olive oil, plus extra to serve
juice of 1 lemon
salt and freshly ground black
  pepper
450 g / 1 lb penne or pennette
freshly grated Parmesan cheese,
  to serve

Food Fact
Fennel is a greenish-white bulbous vegetable that has a distinctive aniseed flavour. It is also known as Florence fennel to distinguish it from the herb. When buying fennel, choose a bulb that is well-rounded and as white as possible; the darker green ones may be bitter. Trim off the feathery leaves, chop them finely and use as a garnish.

Helpful Hint
The vegetables used in this dish are not cooked, but are tossed with the hot pasta. It is important, therefore, that they are chopped finely.

Spaghetti with Fresh Tomatoes, Chilli & Potatoes

1 Preheat the grill to high 5 minutes before using. Cook the potatoes in plenty of boiling water until tender but firm. Allow to cool, then peel and cut into cubes.

2 Blend the garlic, basil and 4 tablespoons of the olive oil in a blender or food processor until the basil is finely chopped, then reserve.

3 Place the tomatoes, basil and oil mixture in a small bowl, add the chilli and season with salt and pepper to taste. Mix together and reserve the sauce.

4 Bring a large pan of salted water to a rolling boil, add the spaghetti and cook according to the packet instructions, or until 'al dente'.

5 Meanwhile, toss the potato cubes with the remaining olive oil and transfer to a baking sheet. Place the potatoes under the preheated grill until they are crisp and golden, turning once or twice, then drain on absorbent kitchen paper.

6 Drain the pasta thoroughly and transfer to a warmed shallow serving bowl. Add the tomato sauce and the hot potatoes. Toss well and adjust the seasoning to taste. Serve immediately with the grated Parmesan cheese, if using.

INGREDIENTS
Serves 6

2 medium potatoes, unpeeled
3 garlic cloves, peeled and crushed
1 small bunch basil, roughly chopped
6 tbsp olive oil
4 large ripe plum tomatoes, skinned, seeded and chopped
1 small red chilli, deseeded and finely chopped
salt and freshly ground black pepper
450 g / 1 lb spaghetti
4 tbsp freshly grated Parmesan cheese, to serve (optional)

Pasta Genovese with Pesto, Green Beans & Potatoes

1 Put the basil leaves, garlic, pine nuts and Parmesan cheese into a food processor and blend until finely chopped. Transfer the mixture in to a small bowl and stir in the olive oil. Season the pesto to taste with salt and pepper and reserve.

2 Bring a pan of salted water to boil and cook the potatoes for 12–14 minutes, or until tender. About 4 minutes before the end of the cooking time, add the beans. Drain well and refresh under cold water. Reserve the beans and slice the potatoes thickly, or halve them if small.

3 Heat the olive oil in a frying pan and add the potatoes. Fry over a medium heat for 5 minutes, or until golden. Add the reserved beans and pesto and cook for a further 2 minutes.

4 Meanwhile, bring a large pan of lightly salted water to a rolling boil. Cook the pasta shapes according to the packet instructions, or until 'al dente'. Drain thoroughly, return to the pan and add the pesto mixture. Toss well and heat through for 1–2 minutes. Tip into a warmed serving bowl and serve immediately with Parmesan cheese.

INGREDIENTS
Serves 6

40 g/1½ oz basil leaves
2 garlic cloves, peeled and crushed
2 tbsp pine nuts, lightly toasted
25 g/1 oz freshly grated Parmesan cheese
75 ml/3 fl oz extra virgin olive oil
salt and freshly ground pepper
175 g/6 oz new potatoes, scrubbed
125 g/4 oz fine French beans, trimmed
2 tbsp olive oil
450 g/1 lb pasta shapes
extra freshly grated Parmesan cheese, to serve

Tasty Tip

Classic pesto, as used in this recipe, is always made with fresh basil and pine nuts, but other herb variations work equally well. For a change try a coriander and chilli pesto, replacing the basil with fresh coriander leaves and adding a deseeded and finely chopped red chilli, or try an almond and mint pesto, replacing the pine nuts with blanched almonds and the basil with equal amounts of fresh mint and fresh parsley leaves.

Tiny Pasta with Fresh Herb Sauce

1 Bring a large pan of lightly salted water to a rolling boil. Add the pasta and cook according to the packet instructions, or until 'al dente'.

2 Meanwhile, place all the herbs, the lemon zest, olive oil, garlic and chilli flakes in a heavy-based pan. Heat gently for 2–3 minutes, or until the herbs turn bright green and become very fragrant. Remove from the heat and season to taste with salt and pepper.

3 Drain the pasta thoroughly, reserving 2–3 tablespoons of the cooking water. Transfer the pasta to a large warmed bowl.

4 Pour the heated herb mixture over the pasta and toss together until thoroughly mixed. Check and adjust the seasoning, adding a little of the pasta cooking water if the pasta mixture seems a bit dry. Transfer to warmed serving dishes and serve immediately with grated Parmesan cheese.

INGREDIENTS
Serves 6

375 g/13 oz tripolini (small bows with rounded ends) or small farfalle
2 tbsp freshly chopped flat-leaf parsley
2 tbsp freshly chopped basil
1 tbsp freshly snipped chives
1 tbsp freshly chopped chervil
1 tbsp freshly chopped tarragon
1 tbsp freshly chopped sage
1 tbsp freshly chopped oregano
1 tbsp freshly chopped marjoram
1 tbsp freshly chopped thyme
1 tbsp freshly chopped rosemary
finely grated zest of 1 lemon
75 ml/3 fl oz extra virgin olive oil
2 garlic cloves, peeled and finely chopped
½ tsp dried chilli flakes
salt and freshly ground black pepper
freshly grated Parmesan cheese, to serve

Helpful Hint

Look out for packets of mixed fresh herbs in the supermarket, if you do not want to buy individual packets or bunches of all the herbs used in this fresh and vibrant sauce. If you cannot find all the herbs listed, you can increase the quantity of some of them as a substitute for others not being used. Do not add more than 1 tablespoon each of thyme or rosemary though, or their flavour may overpower the sauce.

Louisiana Prawns & Fettuccine

1 Heat 2 tablespoons of the olive oil in a large saucepan and add the reserved prawn shells and heads. Fry over a high heat for 2–3 minutes, until the shells turn pink and are lightly browned. Add half the shallots, half the garlic, half the basil and the carrot, onion, celery, parsley and thyme. Season lightly with salt, pepper and cayenne and sauté for 2–3 minutes, stirring often.

2 Pour in the wine and stir, scraping the pan well. Bring to the boil and simmer for 1 minute, then add the tomatoes. Cook for a further 3–4 minutes then pour in 200 ml/7 fl oz water. Bring to the boil, lower the heat and simmer for about 30 minutes, stirring often and using a wooden spoon to mash the prawn shells in order to release as much flavour as possible into the sauce. Lower the heat if the sauce is reducing very quickly.

3 Strain through a sieve, pressing well to extract as much liquid as possible; there should be about 450 ml/¾ pint. Pour the liquid into a clean pan and bring to the boil, then lower the heat and simmer gently until the liquid is reduced by about half.

4 Heat the remaining olive oil over a high heat in a clean frying pan and add the peeled prawns. Season lightly and add the lemon juice. Cook for 1 minute, lower the heat and add the remaining shallots and garlic. Cook for 1 minute. Add the sauce and adjust the seasoning.

5 Meanwhile, bring a large pan of lightly salted water to a rolling boil and add the fettuccine. Cook according to the packet instructions, or until 'al dente', and drain thoroughly. Transfer to a warmed serving dish. Add the sauce and toss well. Garnish with the remaining basil and serve immediately.

INGREDIENTS
Serves 4

4 tbsp olive oil
450 g/1 lb raw tiger prawns, washed and peeled, shells and heads reserved
2 shallots, peeled and finely chopped
4 garlic cloves, peeled and finely chopped
large handful fresh basil leaves
1 carrot, peeled and finely chopped
1 onion, peeled and finely chopped
1 celery stick, trimmed and finely chopped
2–3 sprigs fresh parsley
2–3 sprigs fresh thyme
salt and freshly ground black pepper
pinch cayenne pepper
175 ml/6 fl oz dry white wine
450 g/1 lb ripe tomatoes, roughly chopped
juice of ½ lemon, or to taste
350 g/12 oz fettuccine

Salmon & Roasted Red Pepper Pasta

1 Preheat the grill to high. Place the salmon in a bowl. Add the shallots, parsley, 3 tablespoons of the olive oil and the lemon juice. Reserve.

2 Brush the pepper quarters with a little olive oil. Cook them under the preheated grill for 8–10 minutes, or until the skins have blackened and the flesh is tender. Place the peppers in a plastic bag until cool enough to handle. When cooled, peel the peppers and cut into strips. Put the strips into a bowl with the basil and the remaining olive oil and reserve.

3 Toast the breadcrumbs until dry and lightly browned then toss with the extra virgin olive oil and reserve.

4 Bring a large pan of salted water to a rolling boil and add the pasta. Cook according to the packet instructions, or until 'al dente'.

5 Meanwhile, transfer the peppers and their marinade to a hot frying pan. Add the spring onions and cook for 1–2 minutes, or until they have just softened. Add the salmon and its marinade and cook for a further 1–2 minutes, or until the salmon is just cooked. Season to taste with salt and pepper.

6 Drain the pasta thoroughly and transfer to a warmed serving bowl. Add the salmon mixture and toss gently. Garnish with the breadcrumbs and serve immediately.

INGREDIENTS
Serves 6

225 g/8 oz skinless and boneless salmon fillet, thinly sliced
3 shallots, peeled and finely chopped
1 tbsp freshly chopped parsley
6 tbsp olive oil
juice of ½ lemon
2 red peppers, deseeded and quartered
handful fresh basil leaves, shredded
50 g/2 oz fresh breadcrumbs
4 tbsp extra virgin olive oil
450 g/1 lb fettuccine or linguine
6 spring onions, trimmed and shredded
salt and freshly ground black pepper

Food Fact

Olive oil is graded according to aroma, flavour, colour and acidity - virgin olive oil has less than 2 per cent acidity, extra virgin olive oil less than 1 per cent.

Spaghettini with Peas, Spring Onions & Mint

1 Soak the saffron in 2 tablespoons hot water while you prepare the sauce. Shell the peas if using fresh ones.

2 Heat 50 g/2 oz of the butter in a medium frying pan, add the spring onions and a little salt and cook over a low heat for 2–3 minutes, or until the onions are softened. Add the garlic, then the peas and 100 ml/3 ½ fl oz water. Bring to the boil and cook for 5–6 minutes, or until the peas are just tender. Stir in the mint and keep warm.

3 Blend the remaining butter and the saffron water in a large warmed serving bowl and reserve.

4 Meanwhile, bring a large pan of lightly salted water to a rolling boil and add the spaghettini. Cook according to the packet instructions, or until 'al dente'.

5 Drain thoroughly, reserving 2–3 tablespoons of the pasta cooking water. Tip into a warmed serving bowl, add the pea sauce and toss together gently. Season to taste with salt and pepper. Serve immediately with extra black pepper and grated Parmesan cheese.

INGREDIENTS
Serves 6

pinch saffron strands
700 g/1½ lb fresh peas or
    350 g/12 oz frozen petit
    pois, thawed
75 g/3 oz unsalted butter,
    softened
6 spring onions, trimmed and
    finely sliced
salt and freshly ground black
    pepper
1 garlic clove, peeled and finely
    chopped
2 tbsp freshly chopped mint
1 tbsp freshly snipped chives
450 g/1 lb spaghettini
freshly grated Parmesan cheese,
    to serve

Helpful Hint

To develop the full flavour and deep golden colour of the saffron, it should be soaked for at least 20 minutes, so do this well before you start cooking. Saffron is one of the few spices that can be kept for several years, but you must store it in an airtight container, away from light.

Fusilli with Spicy Tomato & Chorizo Sauce with Roasted Peppers

1 Preheat the grill to high. Brush the pepper quarters with 1 tablespoon of the olive oil, then cook under the pre-heated grill, turning once, for 8–10 minutes, or until the skins have blackened and the flesh is tender. Place the peppers in a plastic bag until cool enough to handle. When cooled, peel the peppers, slice very thinly and reserve.

2 Heat the remaining oil in a frying pan and add the chorizo. Cook over a medium heat for 3–4 minutes, or until starting to brown. Add the garlic and chilli flakes and cook for a further 2–3 minutes.

3 Add the tomatoes, season lightly with salt and pepper then cook gently for about 5 minutes, or until the tomatoes have broken down. Lower the heat and cook for a further 10–15 minutes, or until the sauce has thickened. Add the peppers and heat gently for 1-2 minutes. Adjust the seasoning to taste.

4 Meanwhile, bring a large pan of lightly salted water to a rolling boil. Add the fusilli and cook according to the packet instructions, or until 'al dente'. Drain thoroughly and transfer to a warmed serving dish. Pour over the sauce, sprinkle with basil and serve with Parmesan cheese.

INGREDIENTS
Serves 6

4 tbsp olive oil
1 red pepper, deseeded and
    quartered
1 yellow pepper, deseeded and
    quartered
175 g/6 oz chorizo (outer skin
    removed), roughly chopped
2 garlic cloves, peeled and finely
    chopped
large pinch chilli flakes
700 g/1½ lb ripe tomatoes,
    skinned and roughly chopped
salt and freshly ground black
    pepper
450 g/1 lb fusilli
basil leaves, to garnish
freshly grated Parmesan cheese, to
    serve

Food Fact

There are two types of chorizo sausage; the dried, salami-type, usually about 5 cm/2 in in diameter, and the slightly softer, semi-dried chorizo, which look like short fat sausages. The latter type is preferable for this recipe. Both types of chorizo are pork sausages containing chilli and paprika, which gives them a vibrant orange-red colour.

Pasta with Walnut Sauce

1 Place the toasted walnuts in a blender or food processor with the chopped spring onions, one of the garlic cloves and parsley or basil. Blend to a fairly smooth paste, then gradually add 3 tablespoons of the olive oil, until it is well mixed into the paste. Season the walnut paste to taste with salt and pepper and reserve.

2 Bring a large pan of lightly salted water to a rolling boil. Add the broccoli, return to the boil and cook for 2 minutes. Remove the broccoli, using a slotted draining spoon and refresh under cold running water. Drain again and pat dry on absorbent kitchen paper.

3 Bring the water back to a rolling boil. Add the pasta and cook according to the packet instructions, or until 'al dente'.

4 Meanwhile, heat the remaining oil in a frying pan. Add the remaining garlic and chilli. Cook gently for 2 minutes, or until softened. Add the broccoli and walnut paste. Cook for a further 3–4 minutes, or until heated through.

5 Drain the pasta thoroughly and transfer to a large warmed serving bowl. Pour over the walnut and broccoli sauce. Toss together, adjust the seasoning and serve immediately.

INGREDIENTS
Serves 4

50 g/2 oz walnuts, toasted
3 spring onions, trimmed and
  chopped
2 garlic cloves, peeled and sliced
1 tbsp freshly chopped parsley or
  basil
5 tbsp extra virgin olive oil
salt and freshly ground black
  pepper
450 g/1 lb broccoli, cut into
  florets
350 g/12 oz pasta shapes
1 red chilli, deseeded and finely
  chopped

Helpful Hint

There is no hard-and-fast rule about which shape of pasta to use with this recipe; it is really a matter of personal preference. Spirali have been used here, but rigatoni, farfalle, garganelle or pipe rigate would all work well, or you could choose flavoured pasta, such as tomato, or a wholewheat variety for a change.

Pasta & Bean Soup

1 Heat the olive oil in a heavy-based pan, add the celery and prosciutto and cook gently for 6–8 minutes, or until softened. Add the chopped chilli and potato cubes and cook for a further 10 minutes.

2 Add the garlic to the chilli and potato mixture and cook for 1 minute. Add the chopped tomatoes and simmer for 5 minutes. Stir in two-thirds of the beans, then pour in the chicken or vegetable stock and bring to the boil.

3 Add the pasta shapes to the soup stock and return it to

simmering point. Cook the pasta for about 10 minutes, or until 'al dente'.

4 Meanwhile, place the remaining beans in a food processor or blender and blend with enough of the soup stock to make a smooth, thinnish purée.

5 When the pasta is cooked, stir in the puréed beans with the torn basil. Season the soup to taste with salt and pepper. Ladle into serving bowls, garnish with shredded basil and serve immediately with plenty of crusty bread.

INGREDIENTS
Serves 4–6

3 tbsp olive oil
2 celery sticks, trimmed and finely chopped
100 g/3½ oz prosciutto or prosciutto di speck, cut in pieces
1 red chilli, deseeded and finely chopped
2 large potatoes, peeled and cut into 2.5 cm/1 in cubes
2 garlic cloves, peeled and finely chopped
3 ripe plum tomatoes, skinned and chopped
1 x 400 g cans borlotti beans, drained and rinsed
1 litre/1¾ pints chicken or vegetable stock
100 g/3½ oz pasta shapes
large handful basil leaves, torn
salt and freshly ground black pepper
shredded basil leaves, to garnish
crusty bread, to serve

Food Fact

Oval borlotti beans have red-streaked, pinkish-brown skin. They have a moist texture and a bitter-sweet flavour, which makes them excellent in soups. Other canned beans may be used if preferred. Try pinto beans, a smaller, paler version of the borlotti bean, or cannellini beans, which have a soft creamy texture.

Gnocchetti with Broccoli & Bacon Sauce

1 Bring a large pan of salted water to the boil. Add the broccoli florets and cook for about 8–10 minutes, or until very soft. Drain thoroughly, allow to cool slightly then chop finely and reserve.

2 Heat the olive oil in a heavy-based pan, add the pancetta or bacon and cook over a medium heat for 5 minutes, or until golden and crisp. Add the onion and cook for a further 5 minutes, or until soft and lightly golden. Add the garlic and cook for 1 minute.

3 Transfer the chopped broccoli to the bacon or pancetta mixture and pour in the milk. Bring slowly to the boil and simmer rapidly for about 15 minutes, or until reduced to a creamy texture.

4 Meanwhile, bring a large pan of lightly salted water to a rolling boil. Add the pasta and cook according to the packet instructions, or until 'al dente'.

5 Drain the pasta thoroughly, reserving a little of the cooking water. Add the pasta and the Parmesan cheese to the broccoli mixture. Toss, adding enough of the reserved cooking water to make a creamy sauce. Season to taste with salt and pepper. Serve immediately with extra Parmesan cheese.

INGREDIENTS
Serves 6

450 g / 1 lb broccoli florets
4 tbsp olive oil
50 g / 2 oz pancetta or smoked bacon, finely chopped
1 small onion, peeled and finely chopped
3 garlic cloves, peeled and sliced
200 ml / 7 fl oz milk
450 g / 1 lb gnocchetti (little elongated ribbed shells)
50 g / 2 oz freshly grated Parmesan cheese, plus extra to serve
salt and freshly ground black pepper

Food Fact

Pancetta is an Italian streaky bacon that may be either smoked or unsmoked. You can buy it sliced or in a piece, but it is often sold pre-packed, cut into tiny cubes ready for cooking. Thickly cut, rindless smoked streaky bacon makes a good alternative.

Penne with Artichokes, Bacon & Mushrooms

1 Heat the olive oil in a frying pan and add the pancetta or bacon and the onion. Cook over a medium heat for 8–10 minutes, or until the bacon is crisp and the onion is just golden. Add the mushrooms and garlic and cook for a further 5 minutes, or until softened.

2 Add the artichoke hearts to the mushroom mixture and cook for 3–4 minutes. Pour in the wine, bring to the boil then simmer rapidly until the liquid is reduced and syrupy.

3 Pour in the chicken stock, bring to the boil then simmer rapidly for about 5 minutes, or until slightly reduced. Reduce the heat slightly, then slowly stir in the double cream and Parmesan cheese. Season the sauce to taste with salt and pepper.

4 Meanwhile, bring a large pan of lightly salted water to a rolling boil. Add the pasta and cook according to the packet instructions, or until 'al dente'.

5 Drain the pasta thoroughly and transfer to a large warmed serving dish. Pour over the sauce and toss together. Garnish with shredded basil and serve with extra Parmesan cheese.

INGREDIENTS
Serves 6

2 tbsp olive oil

75 g/3 oz smoked bacon or pancetta, chopped

1 small onion, peeled and finely sliced

125 g/4 oz chestnut mushrooms, wiped and sliced

2 garlic cloves, peeled and finely chopped

400 g/14 oz can artichoke hearts, drained and halved or quartered if large

100 ml/3½ fl oz dry white wine

100 ml/3½ fl oz chicken stock

3 tbsp double cream

50 g/2 oz freshly grated Parmesan cheese, plus extra to serve

salt and freshly ground black pepper

450 g/1 lb penne

shredded basil leaves, to garnish

Tasty Tip

Brown-capped chestnut mushrooms are similar in appearance to cultivated button mushrooms, but they have a rich orange-brown colour and a slightly stronger, nutty flavour. Tiny, baby chestnut mushrooms are sometimes available and could be used whole or halved in this recipe.

Fettuccine with Wild Mushrooms & Prosciutto

1 Place the dried mushrooms in a small bowl and pour over the hot chicken stock. Leave to soak for 15–20 minutes, or until the mushrooms have softened.

2 Meanwhile, heat the olive oil in a large frying pan. Add the onion and cook for 5 minutes over a medium heat, or until softened. Add the garlic and cook for 1 minute, then add the prosciutto and cook for a further minute.

3 Drain the dried mushrooms, reserving the soaking liquid. Roughly chop and add to the frying pan together with the fresh mushrooms. Cook over a high heat for 5 minutes, stirring often, or until softened. Strain the mushroom soaking liquid into the pan.

4 Meanwhile, bring a large pan of lightly salted water to a rolling boil. Add the pasta and cook according to the packet instructions, or until 'al dente'.

5 Stir the crème fraîche and chopped parsley into the mushroom mixture and heat through gently. Season to taste with salt and pepper. Drain the pasta well, transfer to a large warmed serving dish and pour over the sauce. Serve immediately with grated Parmesan cheese.

INGREDIENTS
Serves 6

15 g/½ oz dried porcini mushrooms
150 ml/¼ pint hot chicken stock
2 tbsp olive oil
1 small onion, peeled and finely chopped
2 garlic cloves, peeled and finely chopped
4 slices prosciutto, chopped or torn
225 g/8 oz mixed wild or cultivated mushrooms, wiped and sliced if necessary
450 g/1 lb fettuccine
3 tbsp crème fraîche
2 tbsp freshly chopped parsley
salt and freshly ground black pepper
freshly grated Parmesan cheese, to serve (optional)

Food Fact

Prosciutto is produced from pigs fed on whey, a by-product of the local Parmesan cheese industry. The ham is dry cured, then weighted to flatten it and give it a dense texture. The delicious flavour develops during the year it is allowed to mature. It is always served in paper-thin slices, either raw or lightly fried.

Tagliarini with Broad Beans, Saffron & Crème Fraîche

1 If using fresh broad beans, bring a pan of lightly salted water to the boil. Pod the beans and drop them into the boiling water for 1 minute. Drain and refresh under cold water. Drain again. Remove the outer skin of the beans and discard. If using thawed frozen broad beans, remove and discard the skins. Reserve the peeled beans.

2 Heat the olive oil in a saucepan. Add the peeled broad beans and the garlic and cook gently for 2–3 minutes. Stir in the basil, the crème fraîche

and the pinch of saffron strands and simmer for 1 minute.

3 Meanwhile, bring a large pan of lightly salted water to a rolling boil. Add the pasta and cook according to the packet instructions, or until 'al dente'. Drain the pasta well and add to the sauce. Toss together and season to taste with salt and pepper.

4 Transfer the pasta and sauce to a warmed serving dish. Sprinkle with snipped chives and serve immediately with Parmesan cheese.

INGREDIENTS
Serves 2–3

225 g/8 oz fresh young broad beans in pods or 100 g/3½ oz frozen broad beans, thawed
1 tbsp olive oil
1 garlic clove, peeled and chopped
small handful basil leaves, shredded
200 ml/7 fl oz crème fraîche
large pinch saffron strands
350 g/12 oz tagliarini
salt and freshly ground black pepper
1 tbsp freshly snipped chives
freshly grated Parmesan cheese, to serve

Helpful Hint

If you buy fresh broad beans in their pods (they are available from May to July), look for smooth, plump, bright green pods and use within two days of purchase; they should be cooked the same day as shelling. The skins on the beans become tougher as they age, so if the beans are very young and fresh, there is no need to peel them.

Linguine with Fennel, Crab & Chervil

1 Bring a large pan of lightly salted water to a rolling boil. Add the pasta and cook according to the packet instructions, or until 'al dente'.

2 Meanwhile, heat the butter in a large saucepan. Add the carrots, shallots, celery, fennel and three-quarters of the chopped spring onions. Cook the vegetables gently for 8–10 minutes, or until tender, stirring frequently and ensuring that they do not brown.

3 Add the double cream and chopped chervil to the vegetable mixture. Scrape the crab meat over the sauce, then stir to mix the sauce ingredients.

4 Season the sauce to taste with salt and pepper and stir in the lemon juice. Drain the pasta thoroughly and transfer to a large warmed serving dish. Pour over the sauce and toss. Garnish with extra chervil, the remaining spring onions and a sprig of dill. Serve immediately.

INGREDIENTS
Serves 6

450g/1 lb linguine
25 g/1 oz butter
2 carrots, peeled and finely diced
2 shallots, peeled and finely diced
*2 celery sticks, trimmed and
    finely diced*
*1 bulb fennel, trimmed and
    finely diced*
*6 spring onions, trimmed and
    finely chopped*
300 ml/½ pint double cream
3 tbsp freshly chopped chervil
1 large cooked crab
plus extra for garnish
salt and freshly ground pepper
juice of ½ lemon, or to taste
sprig of dill, to garnish

Helpful Hint

If you prefer to prepare a cooked crab yourself, start by twisting off the legs and claws, then cracking them open and removing the meat. Next, turn the crab on to its back and twist off the bony, pointed flap. Put the tip of a knife between the main shell and where the legs and claws were attached, twist the blade to lift up and remove, then scrape out the brown meat in the main shell. Pull away and discard the grey, soft gills. Split the body in half and, using a skewer, remove all the white meat from the cavities. An average-sized crab should produce about 225 g/8 oz of white and brown meat.

Pea & Prawn Risotto

1 Peel the prawns and reserve the heads and shells. Remove the black vein from the back of each prawn, then wash and dry on absorbent kitchen paper. Melt half the butter in a large frying pan, add the prawns' heads and shells and fry, stirring occasionally for 3–4 minutes, or until golden. Strain the butter, discard the heads and shells and return the butter to the pan.

2 Add a further 25 g/1 oz of butter to the pan and fry the onion and garlic for 5 minutes until softened, but not coloured. Add the rice and stir the grains in the butter for 1 minute, until they are coated

thoroughly. Add the white wine and boil rapidly until the wine is reduced by half.

3 Bring the stock to a gentle simmer, and add to the rice, a ladleful at a time. Stir constantly, adding the stock as it is absorbed, until the rice is creamy, but still has a bite in the centre.

4 Melt the remaining butter and stir-fry the prawns for 3–4 minutes. Stir into the rice, along with all the pan juices and the peas. Add the chopped mint and season to taste with salt and pepper. Cover the pan and leave the prawns to infuse for 5 minutes before serving.

INGREDIENTS
Serves 6

450 g/1 lb whole raw prawns
125 g/4 oz butter
1 red onion, peeled and chopped
4 garlic cloves, peeled and finely
   chopped
225 g/8 oz Arborio rice
150 ml/¼ pint dry white wine
1.1 litres/2 pints vegetable or fish
   stock
375 g/13 oz frozen peas
4 tbsp freshly chopped mint
salt and freshly ground black
   pepper

Tasty Tip

Frying the prawn shells and heads before cooking the dish adds a great deal of flavour to the rice. Alternatively, the shells and heads could be added to the stock and simmered for 10 minutes. Strain the stock, pressing the shells and heads well to extract the maximum flavour.

Stuffed Squid with Romesco Sauce

1 Preheat oven to 230°C/ 450°F/Gas Mark 8, 15 minutes before cooking. Clean the squid if necessary, rinse lightly, pat dry with absorbent kitchen paper and finely chop the tentacles.

2 Heat 2 tablespoons of the olive oil in a large non-stick frying pan and fry the pancetta for 5 minutes, or until crisp. Remove the pancetta and reserve. Add the tentacles, onion, 2 garlic cloves, thyme and sun-dried tomatoes to the oil remaining in the pan and cook gently for 5 minutes, or until softened.

3 Remove the pan from the heat and stir in the diced pancetta. Blend in a food processor if a smoother stuffing is preferred, then stir in the breadcrumbs, basil and lime juice. Season to taste with salt and pepper and reserve. Spoon the stuffing into the cavity of the squid and secure the tops with cocktail sticks.

4 Place the squid in a large roasting tin, and sprinkle over 2 tablespoons each of oil and water. Place in the preheated oven and cook for 20 minutes.

5 Heat the remaining oil in a saucepan and cook the remaining garlic for 3 minutes. Add the tomatoes, chilli flakes and oregano and simmer gently for 15 minutes before stirring in the red pepper. Cook gently for a further 5 minutes. Blend in a food processor to make a smooth sauce and season to taste. Pour the sauce over the squid and serve immediately with some assorted salad leaves.

INGREDIENTS
Serves 4

8 small squid, about 350 g/ 12 oz
5 tbsp olive oil
50 g/2 oz pancetta, diced
1 onion, peeled and chopped
3 garlic cloves, peeled and finely chopped
2 tsp freshly chopped thyme
50 g/2 oz sun-dried tomatoes in oil drained, and chopped
75 g/3 oz fresh white breadcrumbs
2 tbsp freshly chopped basil
juice of ½ lime
salt and freshly ground black pepper
2 vine-ripened tomatoes, peeled and finely chopped
pinch of dried chilli flakes
1 tsp dried oregano
1 large red pepper, skinned and chopped
assorted salad leaves, to serve

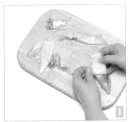

Scallops & Monkfish Kebabs with Fennel Sauce

1 Place the monkfish on a chopping board and remove the skin and the bone that runs down the centre of the tail and discard. Lightly rinse and pat dry with absorbent kitchen paper. Cut the 2 fillets into 12 equal-sized pieces and place in a shallow bowl.

2 Remove the scallops from their shells, if necessary, and clean thoroughly discarding the black vein. Rinse lightly and pat dry with absorbent kitchen paper. Put in the bowl with the fish.

3 Blend the 2 tablespoons of olive oil, the crushed garlic and a pinch of black pepper in a small bowl, then pour the mixture over the monkfish and scallops, making sure they are well coated. Cover lightly and leave to marinate in the refrigerator for at least 30 minutes, or longer if time permits. Spoon over the marinade occasionally.

4 Lightly crush the fennel seeds and chilli flakes in a pestle and mortar. Stir in the 4 tablespoons of olive oil and lemon juice and season to taste with salt and pepper. Cover and leave to infuse for 20 minutes.

5 Drain the monkfish and scallops, reserving the marinade and thread on to 4 skewers.

6 Spray a griddle pan with a fine spray of oil, then heat until almost smoking and cook the kebabs for 5–6 minutes, turning halfway through and brushing with the marinade throughout.

7 Brush the fennel slices with the fennel sauce and cook on the griddle for 1 minute on each side. Serve the fennel slices, topped with the kebabs and drizzled with the fennel sauce. Serve with a few assorted salad leaves.

INGREDIENTS
Serves 4

700 g/1½ lb monkfish tail
8 large fresh scallops
2 tbsp olive oil
1 garlic clove, peeled and crushed
freshly ground black pepper
1 fennel bulb, trimmed and thinly sliced
assorted salad leaves, to serve

FOR THE SAUCE:

2 tbsp fennel seeds
pinch of chilli flakes
4 tbsp olive oil
2 tsp lemon juice
salt and freshly ground black pepper

Red Pesto & Clam Spaghetti

1 To make the red pesto, place the garlic, pine nuts, basil leaves, sun-dried tomatoes and olive oil in a food processor and blend in short, sharp bursts until smooth. Scrape into a bowl, then stir in the Parmesan cheese and season to taste with salt and pepper. Cover and leave in the refrigerator until required.

2 Scrub the clams with a soft brush and remove any beards from the shells, discard any shells that are open or damaged. Wash in plenty of cold water then leave in a bowl covered with cold water in the refrigerator until required. Change the water frequently.

3 Heat the olive oil in a large saucepan and gently fry the garlic and onion for 5 minutes until softened, but not coloured. Add the wine and stock and bring to the boil. Add the clams, cover and cook for 3–4 minutes, or until the clams have opened.

4 Discard any clams that have not opened and stir in the red pesto sauce. Bring a large saucepan of lightly salted water to the boil and cook the spaghetti for 5–7 minutes, or until 'al dente'. Drain and return to the saucepan. Add the sauce to the spaghetti, mix well, then spoon into a serving dish and serve immediately.

INGREDIENTS
Serves 4

FOR THE RED PESTO:
2 garlic cloves, peeled and finely chopped
50 g/2 oz pine nuts
25 g/1 oz fresh basil leaves
4 sun-dried tomatoes in oil, drained
4 tbsp olive oil
4 tbsp Parmesan cheese, grated
salt and freshly ground black pepper

FOR THE CLAM SAUCE:
450 g/1 lb live clams, in their shells
1 tbsp olive oil
2 garlic cloves, peeled and crushed
1 small onion, peeled and chopped
5 tbsp medium dry white wine
150 ml/¼ pint fish or chicken stock
275 g/10 oz spaghetti

Tasty Tip
This dish looks particularly attractive with the clams left in their shells. If you prefer, you could remove the meat from the shells at the end of step 3, leaving just a few in for garnishing and stir back into the saucepan with the pasta.

Sardines in Vine Leaves

1 Preheat the grill and line the grill rack with tinfoil just before cooking. Cut 8 pieces of string about 25.5 cm/10 inches long, and leave to soak in cold water for about 10 minutes. Cover the vine leaves in almost boiling water. Leave for 20 minutes, then drain and rinse thoroughly. Pat the vine leaves dry with absorbent kitchen paper.

2 Trim the spring onions and finely chop, then place into a small bowl. With a balloon whisk beat in the olive oil, lime juice, oregano, mustard powder and season to taste with salt and pepper. Cover with clingfilm and leave in the refrigerator, until required. Stir the mixture before using.

3 Prepare the sardines, by making 2 slashes on both sides of each fish and brush with a little of the lime juice mixture. Place a bay leaf and a dill sprig inside each sardine cavity and wrap with 1–2 vine leaves, depending on size. Brush with the lime mixture and tie the vine leaves in place with string.

4 Grill the fish for 4–5 minutes on each side under a medium heat, brushing with a little more of the lime mixture if necessary. Leave the fish to rest, unwrap and discard the vine leaves. Garnish with lime wedges and sprigs of fresh dill and serve with the remaining lime mixture, olive salad and crusty bread.

INGREDIENTS
Serves 4

8–16 vine leaves in brine, drained
2 spring onions
6 tbsp olive oil
2 tbsp lime juice
2 tbsp freshly chopped oregano
1 tsp mustard powder
salt and freshly ground black pepper
8 sardines, cleaned
8 bay leaves
8 sprigs of fresh dill

TO GARNISH:
lime wedges
sprigs of fresh dill

TO SERVE:
olive salad
crusty bread

Helpful Hint

To clean sardines, first gut the fish. Insert a knife or point of a pair of scissors and make a cut along the belly. Remove the insides and discard. Wash the fish well. Remove the scales by gently rubbing your thumb along the fish from tail to head. Sardines have very delicate skin, so rub gently.

Parmesan & Garlic Lobster

1 Preheat oven to 180°C/ 350°F/Gas Mark 4, 10 minutes before cooking. Halve the lobster and crack the claws. Remove the gills, green sac behind the head and the black vein running down the body. Place the 2 lobster halves in a shallow ovenproof dish.

2 Melt the butter in a small saucepan and gently cook the garlic for 3 minutes, until softened. Add the flour and stir over a medium heat for 1 minute. Draw the saucepan off the heat then gradually stir in the milk, stirring until the sauce thickens. Return to the heat and cook for 2 minutes, stirring throughout until smooth and thickened. Stir in half the cheese and continue to cook for 1 minute, then season to taste with salt and pepper.

3 Pour the cheese sauce over the lobster halves and sprinkle with the remaining Parmesan cheese. Bake in the preheated oven for 20 minutes, or until heated through and the cheese sauce is golden brown. Serve with assorted salad leaves.

INGREDIENTS
Serves 2

1 large cooked lobster
25 g/1 oz unsalted butter
4 garlic cloves, peeled and crushed
1 tbsp plain flour
300 ml/½ pint milk
125 g/4 oz Parmesan cheese, grated
sea salt and freshly ground black pepper
assorted salad leaves, to serve

Food Fact

Nowadays we consider lobster to be a luxury, however, up until the end of 19th century lobster was so plentiful that it was used as fish bait.

Helpful Hint

This impressive-looking dish makes a wonderful starter for two. Make the sauce in advance and cover the surface with a layer of clingfilm. Refrigerate until ready to use.

Roasted Cod with Saffron Aïoli

1 Preheat oven to 180°C/350°F/Gas Mark 4, 10 minutes before cooking. Crush the garlic, saffron and a pinch of salt in a pestle and mortar to form a paste. Place in a blender with the egg yolk and blend for 30 seconds. With the motor running, slowly add the olive oil in a thin, steady stream until the mayonnaise is smooth and thick. Spoon into a small bowl and stir in the lemon juice. Cover and leave in the refrigerator until required.

2 Combine the olive oil, garlic, red onion, rosemary and thyme for the marinade and leave to infuse for about 10 minutes.

3 Place the sprigs of rosemary and slices of lemon in the bottom of a lightly oiled roasting tin. Add the cod, skinned -side up. Pour over the prepared marinade and leave to marinate in the refrigerator for 15–20 minutes. Bake in the preheated oven for 15–20 minutes, or until the cod is cooked and the flesh flakes easily with a fork. Leave the cod to rest for 1 minute before serving with the saffron aïoli and vegetables.

INGREDIENTS
Serves 4

FOR THE SAFFRON AÏOLI:
2 garlic cloves, peeled
¼ tsp saffron strands
sea salt, to taste
1 medium egg yolk
200 ml/7 fl oz extra-virgin olive oil
2 tbsp lemon juice

FOR THE MARINADE:
2 tbsp olive oil
4 garlic cloves, peeled and finely chopped
1 red onion, peeled and finely chopped
1 tbsp freshly chopped rosemary
2 tbsp freshly chopped thyme
4–6 sprigs of fresh rosemary
1 lemon, sliced
4 x 175 g/6 oz thick cod fillets with skin
freshly cooked vegtables, to serve

Helpful Hint

Vulnerable groups, such as the very young, the elderly and pregnant women should avoid eating raw and semi-cooked eggs. Instead, make the garlic and saffron paste as above and stir into a good-quality bought mayonnaise.

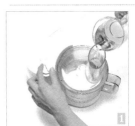

Foil-baked Fish

1 Preheat oven to 180°C/350°F/Gas Mark 4, 10 minutes before cooking. Heat the olive oil and gently fry the garlic and shallots for 2 minutes. Stir in the tomatoes and simmer for 10 minutes, breaking the tomatoes down with the wooden spoon. Add the parsley and basil, season to taste with salt and pepper and cook for a further 2 minutes. Reserve and keep warm.

2 Lightly rinse the fish fillets and cut into 4 portions. Scrub the mussels thoroughly, removing the beard and any barnacles from the shells. Discard any mussels that are open. Clean the squid and cut into rings. Peel the prawns and remove the thin black intestinal vein that runs down the back.

3 Cut 4 large pieces of tinfoil, then place them on a large baking sheet and brush with olive oil. Place 1 fish portion in the centre of each piece of tinfoil. Close the tinfoil to form parcels, and bake in the preheated oven for 10 minutes, then remove.

4 Carefully open up the parcels and add the mussels, squid and prawns. Pour in the wine and spoon over a little of the tomato sauce. Sprinkle with the basil leaves and return to the oven and bake for 5 minutes, or until cooked thoroughly. Disgard any unopened mussels, then garnish with lemon wedges and serve with the extra tomato sauce.

Helpful Hint

This is an excellent basic tomato sauce. Make a large batch and serve it with pasta. Keep covered in the refrigerator until needed or freeze for up to 2 months. Thaw completely and reheat gently before using.

INGREDIENTS
Serves 4

FOR THE TOMATO SAUCE:

125 ml/4 fl oz olive oil
4 garlic cloves, peeled and finely chopped
4 shallots, peeled and finely chopped
400 g can chopped Italian tomatoes
2 tbsp freshly chopped flat-leaf parsley
3 tbsp basil leaves
salt and freshly ground black pepper

700 g/1½ lb red mullet, bass or haddock fillets
450 g/1 lb live mussels
4 squids
8 large raw prawns
2 tbsp olive oil
3 tbsp dry white wine
3 tbsp freshly chopped basil leaves
lemon wedges, to garnish

Roasted Monkfish with Parma Ham

1 Preheat oven to 200°C/
400°F/Gas Mark 6, 15
minutes before cooking. Discard
any skin from the monkfish tail
and cut away and discard the
central bone. Cut the fish into
4 equal-sized pieces and season
to taste with salt and pepper and
lay a bay leaf on each fillet, along
with a slice of cheese.

2 Wrap each fillet with
2 slices of the Parma ham,
so that the fish is covered completely. Tuck the ends of the
Parma ham in and secure with
a cocktail stick.

3 Lightly oil a baking sheet
and place in the preheated
oven for a few minutes. Place
the fish on the preheated baking

sheet, then place in the oven
and cook for 12–15 minutes.

4 Bring a large saucepan of
lightly salted water to the
boil, then slowly add the pasta
and cook for 5 minutes until 'al
dente', or according to packet
directions. Drain, reserving 2
tablespoons of the pasta-cooking
liquor. Return the pasta to the
saucepan and add the reserved
pasta liquor, butter, lemon zest
and juice. Toss until the pasta is
well coated and glistening.

5 Twirl the pasta into small
nests on 4 warmed serving
plates and top with the monkfish
parcels. Garnish with sprigs of
coriander and serve with chargrilled courgettes and tomatoes.

INGREDIENTS
Serves 4

700 g / 1½ lb monkfish tail
sea salt and freshly ground black
  pepper
4 bay leaves
4 slices fontina cheese, rind
  removed
8 slices Parma ham
225 g / 8 oz angel hair pasta
50 g / 2 oz butter
the zest and juice of 1 lemon
sprigs of fresh coriander, to garnish

TO SERVE:

chargrilled courgettes
chargrilled tomatoes

Helpful Hint
Monkfish is also sold in boneless fillets, sometimes
called loins. Remove the skin from the fish before cooking
and if cubes or strips are required, remove the central bone.

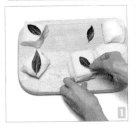

Mussels Arrabbiata

1 Clean the mussels by scrubbing with a small, soft brush, removing the beard and any barnacles from the shells. Discard any mussels that are open or have damaged shells. Place in a large bowl and cover with cold water. Change the water frequently before cooking and leave in the refrigerator until required.

2 Heat the olive oil in a large saucepan and sweat the onion, garlic and chilli until soft, but not coloured. Add the tomatoes and bring to the boil, then simmer for 15 minutes.

3 Add the white wine to the tomato sauce, bring the sauce to the boil and add the mussels. Cover and carefully shake the pan. Cook the mussels for 5–7 minutes, or until the shells have opened.

4 Add the olives to the pan and cook uncovered for about 5 minutes to warm through. Season to taste with salt and pepper and sprinkle in the chopped parsley. Discard any mussels that have not opened and serve immediately with lots of warm crusty bread.

INGREDIENTS
Serves 4

1.8 kg/4 lb mussels
3–4 tbsp olive oil
1 large onion, peeled and sliced
4 garlic cloves, peeled and finely chopped
1 red chilli, deseeded and finely chopped
3 x 400 g cans chopped tomatoes
150 ml/¼ pint white wine
175 g/6 oz black olives, pitted and halved
salt and freshly ground black pepper
2 tbsp freshly chopped parsley
warm crusty bread, to serve

Food Fact

Arrabbiata sauce is a classic Italian tomato-based sauce, usually containing onions, peppers, garlic and fresh herbs. It needs slow simmering to bring out the flavour and is excellent with meat, poultry and pasta as well as seafood.

Tuna Cannelloni

1 Preheat oven to 180°C/ 375°F/Gas Mark 5, 10 minutes before cooking. Heat the olive oil in a frying pan and cook the spring onions and pepper until soft. Remove from the pan with a slotted draining spoon and place in large bowl.

2 Drain the tuna, then stir into the spring onions and pepper. Beat the ricotta cheese with the lemon zest and juice, and the snipped chives and season to taste with salt and pepper until soft and blended. Add to the tuna and mix together. If the mixture is still a little stiff, add a little extra lemon juice.

3 With a teaspoon, carefully spoon the mixture into the cannelloni tubes, then lay the filled tubes in a lightly oiled shallow ovenproof dish. Beat the egg, cottage cheese, natural yogurt and nutmeg together and pour over the cannelloni. Sprinkle with the grated mozzarella cheese and bake in the preheated oven for 15–20 minutes, or until the topping is golden brown and bubbling. Serve immediately with a tossed green salad.

INGREDIENTS
Serves 4

1 tbsp olive oil
6 spring onions, trimmed and finely sliced
1 sweet Mediterranean red pepper, deseeded and finely chopped
200 g can tuna in brine
250 g tub ricotta cheese
zest and juice of 1 lemon
1 tbsp freshly snipped chives
salt and freshly ground black pepper
8 dried cannelloni tubes
1 medium egg, beaten
125 g/4 oz cottage cheese
150 ml/¼ pint natural yogurt
pinch of freshly grated nutmeg
50 g/2 oz mozzarella cheese, grated
tossed green salad, to serve

Helpful Hint

It may seem tempting to part cook the cannelloni tubes before stuffing them but this makes them too slippery to handle. The moisture in the sauce is sufficient to cook them thoroughly while they are baking in the oven.

Seared Tuna with Italian Salsa

1 Wipe the fish and season lightly with salt and pepper, then place in a shallow dish. Mix together the Pernod, olive oil, lemon zest and juice, thyme, fennel seeds, sun-dried tomatoes and chilli flakes and pour over the fish. Cover lightly and leave to marinate in a cool place for 1–2 hours, occasionally spooning the marinade over the fish.

2 Meanwhile, mix all the ingredients for the salsa together in a small bowl. Season to taste with salt and pepper, then cover and leave for about 30 minutes to allow all the flavours to develop.

3 Lightly oil a griddle pan and heat until hot. When the pan is very hot, drain the fish, reserving the marinade. Cook the fish for 3–4 minutes on each side, taking care not to overcook them – the tuna steaks should be a little pink inside. Pour any remaining marinade into a small saucepan, bring to the boil and boil for 1 minute. Serve the steaks hot with the marinade, chilled salsa and a few assorted salad leaves.

INGREDIENTS
Serves 4

4 x 175 g/6 oz tuna or swordfish steaks
salt and freshly ground black pepper
3 tbsp Pernod
2 tbsp olive oil
zest and juice of 1 lemon
2 tsp fresh thyme leaves
2 tsp fennel seeds, lightly roasted
4 sun-dried tomatoes, chopped
1 tsp dried chilli flakes
assorted salad leaves, to serve

FOR THE SALSA:

1 white onion, peeled and finely chopped
2 tomatoes, deseeded and sliced
2 tbsp freshly shredded basil leaves
1 red chilli, deseeded and finely sliced
3 tbsp extra-virgin olive oil
2 tsp balsamic vinegar
1 tsp caster sugar

Food Fact

The word salsa simply means sauce but is generally used to indicate a chunky sauce of uncooked vegetables or fruit. If tightly covered and stored in the refrigerator this salsa should last for five days.

Mediterranean Fish Stew

1 Heat the olive oil in a large saucepan. Add the onion, garlic, fennel and celery and cook over a low heat for 15 minutes, stirring frequently until the vegetables are soft and just beginning to turn brown.

2 Add the canned tomatoes with their juice, oregano, bay leaf, orange zest and juice with the saffron strands. Bring to the boil, then reduce the heat and simmer for 5 minutes. Add the fish stock, vermouth and season to taste with salt and pepper. Bring to the boil. Reduce the heat and simmer for 20 minutes.

3 Wipe or rinse the haddock and bass fillets and remove as many of the bones as possible. Place on a chopping board and cut into 5 cm/2 inch cubes. Add to the saucepan and cook for 3 minutes. Add the prawns and cook for a further 5 minutes. Adjust the seasoning to taste and serve with crusty bread.

INGREDIENTS
Serves 4–6

4 tbsp olive oil
1 onion, peeled and finely sliced
5 garlic cloves, peeled and finely sliced
1 fennel bulb, trimmed and finely chopped
3 celery sticks, trimmed and finely chopped
400 g can chopped tomatoes with Italian herbs
1 tbsp freshly chopped oregano
1 bay leaf
zest and juice of 1 orange
1 tsp saffron strands
750 ml/1¼ pints fish stock
3 tbsp dry vermouth
salt and freshly ground black pepper
225 g/8 oz thick haddock fillets
225 g/8 oz sea bass or bream fillets
225 g/8 oz raw tiger prawns, peeled
crusty bread, to serve

Food Fact

In this recipe saffron is used to colour and flavour this dish. Saffron may seem to be considerably overpriced, however, the flower from which it is grown provides only three stigmas, which must be carefully handpicked and dried. It is no wonder that it is the world's most expensive spice.

Helpful Hint

Use the list of fish here as a guideline – any combination of fish and shellfish that you prefer will work well in a stew such as this. Try serving with toasted French bread and some homemade mayonnaise or aïoli.

Plaice with Parmesan & Anchovies

1 Preheat oven to 220°C/ 425°F/Gas Mark 7, 15 minutes before cooking. Put the plaice on a chopping board and holding the tail, strip off the skin from both sides. With a filleting knife, fillet the fish, then wipe and reserve.

2 Place the fillets on a large chopping board, skinned-side up and halve lengthways along the centre. Dot each one with some of the chopped anchovies, then roll up from the thickest end and reserve.

3 Pour boiling water over the spinach, leave for 2 minutes, drain, squeezing out as much moisture as possible, then place in the base of an ovenproof dish. Arrange the tomatoes on top of the spinach. Arrange the rolled-up fillets standing up in the dish and pour over the cream.

4 Place the ciabatta and rocket in a food processor and blend until finely chopped, then stir in the grated Parmesan cheese.

5 Sprinkle the topping over the fish and bake in the preheated oven for 8–10 minutes, or until the fish is cooked and has lost its translucency and the topping is golden brown. Serve with freshly cooked pasta.

INGREDIENTS
Serves 4

4 plaice fillets
4 anchovy fillets, finely chopped
450 g/1 lb spinach, rinsed
3 firm tomatoes, sliced
200 ml/7 fl oz double cream
5 slices of olive ciabatta bread
50 g/2 oz wild rocket
8 tbsp Parmesan cheese, grated
freshly cooked pasta, to serve

Helpful Hint

Anchovies can either be preserved in oil (usually olive oil) or salt. If you buy them preserved in oil, simply lift them from the oil and drain on kitchen paper before using. If you buy salted anchovies, soak them in several changes of water to remove most of the salt before using. Also, season dishes containing anchovies carefully to avoid oversalting.

Grilled Red Mullet with Orange & Anchovy Sauce

1 Preheat the grill and line the grill rack with tinfoil just before cooking. Peel the oranges with a sharp knife, over a bowl in order to catch the juice. Cut into thin slices and reserve. If necessary, make up the juice to 150 ml/¼ pint with extra juice.

2 Place the fish on a chopping board and make 2 diagonal slashes across the thickest part of both sides of the fish. Season well, both inside and out, with salt and pepper. Tuck a rosemary sprig and a few lemon slices inside the cavity of each fish. Brush the fish with a little of

the olive oil and then cook under the preheated grill for 4–5 minutes on each side. The flesh should just fall away from the bone.

3 Heat the remaining oil in a saucepan and gently fry the garlic and anchovies for 3–4 minutes. Do not allow to brown. Add the chopped rosemary and plenty of black pepper. The anchovies will be salty enough, so do not add any salt. Stir in the orange slices with their juice and the lemon juice. Simmer gently until heated through. Spoon the sauce over the red mullet and serve immediately.

INGREDIENTS
Serves 4

2 oranges
4 x 175 g/6 oz red mullet, cleaned and descaled
salt and freshly ground black pepper
4 sprigs of fresh rosemary
1 lemon, sliced
2 tbsp olive oil
2 garlic cloves, peeled and crushed
6 anchovies fillets in oil, drained and roughly chopped
2 tsp freshly chopped rosemary
1 tsp lemon juice

Helpful Hint

Red mullet is a fairly common fish but size can vary enormously – often only very large fish are available. Substitute with grey mullet or snapper, if necessary.

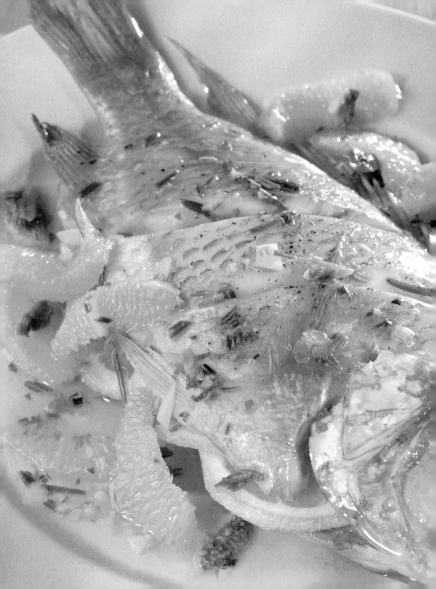

Grilled Snapper with Roasted Pepper

1 Preheat the grill to a high heat and line the grill rack with tinfoil. Cut the tops off the peppers and divide into quarters. Remove the seeds and the membrane, then place on the foil-lined grill rack and cook for 8–10 minutes, turning frequently, until the skins have become charred and blackened. Remove from the grill rack, place in a polythene bag and leave until cool. When the peppers are cool, strip off the skin, slice thinly and reserve.

2 Cover the grill rack with another piece of tinfoil, then place the snapper fillets skin-side up on the grill rack. Season to taste with salt and pepper and brush with a little of the olive oil. Cook for 10–12 minutes, turning over once and brushing again with a little olive oil.

3 Pour the cream and wine into a small saucepan, bring to the boil and simmer for about 5 minutes until the sauce has thickened slightly. Add the dill, season to taste and stir in the sliced peppers. Arrange the cooked snapper fillets on warm serving plates and pour over the cream and pepper sauce. Garnish with sprigs of dill and serve immediately with freshly cooked tagliatelle.

INGREDIENTS
Serves 4

1 medium red pepper
1 medium green pepper
4–8 snapper fillets, depending on size, about 450 g / 1 lb
sea salt and freshly ground black pepper
1 tbsp olive oil
5 tbsp double cream
125 ml / 4 fl oz white wine
1 tbsp freshly chopped dill
sprigs of fresh dill, to garnish
freshly cooked tagliatelle, to serve

Tasty Tip

This dish would be just as tasty with a variety of grilled vegetables – try different coloured peppers, red onions, courgettes and aubergines. Cut into slices or wedges and grill as above. Chop or slice when cool enough to handle.

Pan-fried Salmon with Herb Risotto

1 Wipe the salmon fillets with a clean, damp cloth. Mix together the flour, mustard powder and seasoning on a large plate and use to coat the salmon fillets and reserve.

2 Heat half the olive oil in a large frying pan and fry the shallots for 5 minutes until softened, but not coloured. Add the rice and stir for 1 minute, then slowly add the wine, bring to the boil and boil rapidly until reduced by half.

3 Bring the stock to a gentle simmer, then add to the rice, a ladleful at a time. Cook, stirring frequently, until all the stock has been added and the rice is cooked but still retains a bite. Stir in the butter and freshly chopped herbs and season to taste with salt and pepper.

4 Heat the remaining olive oil and the knob of butter in a large griddle pan, add the salmon fillets and cook for 2–3 minutes on each side, or until cooked. Arrange the herb risotto on warm serving plates and top with the salmon. Garnish with slices of lemon and sprigs of dill and serve immediately with a tomato salad.

INGREDIENTS
Serves 4

4 x 175 g/6 oz salmon fillets
3–4 tbsp plain flour
1 tsp dried mustard powder
salt and freshly ground black pepper
2 tbsp olive oil
3 shallots, peeled and chopped
225 g/8 oz Arborio rice
150 ml/¼ pint dry white wine
1.4 litres/2½ pints vegetable or fish stock
50 g/2 oz butter
2 tbsp freshly snipped chives
2 tbsp freshly chopped dill
2 tbsp freshly chopped flat-leaf parsley
knob of butter

TO GARNISH:
slices of lemon
sprigs of fresh dill
tomato salad, to serve

Helpful Hint

Stirring the butter into the risotto at the end is an important step – in Italian it is called *mantecare*, possibly from the Spanish *mantequilla*, which means butter. This final addition of butter gives the risotto its fine texture and a beautiful shine. Serve risotto as soon as it is cooked.

Sea Bass in Creamy Watercress & Prosciutto Sauce

1 Remove the leaves from the watercress stalks and reserve. Chop the stalks roughly and put in a large pan with the stock. Bring to the boil slowly, cover, and simmer for 20 minutes. Strain, and discard the stalks. Make the stock up to 300 ml/½ pint with the wine.

2 Bring a large saucepan of lightly salted water to the boil and cook the pasta for 8–10 minutes or until 'al dente'. Drain and reserve.

3 Melt the butter in a saucepan, and cook the prosciutto gently for 3 minutes. Remove with a slotted spoon. Stir the flour into the saucepan and cook on a medium heat for 2 minutes. Remove from the

heat and gradually pour in the hot watercress stock, stirring continuously. Return to the heat and bring to the boil, stirring throughout. Simmer for 3 minutes, or until the sauce has thickened and is smooth. Purée the watercress leaves and cream in a food processor then add to the sauce with the prosciutto. Season to taste with salt and pepper, add the pasta, toss lightly and keep warm.

4 Meanwhile, spray a griddle pan lightly with olive oil, then heat until hot. When hot, cook the fillets for 3–4 minutes on each side, or until cooked. Arrange the sea bass on a bed of pasta and drizzle with a little sauce. Garnish with watercress and serve immediately.

INGREDIENTS
Serves 4

75 g/3 oz watercress
450 ml/¾ pint fish or chicken
  stock
150 ml/¼ pint dry white wine
225 g/8 oz tagliatelle pasta
40 g/1½ oz butter
75 g/3 oz prosciutto ham
2 tbsp plain flour
300 ml/½ pint single cream
salt and freshly ground black
  pepper
olive oil, for spraying
4 x 175 g/6 oz sea bass fillets
fresh watercress, to garnish

Helpful Hint

Always wash watercress thoroughly before using, then either dry in a clean tea towel or a salad spinner to remove all the excess moisture.

Marinated Mackerel with Tomato & Basil Salad

1 Remove as many of the fine pin bones as possible from the mackerel fillets, lightly rinse and pat dry with absorbent kitchen paper and place in a shallow dish.

2 Blend the marinade ingredients together and pour over the mackerel fillets. Make sure the marinade has covered the fish completely. Cover and leave in a cool place for at least 8 hours, but preferably overnight. As the fillets marinate, they will loose the translucency and look as if they are cooked.

3 Place the tomatoes, watercress, oranges and mozzarella cheese in a large bowl and toss.

4 To make the dressing, whisk the lemon juice with the mustard, sugar and seasoning in a bowl. Pour over half the dressing, toss again and then arrange on a serving platter. Remove the mackerel from the marinade, cut into bite-sized pieces and sprinkle with the shredded basil. Arrange on top of the salad, drizzle over the remaining dressing, scatter with basil leaves and garnish with a basil sprig. Serve.

INGREDIENTS
Serves 3

3 mackerel, filleted
3 beefsteak tomatoes, sliced
50 g/2 oz watercress
2 oranges, peeled and segmented
75 g/3 oz mozzarella cheese, sliced
2 tbsp basil leaves, shredded
sprig of fresh basil, to garnish

FOR THE MARINADE:
juice of 2 lemons
4 tbsp olive oil
4 tbsp basil leaves

FOR THE DRESSING:
1 tbsp lemon juice
1 tsp Dijon mustard
1 tsp caster sugar
salt and freshly ground black pepper
5 tbsp olive oil

Food Fact

This dish is based on ceviche, which is a dish of thinly sliced raw fish marinated in lemon juice with other flavourings. Make sure that the fish is absolutely fresh for this dish – use a busy fishmonger, who will have a high turnover and therefore a fresh supply.

Seafood Special

1 Heat the olive oil in a saucepan. Chop half of the garlic, add to the saucepan and gently cook for 1–2 minutes. Add the squid, 150 ml/¼ pint of the wine together with the tomatoes and simmer for 10–15 minutes.

2 Chop the remaining garlic and place with the remaining wine and 2 tablespoons of the parsley in another saucepan. Add the cleaned mussels to the pan, cover and cook for 7–8 minutes. Discard any mussels that have not opened, then remove the remaining mussels with a slotted spoon and add to the squid and tomato mixture. Reserve the liquor.

3 Cut the monkfish and tuna into chunks and place in the saucepan with the mussels' cooking liquor. Simmer for about 5 minutes, or until the fish is just tender.

4 Mix all the cooked fish and shellfish, with the exception of the prawns and langoustines, with the tomato mixture and cooking liquor in a large saucepan. Heat everything through until piping hot.

5 Toast the slices of bread and place in the base of a large, shallow serving dish.

6 Pour the fish mixture over the toasted bread and garnish with the prawns, langoustines and chopped parsley. Serve immediately.

INGREDIENTS
Serves 4

2 tbsp olive oil
4 garlic cloves, peeled
125 g/4 oz squid, cut into rings
300 ml/½ pint medium-dry
 white wine
400 g can chopped tomatoes
2 tbsp fresh parsley, finely chopped
225 g/8 oz live mussels, cleaned
 and beards removed
125 g/4 oz monkfish fillet
125 g/4 oz fresh tuna
4 slices of Italian bread

TO GARNISH:

225 g/8 oz large, unpeeled
 prawns, cooked
4 langoustines, cooked
3 tbsp freshly chopped parsley

Tasty Tip

This dish requires a well-flavoured bread – use a good-quality ciabatta or Pugliese loaf from an Italian delicatessen.

Farfalle with Smoked Trout in a Dill & Vodka Sauce

1 Bring a large pan of lightly salted water to a rolling boil. Add the pasta and cook according to the packet instructions, or until 'al dente'.

2 Meanwhile, cut the smoked trout into thin slivers, using scissors. Sprinkle lightly with the lemon juice and reserve.

3 Place the cream, mustard, chopped dill and vodka in a small pan. Season lightly with salt and pepper. Bring the contents of the pan to the boil and simmer gently for 2–3 minutes, or until slightly thickened.

4 Drain the cooked pasta thoroughly, then return to the pan. Add the smoked trout to the dill and vodka sauce, then pour over the pasta. Toss gently until the pasta is coated and the trout evenly mixed.

5 Spoon into a warmed serving dish or on to individual plates. Garnish with sprigs of dill and serve immediately.

INGREDIENTS
Serves 4

400 g / 14 oz farfalle
150 g / 5 oz smoked trout
2 tsp lemon juice
200 ml / 7 fl oz double cream
2 tsp wholegrain mustard
2 tbsp freshly chopped dill
4 tbsp vodka
salt and freshly ground black pepper
sprigs of dill, to garnish

Food Fact

Two types of smoked trout are available. One resembles smoked salmon in colour, texture and flavour, and can be cut into thin slivers as shown here. Equally delicious is hot smoked rainbow trout, which is available as a whole fish or in fillets. These should be skinned and the bones should be removed before use. The flesh can then be broken into large flakes. Smoked trout is fairly salty, so the sauce requires a minimal amount of seasoning with salt.

Pappardelle with Smoked Haddock & Blue Cheese Sauce

1 Place the smoked haddock in a saucepan with 1 bay leaf and pour in the milk. Bring to the boil slowly, cover and simmer for 6–7 minutes, or until the fish is opaque. Remove and roughly flake the fish, discarding the skin and any bones. Strain the milk and reserve.

2 Bring a large pan of lightly salted water to a rolling boil. Add the pasta and cook according to the packet instructions, or until 'al dente'.

3 Meanwhile, place the butter, flour and single cream or milk if preferred, in a pan and stir to mix. Stir in the reserved warm milk and add the remaining bay leaf. Bring to the boil, whisking all the time until smooth and thick. Gently simmer for 3–4 minutes, stirring frequently. Discard the bay leaf.

4 Add the Dolcelatte or Gorgonzola cheese to the sauce. Heat gently, stirring until melted. Add the flaked haddock and season to taste with nutmeg and salt and pepper.

5 Drain the pasta thoroughly and return to the pan. Add the sauce and toss gently to coat, taking care not to break up the flakes of fish. Tip into a warmed serving bowl, sprinkle with toasted walnuts and parsley and serve immediately.

INGREDIENTS
Serves 4

350 g / 12 oz smoked haddock
2 bay leaves
300 ml / ½ pint milk
400 g / 14 oz pappardelle or tagliatelle
25 g / 1 oz butter
25 g / 1 oz plain flour
150 ml / ¼ pint single cream or extra milk
125 g / 4 oz Dolcelatte cheese or Gorgonzola, cut into small pieces
¼ tsp freshly grated nutmeg
salt and freshly ground black pepper
40 g / 1½ oz toasted walnuts, chopped
1 tbsp freshly chopped parsley

Tasty Tip

Dolcelatte is an Italian, semi-soft, blue-veined cheese made from cows' milk. It has a smooth creamy texture and a delicate taste. For a more strongly flavoured blue cheese sauce, a young Gorgonzola, Roquefort or blue Stilton can be used instead.

Special Seafood Lasagne

1 Preheat the oven to 200°C/400°F/Gas Mark 6, 15 minutes before cooking. Place the haddock in a pan with the wine, fish stock, onion and bay leaf. Bring to the boil slowly, cover and simmer gently for 5 minutes, or until the fish is opaque. Remove and flake the fish, discarding any bones. Strain the cooking juices and reserve.

2 Melt 50 g/2 oz of the butter in a large saucepan. Add the leeks and garlic and cook gently for 10 minutes. Remove from the pan, using a slotted draining spoon, and reserve.

3 Melt the remaining butter in a small saucepan. Stir in the flour, then gradually whisk in the cream, off the heat, followed by the reserved cooking juices. Bring to the boil slowly, whisking until thickened. Stir in the dill and season to taste with salt and pepper.

5 Spoon a little of the sauce into the base of a buttered 2.8 litre/5 pint shallow oven-proof dish. Top with a layer of lasagne, followed by the haddock, seafood cocktail and leeks. Spoon over enough sauce to cover. Continue layering up, finishing with sheets of lasagne topped with sauce.

6 Sprinkle over the grated Gruyère cheese and bake in the preheated oven for 40–45 minutes, or until golden-brown and bubbling. Serve immediately.

INGREDIENTS
Serves 4–6

450 g/1 lb fresh haddock fillet, skinned
150 ml/¼ pint dry white wine
150 ml/¼ pint fish stock
½ onion, peeled and thickly sliced
1 bay leaf
75 g/3 oz butter
350 g/12 oz leeks, trimmed and thickly sliced
1 garlic clove, peeled and crushed
25 g/1 oz plain flour
150 ml/¼ pint single cream
2 tbsp freshly chopped dill
salt and freshly ground black pepper
8–12 sheets dried lasagne verde, cooked
225 g/8 oz ready-cooked seafood cocktail
50 g/2 oz Gruyère cheese, grated

Helpful Hint

Cook the lasagne in a large pan of boiling salted water with 1 teaspoon olive oil for about 7 minutes, or according to the packet instructions. Do this even if using pasta labelled pre-cooked. Drain thoroughly and rinse briefly under cold water.

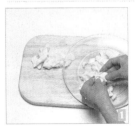

Grand Almonds
Pistachios
Blanched Almonds
80g plain flour .

Mixed Almonds , Hazelnuts 360g
Aniseed .
Cherry Tomatoes

Streaky Bacon
mushrooms
Celery
Courgettes
Can Tomatoes
White wine
~~Feta~~

Cod Fillets - 8.
Pasta shells
Milk
Greek yogurt - double cream

Tuna & Macaroni Timbales

1 Preheat the oven to 180° C/ 350°F/Gas Mark 4, 10 minutes before cooking. Oil and line the bases of 4 individual 150 ml/ ¼ pint timbales or ovenproof cups with non-stick baking parchment and stand in a small roasting tin.

2 Bring a large pan of lightly salted water to a rolling boil. Add the macaroni and cook according to the packet instructions, or until 'al dente'. Drain the cooked pasta thoroughly.

3 Flake the tuna fish and mix with the macaroni. Divide between the timbales or cups.

4 Pour the single and double cream into a small saucepan. Bring to the boil slowly, remove from the heat and stir in the Gruyère cheese until melted. Allow to cool for 1–2 minutes, then whisk into the beaten egg and season lightly with salt and

pepper. Pour the mixture over the tuna fish and macaroni and cover each timbale with a small piece of tinfoil.

5 Pour enough hot water into the roasting tin to come halfway up the timbales. Place in the preheated oven and cook for 25 minutes. Remove the timbales from the water and allow to stand for 5 minutes.

6 For the tomato dressing, whisk together the mustard and vinegar in a small bowl, using a fork. Gradually whisk in the sunflower and nut oils, then stir in the chopped tomatoes and the snipped chives.

7 Unmould the timbales on to warmed serving plates and spoon the tomato dressing over the top and around the bottom. Garnish with fresh chives and serve immediately.

INGREDIENTS
Serves 4

125 g/4 oz macaroni
200 g can tuna in brine, drained
150 ml/¼ pint single cream
150 ml/¼ pint double cream
50 g/2 oz Gruyère cheese, grated
3 medium eggs, lightly beaten
salt and freshly ground black pepper
fresh chives, to garnish

FRESH TOMATO DRESSING:

1 tsp Dijon mustard
1 tsp red wine vinegar
2 tbsp sunflower oil
1 tbsp hazelnut or walnut oil
350 g/12 oz firm ripe tomatoes, skinned, deseeded and chopped
2 tbsp freshly snipped chives

Tasty Tip

Other fish can be used to make these pasta timbales. Try a 200 g can of white crab meat, rinsed and drained, or pink salmon with all the bones removed.

Saucy Cod & Pasta Bake

1 Preheat the oven to 200°C/400°F/Gas Mark 6, 15 minutes before cooking. Cut the cod into bite-sized pieces and reserve.

2 Heat the sunflower oil in a large saucepan, add the onion and bacon and cook for 7–8 minutes. Add the mushrooms and celery and cook for 5 minutes, or until fairly soft.

3 Add the courgettes and tomatoes to the bacon mixture and pour in the fish stock or wine. Bring to the boil, then simmer uncovered for 5 minutes, or until the sauce has thickened slightly. Remove from the heat and stir in the cod pieces and the tarragon. Season to taste

with salt and pepper, then spoon into a large oiled baking dish.

4 Meanwhile, bring a large pan of lightly salted water to a rolling boil. Add the pasta shells and cook, according to the packet instructions, or until 'al dente'.

5 For the topping, place the butter and flour in a saucepan and pour in the milk. Bring to the boil slowly, whisking until thickened and smooth.

6 Drain the pasta thoroughly, and stir into the sauce. Spoon carefully over the fish and vegetables. Place in the preheated oven and bake for 20–25 minutes, or until the top is lightly browned and bubbling.

INGREDIENTS
Serves 4

450 g/1 lb cod fillets, skinned
2 tbsp sunflower oil
1 onion, peeled and chopped
4 rashers smoked streaky bacon, rind removed and chopped
150 g/5 oz baby button mushrooms, wiped
2 celery sticks, trimmed and thinly sliced
2 small courgettes, halved lengthwise and sliced
400 g can chopped tomatoes
100 ml/3½ fl oz fish stock or dry white wine
1 tbsp freshly chopped tarragon
salt and freshly ground black pepper

PASTA TOPPING:
225–275 g/8–10 oz pasta shells
25 g/1 oz butter
4 tbsp plain flour
450 ml/¾ pint milk

Helpful Hint

If you are short of time, you can make a simpler topping. Beat together 2 eggs, 3 tablespoons Greek-style yogurt and 3 tablespoons double cream; season to taste with salt and pepper. Add the drained pasta and mix well. Spoon on top of the fish and vegetables and bake as above for 15–20 minutes, or until the top is set and golden brown.

Pasta Provençale

1 Heat the olive oil in a large saucepan, add the garlic and onion and cook gently for 5 minutes. Add the fennel and cook for a further 5 minutes. Stir in the chopped tomatoes and rosemary sprig. Half-cover the pan and simmer for 10 minutes.

2 Cut the monkfish into bite-sized pieces and sprinkle with the lemon juice. Add to the tomatoes, cover and simmer gently for 5 minutes, or until the fish is opaque.

3 Meanwhile, bring a large pan of lightly salted water to a rolling boil. Add the pasta and cook according to the packet instructions, or until 'al dente'. Drain the pasta thoroughly and return to the saucepan.

4 Remove the rosemary from the tomato sauce. Stir in the black olives, flageolet beans and chopped oregano, then season to taste with salt and pepper. Add the sauce to the pasta and toss gently together to coat, taking care not to break up the monk-fish. Tip into a warmed serving bowl. Garnish with rosemary and oregano sprigs and serve immediately.

INGREDIENTS
Serves 4

2 tbsp olive oil
1 garlic clove, peeled and crushed
1 onion, peeled and finely chopped
1 small fennel bulb, trimmed and halved and thinly sliced
400 g can chopped tomatoes
1 rosemary sprig, plus extra sprig to garnish
350 g/12 oz monkfish, skinned
2 tsp lemon juice
400 g/14 oz gnocchi pasta
50 g/2 oz pitted black olives
200 g can flageolet beans, drained and rinsed
1 tbsp freshly chopped oregano, plus sprig to garnish
salt and freshly ground black pepper

Helpful Hint

Only the tail of the monkfish is eaten and this is usually sold skinned. It has a firm, very white, almost meaty flesh and just one bone running down the middle. It may still have a tough transparent membrane covering it, which should be carefully removed before cooking. A less expensive firm white fish, such as haddock, may be used if preferred.

Seared Salmon & Lemon Linguine

1 Brush the salmon fillets with the sunflower oil, sprinkle with crushed peppercorns and press on firmly and reserve.

2 Bring a large pan of lightly salted water to a rolling boil. Add the linguine and cook according to the packet instructions, or until 'al dente'.

3 Meanwhile, melt the butter in a saucepan and cook the shredded spring onions gently for 2–3 minutes, or until soft. Stir in the soured cream and the lemon zest and remove from the heat.

4 Preheat a griddle or heavy-based frying pan until very hot. Add the salmon and sear for 1½–2 minutes on each side. Remove from the pan and allow to cool slightly.

5 Bring the soured cream sauce to the boil and stir in the Parmesan cheese and lemon juice. Drain the pasta thoroughly and return to the pan. Pour over the sauce and toss gently to coat.

6 Spoon the pasta on to warmed serving plates and top with the salmon fillets. Serve immediately with sprigs of dill and lemon slices.

Helpful Hint

If you are unable to find soured cream, stir 1 teaspoon lemon juice into 300 ml/½ pint of double cream and leave at room temperature for 20 minutes before using. For a less rich and lower fat version of the sauce, use Greek-style yogurt instead, but do not boil as in step 5. Instead, heat gently with the Parmesan cheese until the cheese melts, then pour over the pasta and toss to coat in the sauce, as above.

INGREDIENTS
Serves 4

4 small skinless salmon fillets, each about 75 g/3 oz
2 tsp sunflower oil
½ tsp mixed or black peppercorns, crushed
400 g/14 oz linguine
15 g/½ oz unsalted butter
1 bunch spring onions, trimmed and shredded
300 ml/½ pint soured cream
zest of 1 lemon, finely grated
50 g/2 oz freshly grated Parmesan cheese
1 tbsp lemon juice
pinch of salt

TO GARNISH:
dill sprigs
lemon slices

Tagliatelle with Tuna & Anchovy Tapenade

1 Bring a large pan of lightly salted water to a rolling boil. Add the tagliatelle and cook according to the packet instructions, or until 'al dente'.

2 Meanwhile, place the tuna fish, anchovy fillets, olives and capers in a food processor with the lemon juice and 2 tablespoons of the olive oil and blend for a few seconds until roughly chopped.

3 With the motor running, pour in the remaining olive oil in a steady stream; the resulting mixture should be slightly chunky rather than smooth.

4 Spoon the sauce into a bowl, stir in the chopped parsley and season to taste with black pepper. Check the taste of the sauce and add a little more lemon juice, if required.

5 Drain the pasta thoroughly. Pour the sauce into the pan and cook over a low heat for 1–2 minutes to warm through.

6 Return the drained pasta to the pan and mix together with the sauce. Tip into a warmed serving bowl or spoon on to warm individual plates. Garnish with sprigs of flat-leaf parsley and serve immediately.

INGREDIENTS
Serves 4

400 g / 14 oz tagliatelle
125 g can tuna fish in oil, drained
45 g / 1¼ oz can anchovy fillets, drained
150 g / 5 oz pitted black olives
2 tbsp capers in brine, drained
2 tsp lemon juice
100 ml / 3½ fl oz olive oil
2 tbsp freshly chopped parsley
freshly ground black pepper
sprigs of flat-leaf parsley, to garnish

Food Fact

Capers are the flower buds of the caper bush, which grows throughout the Mediterranean region. The buds are picked before they open and preserved in vinegar and salt. The word tapenade (a mixture of capers, olives and fish, usually anchovies, pounded to a paste with olive oil) comes from the Provençal word for capers – *tapeno*.

Hot Prawn Noodles with Sesame Dressing

1 Pour the vegetable stock into a large saucepan and bring to the boil. Add the egg noodles, stir once, then cook according to the packet instructions, usually about 3 minutes.

2 Meanwhile, heat the sunflower oil in a small frying pan. Add the chopped garlic and chilli and cook gently for a few seconds. Add the sesame seeds and cook, stirring continuously, for 1 minute, or until golden.

3 Add the soy sauce, sesame oil and prawns to the frying pan. Continue cooking for a few seconds, until the mixture is just starting to bubble, then remove immediately from the heat.

4 Drain the noodles thoroughly and return to the pan. Add the prawns in the dressing mixture, and the chopped coriander and season to taste with black pepper. Toss gently to coat the noodles with the hot dressing.

5 Tip into a warmed serving bowl or spoon on to individual plates and serve immediately, garnished with sprigs of fresh coriander.

INGREDIENTS
Serves 4

600 ml/1 pint vegetable stock
350 g/12 oz Chinese egg noodles
1 tbsp sunflower oil
1 garlic clove, peeled and very
  finely chopped
1 red chilli, deseeded and finely
  chopped
3 tbsp sesame seeds
3 tbsp dark soy sauce
2 tbsp sesame oil
175 g/6 oz shelled cooked
  prawns
3 tbsp freshly chopped coriander
freshly ground black pepper
fresh coriander sprigs, to garnish

Food Fact

There are two types of sesame oil that feature frequently in Oriental cooking – the pale and light version, made from untoasted seeds, and the rich dark kind, made from toasted seeds. The latter has a very strong nutty flavour, which can be overpowering in large quantities. If you use the toasted variety in the dressing for this dish, use just 1 tablespoon mixed together with 1 tablespoon of groundnut or sunflower oil.

Pan-fried Scallops & Pasta

1 Rinse the scallops and pat dry on absorbent kitchen paper. Place in a bowl and add the olive oil, crushed garlic and thyme. Cover and chill in the refrigerator until ready to cook.

2 Bring a large pan of lightly salted water to a rolling boil. Add the penne and cook according to the packet instructions, or until 'al dente'.

3 Meanwhile, make the dressing. Place the sun-dried tomatoes into a small bowl or glass jar and add the vinegars, tomato paste, sugar, salt and pepper. Whisk well, then pour into a food processor.

4 With the motor running, pour in the sun-dried tomato oil and olive oil in a steady stream to make a thick, smooth dressing.

5 Preheat a large, dry cast-iron griddle pan over a high heat for about 5 minutes. Lower the heat to medium then add the scallops to the pan. Cook for 1½ minutes on each side. Remove from the pan.

6 Drain the pasta thoroughly and return to the pan. Add the sliced sun-dried tomatoes and dressing and toss. Divide between individual serving plates, top each portion with 4 scallops, garnish with fresh thyme or oregano sprigs and serve immediately.

INGREDIENTS
Serves 4

16 large scallops, shelled
1 tbsp olive oil
1 garlic clove, peeled and crushed
1 tsp freshly chopped thyme
400 g/14 oz penne
4 sun-dried tomatoes in oil, drained and thinly sliced
thyme or oregano sprigs, to garnish

TOMATO DRESSING:

2 sun-dried tomatoes in oil, drained and chopped
1 tbsp red wine vinegar
2 tsp balsamic vinegar
1 tsp sun-dried tomato paste
1 tsp caster sugar
salt and freshly ground black pepper
2 tbsp oil from a jar of sun-dried tomatoes
2 tbsp olive oil

Handy Hint

Try to buy ready-shelled fresh scallops. If you buy in shells, follow this quick and simple method of opening them. Preheat the oven to 150°C/300°F/Gas Mark 2. Place the scallops on a baking sheet, rounded-sided down and put this in the oven for about 10 minutes, or until the shells just open. When pan-frying the scallops, take care not to overcook them, or they will lose their moist, tender texture.

Smoked Mackerel & Pasta Frittata

1 Preheat the grill to high just before cooking. Bring a pan of lightly salted water to a rolling boil. Add the pasta and cook according to the packet instructions, or until 'al dente'. Drain thoroughly and reserve.

2 Remove the skin from the mackerel and break the fish into large flakes, discarding any bones, and reserve.

3 Place the eggs, milk, mustard and parsley in a bowl and whisk together. Season with just a little salt and plenty of freshly ground black pepper and reserve.

4 Melt the butter in a large, heavy-based frying pan.

Cook the spring onions gently for 3–4 minutes, until soft. Pour in the egg mixture, then add the drained pasta, peas and half of the mackerel.

5 Gently stir the mixture in the pan for 1–2 minutes, or until beginning to set. Stop stirring and cook for about 1 minute until the underneath is golden-brown.

6 Scatter the remaining mackerel over the frittata, followed by the grated cheese. Place under the preheated grill for about 1½ minutes, or until golden-brown and set. Cut into wedges and serve immediately with salad and crusty bread.

INGREDIENTS
Serves 4

25 g/1 oz tricolore pasta spirals
   or shells
225 g/8 oz smoked mackerel
6 medium eggs
3 tbsp milk
2 tsp wholegrain mustard
2 tbsp freshly chopped parsley
salt and freshly ground black
   pepper
25 g/1 oz unsalted butter
6 spring onions, trimmed and
   diagonally sliced
50 g/2 oz frozen peas, thawed
75 g/3 oz mature Cheddar
   cheese, grated

TO SERVE:
green salad
warm crusty bread

Food Fact

A frittata is a thick-set Italian omelette, similar to the Spanish tortilla, which may be served hot or cold cut into wedges or fingers. To ensure even cooking, it should be cooked very slowly over a low heat and gently stirred only until the mixture starts to set.

Crispy Cod Cannelloni

1 Add 1 teaspoon of the olive oil to a large pan of lightly salted water and bring to a rolling boil. Add the cannelloni tubes and cook, uncovered, for 5 minutes. Drain and leave in a bowl of cold water.

2 Melt the butter with the remaining oil in a saucepan. Add the mushrooms and leeks and cook gently for 5 minutes. Turn up the heat and cook for 1–2 minutes, or until the mixture is fairly dry. Add the cod and cook, stirring, for 2–3 minutes, or until the fish is opaque.

3 Add the cream cheese to the pan and stir until melted. Season to taste with salt and pepper, then leave the cod mixture to cool.

4 Drain the cannelloni. Using a piping bag without a nozzle or a spoon, fill the cannelloni with the cod mixture.

5 Mix the Parmesan cheese and breadcrumbs together on a plate. Dip the filled cannelloni into the flour, then into the beaten egg and finally into the breadcrumb mixture. Dip the ends twice to ensure they are thoroughly coated. Chill in the refrigerator for 30 minutes.

6 Heat the oil for deep frying to 180°C/350°F. Fry the stuffed cannelloni in batches for 2–3 minutes, or until the coating is crisp and golden-brown. Drain on absorbent kitchen paper and serve immediately with fresh herbs or salad leaves.

INGREDIENTS
Serves 4

1 tbsp olive oil
8 dried cannelloni tubes
25 g / 1 oz unsalted butter
225 g / 8 oz button mushrooms, thinly sliced
175 g / 6 oz leeks, trimmed and finely chopped
175 g / 6 oz cod, skinned and diced
175 g / 6 oz cream cheese
salt and freshly ground black pepper
15 g / ½ oz Parmesan cheese, grated
50 g / 2 oz fine fresh white breadcrumbs
3 tbsp plain flour
1 medium egg, lightly beaten
oil for deep frying
fresh herbs or salad leaves, to serve

Handy Hint

Use a deep, heavy-based pan or a deep-fat fryer for deep-frying. Fill the pan to no more than one-third full with oil. If you do not have a food thermometer to check the oil's temperature, test by dropping in a cube of stale bread; it will turn golden-brown in 40 seconds, when the oil is hot enough.

Spaghetti alle Vongole

1 Soak the clams in lightly salted cold water for 8 hours before required, changing the water once or twice. Scrub the clams, removing any that have broken shells or that remain open when tapped.

2 Place the prepared clams in a large saucepan and pour in the wine. Cover with a tight-fitting lid and cook over a medium heat for 5–6 minutes, shaking the pan occasionally, until the shells have opened.

3 Strain the clams and cooking juices through a sieve lined with muslin and reserve. Discard any clams that have remained unopened.

4 Heat the olive oil in a saucepan and fry the onion

and garlic gently for 10 minutes, or until very soft.

5 Meanwhile, bring a large pan of lightly salted water to a rolling boil. Add the spaghetti and cook according to the packet instructions, or until 'al dente'.

6 Add the cooked clams to the onions and garlic and pour in the reserved cooking juices. Bring to the boil, then add the parsley and basil and season to taste with salt and black pepper.

7 Drain the spaghetti thoroughly. Return to the pan and add the clams with their sauce. Toss together gently, then tip into a large warmed serving bowl or into individual bowls. Serve immediately, sprinkled with oregano leaves.

INGREDIENTS
Serves 4

1.8 kg/4 lb small fresh clams
6 tbsp dry white wine
2 tbsp olive oil
1 small onion, peeled and finely chopped
2 garlic cloves, peeled and crushed
400 g/14 oz spaghetti
2 tbsp freshly chopped parsley
2 tbsp freshly chopped or torn basil
salt and freshly ground black pepper
oregano leaves, to garnish

Handy Hint
Cook and eat clams within 24 hours of buying them. Steam them until the shells have just opened, as overcooking will toughen them.

Seafood Parcels with Pappardelle & Coriander Pesto

1 Preheat the oven to 180°C/ 350° F/Gas Mark 4, 10 minutes before cooking. To make the pesto, blend the coriander leaves, garlic, pine nuts and lemon juice with 1 tablespoon of the olive oil to a smooth paste in a food processor. With the motor running slowly add the remaining oil. Stir the Parmesan cheese into the pesto and season to taste with salt and pepper.

2 Bring a pan of lightly salted water to a rolling boil. Add the pasta and cook for 3 minutes only. Drain thoroughly, return to the pan and spoon over two-thirds of the pesto. Toss to coat.

3 Cut out 4 circles, about 30 cm/12 in in diameter, from non-stick baking parchment. Spoon the pasta on to one half of each circle. Top each pile of pasta with 2 prawns, 3 scallops and a few squid rings. Spoon 1 tablespoon of wine over each serving, then drizzle with the remaining coriander pesto and top with a slice of lemon.

4 Close the parcels by folding over the other half of the paper, to make a semi-circle, then turn and twist the edges of the paper to secure.

5 Place the parcels on a baking tray and bake in the preheated oven for 15 minutes, or until cooked. Serve the parcels immediately, allowing each person to open their own.

INGREDIENTS
Serves 4

300 g/11 oz pappardelle or tagliatelle
8 raw tiger prawns, shelled
12 raw queen scallops
225 g/8oz baby squid, cleaned and cut into rings
4 tbsp dry white wine
4 thin slices of lemon

CORIANDER PESTO:
50 g/2 oz fresh coriander leaves
1 garlic clove, peeled
25 g/1 oz pine nuts, toasted
1 tsp lemon juice
5 tbsp olive oil
1 tbsp grated Parmesan cheese
salt and freshly ground black pepper

Helpful Hint

Prepare whole squid by firmly pulling the pouch and tentacles apart. Remove the transparent quill from the pouch and discard. Rinse the pouch under cold running water, then peel off the dark skin and discard. Slice the pouch and tentacles into rings.

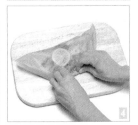

Pasta & Mussels in Tomato & Wine Sauce

1 Scrub the mussels and remove any beards. Discard any that do not close when lightly tapped. Place in a large pan with the bay leaf and pour in the wine. Cover with a tight-fitting lid and steam, shaking the pan occasionally, for 3–4 minutes, or until the mussels open. Remove the mussels with a slotted spoon, discarding any that have not opened, and reserve. Strain the cooking liquid through a muslin-lined sieve and reserve.

2 Melt the butter with the oil in a large saucepan and gently cook the onion and garlic for 10 minutes, until soft. Add the reserved cooking liquid and the tomatoes and simmer, uncovered, for 6–7 minutes, or until very soft and the sauce has reduced slightly.

3 Meanwhile, bring a large pan of lightly salted water to a rolling boil. Add the pasta and cook acording to the packet instructions, or until 'al dente'.

4 Drain the pasta thoroughly and return to the pan. Add the mussels, removing the shells if you prefer, with the tomato sauce. Stir in the basil and season to taste with salt and pepper. Toss together gently. Tip into warmed serving bowls, garnish with basil leaves and serve with crusty bread.

INGREDIENTS
Serves 4

900 g / 2 lb fresh live mussels
1 bay leaf
150 ml / ¼ pint light red wine
15 g / ½ oz unsalted butter
1 tbsp olive oil
1 red onion, peeled and thinly sliced
2 garlic cloves, peeled and crushed
550 g / 1¼ lb ripe tomatoes, skinned, deseeded and chopped
400 g / 14 oz fiochetti or penne
3 tbsp freshly chopped or torn basil
salt and freshly ground black pepper
basil leaves, to garnish
crusty bread, to serve

Helpful Hint

Some fishmongers still sell mussels by volume rather than weight: 1.1 litres / 2 pints is the equivalent of 900 g / 2 lb. If you are not cooking mussels within a few hours of buying them, store in a bowl of water in a cold place or in the warmest part of the refrigerator on a hot day. Do not add salt, flour or oatmeal to the water.

Salmon & Spaghetti in a Creamy Egg Sauce

1 Beat the eggs in a bowl with the parsley, dill, half of the Parmesan and pecorino cheeses and the white wine. Season to taste with freshly ground black pepper and reserve.

2 Bring a large pan of lightly salted water to a rolling boil. Add the spaghetti and cook according to the packet instructions, or until 'al dente'.

3 Meanwhile, cut the salmon into bite-sized pieces. Melt the butter in a large frying pan with the oil and cook the salmon pieces for 3–4 minutes, or until opaque.

4 Drain the spaghetti thoroughly, return to the pan and immediately add the egg mixture. Remove from the heat and toss well; the eggs will cook in the heat of the spaghetti to make a creamy sauce.

5 Stir in the remaining cheeses and the cooked pieces of salmon and toss again. Tip into a warmed serving bowl or on to individual plates. Garnish with sprigs of flat-leaf parsley and serve immediately.

INGREDIENTS
Serves 4

3 medium eggs
1 tbsp freshly chopped parsley
1 tbsp freshly chopped dill
40 g/1½ oz freshly grated
  Parmesan cheese
40 g/1½ oz freshly grated
  pecorino cheese
2 tbsp dry white wine
freshly ground black pepper
400 g/14 oz spaghetti
350 g/12 oz salmon fillet,
  skinned
25 g/1 oz butter
1 tsp olive oil
flat-leaf parsley sprigs, to garnish

Food Fact

This recipe is based on the classic Spaghetti alla Carbonara, which is made with smoked bacon or pancetta. Here, fresh salmon makes an equally delicious alternative. Make sure that you remove the spaghetti from the heat before adding the egg mixture and keep turning the spaghetti until the eggs cook to a light creamy sauce.

Helpful Hint

You will not need to add salt in this recipe as the pecorino cheese is very salty.

Creamy Coconut Seafood Pasta

1 Bring a large pan of lightly salted water to a rolling boil. Add the pasta and cook according to the packet instructions, or until 'al dente'.

2 Meanwhile, heat the sunflower and sesame oils together in a saucepan. Add the spring onions, garlic, chilli and ginger and cook for 3–4 minutes, or until softened.

3 Blend the coconut milk and cream together in a jug. Add the prawns and crab meat to the pan and stir over a low heat for a few seconds to heat through.

Gradually pour in the coconut cream, stirring all the time.

4 Stir the chopped coriander into the seafood sauce and season to taste with salt and pepper. Continue heating the sauce gently until piping hot, but do not allow to boil.

5 Drain the pasta thoroughly and return to the pan. Add the seafood sauce and gently toss together to coat the pasta. Tip into a warmed serving dish or spoon on to individual plates. Serve immediately, garnished with fresh coriander sprigs.

INGREDIENTS
Serves 4

400 g / 14 oz egg tagliatelle
1 tsp sunflower oil
1 tsp sesame oil
4 spring onions, trimmed and sliced diagonally
1 garlic clove, peeled and crushed
1 red chilli, deseeded and finely chopped
2.5 cm / 1 inch piece fresh root ginger, peeled and grated
150 ml / ¼ pint coconut milk
100 ml / 3½ fl oz double cream
225 g / 8 oz cooked peeled tiger prawns
185 g / 6½ oz fresh white crab meat
2 tbsp freshly chopped coriander, plus sprigs to garnish
salt and freshly ground black pepper

Helpful Hint

Coconut milk can be bought either in cans or long-life cartons, or you can make it yourself if you prefer. Put 125 g/4 oz desiccated coconut into a food processor or blender with 225 ml/8 fl oz boiling water and process for 30 seconds. Leave to cool for 5 minutes, then tip into a sieve lined with muslin over a bowl. Allow to drain for a few minutes, then squeeze out as much liquid as possible. Discard the coconut.

Fettuccine with Sardines & Spinach

1 Drain the sardines and cut in half lengthwise. Remove the bones, then cut the fish into 2.5 cm/1 inch pieces and reserve.

2 Bring a large pan of lightly salted water to a rolling boil. Add the pasta and cook according to the packet instructions, or until 'al dente'.

3 Meanwhile, melt half the butter with the olive oil in a large saucepan, add the bread-crumbs and fry, stirring, until they begin to turn crisp. Add the garlic and pine nuts and continue to cook until golden-brown. Remove from the pan and reserve. Wipe the pan clean.

4 Melt the remaining butter in the pan, add the mushrooms and cook for 4–5 minutes, or until soft. Add the spinach and cook, stirring, for 1 minute, or until beginning to wilt. Stir in the crème fraîche and lemon rind and bring to the boil. Simmer gently until the spinach is just cooked. Season the sauce to taste with salt and pepper.

5 Drain the pasta thoroughly and return to the pan. Add the spinach sauce and sardine pieces and gently toss together. Tip into a warmed serving dish. Sprinkle with the toasted bread-crumbs and pine nuts and serve immediately.

INGREDIENTS
Serves 4

120g can sardines in olive oil

400 g/14 oz fettuccine or tagliarini

40 g/1½ oz butter

2 tbsp olive oil

50 g/2 oz one-day-old white breadcrumbs

1 garlic clove, peeled and finely chopped

50 g/2 oz pine nuts

125 g/4 oz chestnut mushrooms, wiped and sliced

125 g/4 oz baby spinach leaves, rinsed

150 ml/¼ pint crème fraîche

rind of 1 lemon, finely grated

salt and freshly ground black pepper

Helpful Hint

Choose a full-fat crème fraîche for this recipe rather than half-fat, otherwise it may curdle. Alternatively, use soured cream if you prefer. Other canned fish such as sild or mackerel fillets may be substituted for the sardines, but check that they are in oil, and not tomato sauce, when you buy.

Sweet-&-Sour Fish with Crispy Noodles

1 Cut the plaice fillets into 5 cm/2 inch slices. Mix the flour with the five-spice powder in a bowl. Add the fish, a few pieces at a time, and toss to coat thoroughly. Reserve.

2 Place the ginger, spring onions, sherry, soy sauce, sugar, vinegar and chilli sauce in a small saucepan and season lightly with salt and pepper. Heat gently until the sugar has dissolved, then bubble the sauce for 2–3 minutes.

3 Break the noodles into pieces about 7.5 cm/3 inch long. Heat the oil in a deep fryer to 180°C/350°F. Deep-fry small handfuls of noodles for about 30 seconds, until puffed up and crisp. Remove and drain on absorbent kitchen paper.

4 Deep-fry the plaice for 1–2 minutes, or until firm and cooked. Remove and drain on absorbent kitchen paper.

5 Place the cooked fish in a warmed serving bowl, drizzle over the sauce and garnish with spring onion tassels and slices of red chilli. Pile the noodles into another bowl and serve.

INGREDIENTS
Serves 4

350 g/12 oz plaice fillets, skinned
3 tbsp plain flour
pinch of Chinese five-spice powder
2.5 cm/1 inch piece fresh root ginger, peeled and grated
4 spring onions, trimmed and finely sliced
3 tbsp dry sherry
1 tbsp dark soy sauce
2 tsp soft light brown sugar
1 tsp rice or sherry vinegar
1 tsp chilli sauce
salt and freshly ground black pepper
125 g/4 oz thin, transparent rice noodles or rice sticks
oil for deep frying

TO GARNISH:
spring onion tassels
slices of red chilli

Food Fact

Chinese five-spice powder adds a taste not unlike liquorice to this dish. It is made from a mixture of Szechuan pepper, cloves, cassia, fennel and star anise, ground together to make a golden-brown powder. Add just a tiny pinch, as it has a powerful flavour.

Warm Swordfish Niçoise

1 Place the swordfish steaks in a shallow dish. Mix the lime juice with the oil, season to taste with salt and pepper and spoon over the steaks. Turn the steaks to coat them evenly. Cover and place in the refrigerator to marinate for 1 hour.

2 Bring a large pan of lightly salted water to a rolling boil. Add the farfalle and cook according to the packet instructions, or until 'al dente'. Add the French beans about 4 minutes before the end of cooking time.

3 Mix the mustard, vinegar and sugar together in a small jug. Gradually whisk in the olive oil to make a thick dressing.

4 Cook the swordfish in a griddle pan or under a hot preheated grill for 2 minutes on each side, or until just cooked through; overcooking will make it tough and dry. Remove and cut into 2 cm/¾ inch chunks.

5 Drain the pasta and beans thoroughly and place in a large bowl. Pour over the dressing and toss to coat. Add the cooked swordfish, tomatoes, olives, hard-boiled eggs and anchovy fillets. Gently toss together, taking care not to break up the eggs.

6 Tip into a warmed serving bowl or divide the pasta between individual plates. Serve immediately.

INGREDIENTS
Serves 4

4 swordfish steaks, about 2.5 cm/1 inch thick, weighing about 175 g/6 oz each
juice of 1 lime
2 tbsp olive oil
salt and freshly ground black pepper
400 g/14 oz farfalle
225 g/8 oz French beans, topped and cut in half
1 tsp Dijon mustard
2 tsp white wine vinegar
pinch caster sugar
3 tbsp olive oil
225 g/8 oz ripe tomatoes, quartered
50 g/2 oz pitted black olives
2 medium eggs, hard boiled and quartered
8 anchovy fillets, drained and cut in half lengthways

Helpful Hint

This dish can also be made with fresh tuna fish steaks. Prepare and cook in exactly the same way as the swordfish, although tuna can be served slightly rare, if wished. Do not marinate the fish for more than the time suggested, or it may become over-tenderised and lose its firm texture.

Oven-roasted Vegetables with Sausages

1 Preheat oven to 200°C/ 400°F/Gas Mark 6, 15 minutes before cooking. Cut the aubergines and courgettes into bite-sized chunks. Place the olive oil in a large roasting tin and heat in the preheated oven for 3 minutes, or until very hot. Add the aubergines, courgettes and garlic cloves, then stir until coated in the hot oil and cook in the oven for 10 minutes.

2 Remove the roasting tin from the oven and stir. Lightly prick the sausages, add to the roasting tin and return to the oven. Continue to roast for a further 20 minutes, turning once during cooking, until the vegetables are tender and the sausages are golden brown.

3 Meanwhile, roughly chop the plum tomatoes and drain the cannellini beans. Remove the sausages from the oven and stir in the tomatoes and cannellini beans. Season to taste with salt and pepper, then return to the oven for 5 minutes, or until heated thoroughly.

4 Scatter over the basil leaves and sprinkle with plenty of Parmesan cheese and extra freshly ground black pepper. Serve immediately.

INGREDIENTS
Serves 4

2 medium aubergines, trimmed
3 medium courgettes, trimmed
4 tbsp olive oil
6 garlic cloves
8 Tuscany-style sausages
4 plum tomatoes
2 x 300 g cans cannellini beans
salt and freshly ground black pepper
1 bunch of fresh basil, torn into coarse pieces
4 tbsp Parmesan cheese, grated

Helpful Hint

Although it is worth seeking out Tuscany-style sausages for this dish, a good alternative would be to use Toulouse sausages instead, as these are more readily available from large supermarkets and from selected butchers.

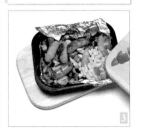

Hot Salami & Vegetable Gratin

1 Preheat oven to 200°C/ 400°F/Gas Mark 6. Peel and slice the carrots, trim the beans and asparagus and reserve. Cook the carrots in a saucepan of lightly salted, boiling water for 5 minutes. Add the remaining vegetables, except the spinach, and cook for about a further 5 minutes, or until tender. Drain and place in an ovenproof dish.

2 Discard any skin from the outside of the salami, if necessary, then chop roughly. Heat the oil in a frying pan and fry the salami for 4–5 minutes, stirring occasionally, until golden. Using a slotted spoon, transfer the salami to the ovenproof dish and scatter over the mint.

3 Add the butter to the frying pan and cook the spinach for 1–2 minutes, or until just wilted. Stir in the double cream and season well with salt and pepper. Spoon the mixture over the vegetables.

4 Whiz the ciabatta loaf in a food processor to make breadcrumbs. Stir in the Parmesan cheese and sprinkle over the vegetables. Bake in the preheated oven for 20 minutes, until golden and heated through. Serve with a green salad.

INGREDIENTS
Serves 4

350 g/12 oz carrots
175 g/6 oz fine green beans
250 g/9 oz asparagus tips
175 g/6 oz frozen peas
225 g/8 oz Italian salami
1 tbsp olive oil
1 tbsp freshly chopped mint
25 g/1 oz butter
150 g/5 oz baby spinach leaves
150 ml/¼ pint double cream
salt and freshly ground black pepper
1 small or ½ an olive ciabatta loaf
75 g/3 oz Parmesan cheese, grated
green salad, to serve

Tasty Tip

Prepare this dish ahead up to the end of step 3 and refrigerate until ready to cook, then top with breadcrumbs and bake, adding about 5 minutes to the final cooking time.

Antipasto Penne

1 Preheat the grill just before cooking. Cut the courgettes into thick slices. Rinse the tomatoes and cut into quarters, then cut the ham into strips. Pour the oil into a baking dish and place under the grill for 2 minutes, or until almost smoking. Remove from the grill and stir in the courgettes. Return to the grill and cook for 8 minutes, stirring occasionally. Remove from the grill and add the tomatoes and cook for a further 3 minutes.

2 Add the ham to the baking dish and cook under the grill for 4 minutes, until all the vegetables are charred and the ham is brown. Season to taste with salt and pepper.

3 Meanwhile, plunge the pasta into a large saucepan of lightly salted, boiling water, return to a rolling boil, stir and cook for 8 minutes, or until 'al dente'. Drain well and return to the saucepan.

4 Stir the antipasto into the vegetables and cook under the grill for 2 minutes, or until heated through. Add the cooked pasta and toss together gently with the remaining ingredients. Grill for a further 4 minutes, then serve immediately.

INGREDIENTS
Serves 4

3 medium courgettes, trimmed
4 plum tomatoes
175 g/6 oz Italian ham
2 tbsp olive oil
salt and freshly ground black pepper
350 g/12 oz dried penne pasta
285 g jar antipasto
125 g/4 oz mozzarella cheese, drained and diced
125 g/4 oz Gorgonzola cheese, crumbled
3 tbsp freshly chopped flat-leaf parsley

Food Fact

The term antipasto refers to the course served before the *pasto* or meal begins and its purpose is to whet the appetite for the following courses. In Italy, these are served in small quantities, though 2 or 3 different dishes may be served at once. There are no hard and fast rules as to what constitutes a suitable dish for antipasti – there are literally thousands of regional variations.

Italian Risotto

1 Chop the onion and garlic and reserve. Heat the olive oil in a large frying pan and cook the salami for 3–5 minutes, or until golden. Using a slotted spoon, transfer to a plate and keep warm. Add the asparagus and stir-fry for 2–3 minutes, until just wilted. Transfer to the plate with the salami. Add the onion and garlic and cook for 5 minutes, or until softened.

2 Add the rice to the pan and cook for about 2 minutes. Add the wine, bring to the boil, then simmer, stirring until the wine has been absorbed. Add

half the stock and return to the boil. Simmer, stirring until the liquid has been absorbed.

3 Add half of the remaining stock and the broad beans to the rice mixture. Bring to the boil, then simmer for a further 5–10 minutes, or until all of the liquid has been absorbed.

4 Add the remaining stock, bring to the boil, then simmer until all the liquid is absorbed and the rice is tender. Stir in the remaining ingredients until the cheese has just melted. Serve immediately.

INGREDIENTS
Serves 4

1 onion, peeled
2 garlic cloves, peeled
1 tbsp olive oil
125 g/4 oz Italian salami or speck, chopped
125 g/4 oz asparagus
350 g/12 oz risotto rice
300 ml/½ pt dry white wine
1 litre/1¼ pints chicken stock, warmed
125g/4 oz frozen broad beans, defrosted
125g/4 oz Dolcelatte cheese, diced
3 tbsp freshly chopped mixed herbs, such as parsley and basil
salt and freshly ground black pepper

Food Fact

Cheese is a common constituent in the making of risotto and in fact helps to provide some of its creamy texture. Usually Parmesan cheese is added at the end of cooking but here a good-quality Dolcelatte is used instead.

Pan-fried Beef with Creamy Mushrooms

1 Cut the shallots in half if large, then chop the garlic. Heat the oil in a large frying pan and cook the shallots for about 8 minutes, stirring occasionally, until almost softened. Add the garlic and beef and cook for 8–10 minutes, turning once during cooking until the meat is browned all over. Using a slotted spoon, transfer the beef to a plate and keep warm.

2 Rinse the tomatoes and cut into eighths, then wipe the mushrooms and slice. Add to the pan and cook for 5 minutes, stirring frequently until the mushrooms have softened.

3 Pour in the brandy and heat through. Draw the pan off the heat and carefully ignite. Allow the flames to subside. Pour in the wine, return to the heat and bring to the boil. Boil until reduced by one-third. Draw the pan off the heat, season to taste with salt and pepper, add the cream and stir.

4 Arrange the beef on serving plates and spoon over the sauce. Serve with baby new potatoes and a few green beans.

INGREDIENTS
Serves 4

225 g/8 oz shallots, peeled
2 garlic cloves, peeled
2 tbsp olive oil
4 medallions of beef
4 plum tomatoes
125 g/4 oz flat mushrooms
3 tbsp brandy
150 ml/¼ pint red wine
salt and freshly ground black pepper
4 tbsp double cream

TO SERVE:
baby new potatoes
freshly cooked green beans

Helpful Hint

To prepare medallions of beef, buy a piece of fillet weighing approximately 700 g/1½lb. Cut crosswise into 4 pieces.

Oven-baked Pork Balls with Peppers

1 Preheat oven to 200°C/ 400°F/Gas Mark 6, 15 minutes before cooking. Crush the garlic, then blend with the softened butter, the parsley and enough lemon juice to give a soft consistency. Shape into a roll, wrap in baking parchment paper and chill in the refrigerator for at least 30 minutes.

2 Mix together the pork, basil, 1 chopped garlic clove, sun-dried tomatoes and seasoning until well combined. With damp hands, divide the mixture into 16, roll into balls and reserve.

3 Spoon the olive oil in a large roasting tin and place

in the preheated oven for about 3 minutes, until very hot. Remove from the heat and stir in the pork balls, the remaining chopped garlic and peppers. Bake for about 15 minutes. Remove from the oven and stir in the cherry tomatoes and season to taste with plenty of salt and pepper. Bake for about a further 20 minutes.

4 Just before the pork balls are ready, slice the bread, toast lightly and spread with the prepared garlic butter. Remove the pork balls from the oven, stir in the vinegar and serve immediately with garlic bread.

INGREDIENTS
Serves 4

FOR THE GARLIC BREAD:
2–4 garlic cloves, peeled
50 g/2 oz butter, softened
1 tbsp freshly chopped parsley
2–3 tsp lemon juice
1 focaccia loaf

FOR THE PORK BALLS:
450 g/1 lb fresh pork mince
4 tbsp freshly chopped basil
2 garlic cloves, peeled and chopped
3 sun-dried tomatoes, chopped
salt and freshly ground black pepper
3 tbsp olive oil
1 medium red pepper, deseeded and cut into chunks
1 medium green pepper, deseeded and cut into chunks
1 medium yellow pepper, deseeded and cut into chunks
225 g/8 oz cherry tomatoes
2 tbsp balsamic vinegar

Helpful Hint
Prepare the garlic butter ahead to the end of step 1.
Refrigerate for up to 1 week or freeze for up to 2 months.

Pork Chop Hotpot

1 Preheat oven to 190°C/ 375°F/Gas Mark 5, 10 minutes before cooking. Trim the pork chops, removing any excess fat, wipe with a clean, damp cloth, then dust with a little flour and reserve. Cut the shallots in half if large. Chop the garlic and slice the sun-dried tomatoes.

2 Heat the olive oil in a large casserole dish and cook the pork chops for about 5 minutes, turning occasionally during cooking, until browned all over. Using a slotted spoon, carefully lift out of the dish and reserve. Add the shallots and cook for 5 minutes, stirring occasionally.

3 Return the pork chops to the casserole dish and scatter with the garlic and sun-dried tomatoes, then pour over the can of tomatoes with their juice.

4 Blend the red wine, stock and tomato purée together and add the chopped oregano. Season to taste with salt and pepper, then pour over the pork chops and bring to a gentle boil. Cover with a close-fitting lid and cook in the preheated oven for 1 hour, or until the pork chops are tender. Adjust the seasoning to taste, then scatter with a few oregano leaves and serve immediately with freshly cooked potatoes and French beans.

INGREDIENTS
Serves 4

4 pork chops
flour for dusting
225 g/8 oz shallots, peeled
2 garlic cloves, peeled
50 g/2 oz sun-dried tomatoes
2 tbsp olive oil
400 g can plum tomatoes
150 ml/¼ pint red wine
150 ml/¼ pint chicken stock
3 tbsp tomato purée
2 tbsp freshly chopped oregano
salt and freshly ground black pepper
fresh oregano leaves, to garnish

TO SERVE:
freshly cooked new potatoes
French beans

Tasty Tip

Choose bone-in chops for this recipe. Remove any excess fat and rind before cooking.

Rabbit Italian

1 Trim the rabbit if necessary. Chop the bacon and reserve. Chop the garlic and onion and slice the carrot thinly, then trim the celery and chop.

2 Heat the butter and 1 tablespoon of the oil in a large saucepan and brown the rabbit for 5 minutes, stirring frequently, until sealed all over. Transfer the rabbit to a plate and reserve.

3 Add the garlic, bacon, celery, carrot and onion to the saucepan and cook for a further 5 minutes, stirring occasionally, until softened, then return the rabbit to the saucepan and pour over the tomatoes with their juice and the wine. Season to taste with salt and pepper. Bring to the boil, cover, reduce the heat and simmer for 45 minutes.

4 Meanwhile, wipe the mushrooms and if large, cut in half. Heat the remaining oil in a small frying pan and sauté the mushrooms for 2 minutes. Drain, then add to the rabbit and cook for 15 minutes, or until the rabbit is tender. Season to taste and serve immediately with freshly cooked pasta and a green salad.

INGREDIENTS
Serves 4

450 g/1 lb diced rabbit, thawed
   if frozen
6 rashers streaky bacon
1 garlic clove, peeled
1 onion, peeled
1 carrot, peeled
1 celery stalk
25 g/1 oz butter
2 tbsp olive oil
400 g can chopped tomatoes
150 ml/¼ pint red wine
salt and freshly ground black
   pepper
125 g/4 oz mushrooms

TO SERVE:
freshly cooked pasta
green salad

Helpful Hint

If you prefer to buy a whole rabbit, have your butcher joint it for you into 8 pieces. The method and cooking time will remain the same.

Roasted Lamb
with Rosemary & Garlic

1 Preheat oven to 200°C/ 400°F/Gas Mark 6, 15 minutes before roasting. Wipe the leg of lamb with a clean damp cloth, then place the lamb in a large roasting tin. With a sharp knife, make small, deep incisions into the meat. Cut 2–3 garlic cloves into small slivers, then insert with a few small sprigs of rosemary into the lamb. Season to taste with salt and pepper and cover the lamb with the slices of pancetta.

2 Drizzle over 1 tablespoon of the olive oil and lay a few more rosemary sprigs across the

lamb. Roast in the preheated oven for 30 minutes, then pour over the vinegar.

3 Peel the potatoes and cut into large dice. Peel the onion and cut into thick wedges then thickly slice the remaining garlic. Arrange around the lamb. Pour the remaining olive oil over the potatoes, then reduce the oven temperature to 180°C/ 350°F/Gas Mark 4 and roast for a further 1 hour, or until the lamb is tender. Garnish with fresh sprigs of rosemary and serve immediately with the roast potatoes and ratatouille.

INGREDIENTS
Serves 6

1.6 kg/3½ lb leg of lamb
8 garlic cloves, peeled
few sprigs of fresh rosemary
salt and freshly ground black pepper
4 slices pancetta
4 tbsp olive oil
4 tbsp red wine vinegar
900 g/2 lb potatoes
1 large onion
sprigs of fresh rosemary, to garnish
freshly cooked ratatouille, to serve

Helpful Hint

If you are unable to get a leg of lamb weighing exactly 1.6 kg/3½ lb, calculate the cooking time as follows: 20 minutes per 450 g/lb plus 30 minutes for rare, 25 minutes per 450 g/lb plus 30 minutes for medium and 30 minutes per 450 g/lb plus 30 minutes for well done.

Braised Lamb with Broad Beans

1 Trim the lamb, discarding any fat or gristle, then place the flour in a polythene bag, add the lamb and toss until coated thoroughly. Peel and slice the onion and garlic and reserve. Heat the olive oil in a heavy-based saucepan and when hot, add the lamb and cook, stirring until the meat is sealed and browned all over. Using a slotted spoon transfer the lamb to a plate and reserve.

2 Add the onion and garlic to the saucepan and cook for 3 minutes, stirring frequently until softened, then return the lamb to the saucepan. Add the chopped tomatoes with their juice, the stock, the chopped thyme and oregano to the pan and season to taste with salt and pepper. Bring to the boil, then cover with a close-fitting lid, reduce the heat and simmer for 1 hour.

3 Add the broad beans to the lamb and simmer for 20–30 minutes, or until the lamb is tender. Garnish with fresh oregano and serve with creamy mashed potatoes.

INGREDIENTS
Serves 4

700 g/1½ lb lamb, cut into large chunks
1 tbsp plain flour
1 onion
2 garlic cloves
1 tbsp olive oil
400 g can chopped tomatoes with basil
300 ml/½ pint lamb stock
2 tbsp freshly chopped thyme
2 tbsp freshly chopped oregano
salt and freshly ground black pepper
150 g/5 oz frozen broad beans
fresh oregano, to garnish
creamy mashed potatoes, to serve

Tasty Tip

If you want to use fresh broad beans in season, you will need about 450 g/1 lb of beans in their pods for this recipe. If you prefer to peel the beans, plunge them first into boiling salted water for about 30 seconds, drain and refresh under cold water. The skins will come off very easily.

Spaghetti Bolognese

1 Peel and chop the carrot, trim and chop the celery, then peel and chop the onion and garlic. Heat a large non-stick frying pan and sauté the beef and bacon for 5–10 minutes, stirring occasionally, until browned. Add the prepared vegetables to the frying pan and cook for about 3 minutes, or until softened, stirring occasionally.

2 Add the flour and cook for 1 minute. Stir in the red wine, tomatoes, tomato purée, mixed herbs, seasoning to taste and sugar. Bring to the boil, then cover and simmer for 45 minutes, stirring occasionally.

3 Meanwhile, bring a large saucepan of lightly salted water to the boil and cook the spaghetti for 10–12 minutes, or until 'al dente'. Drain well and divide between 4 serving plates. Spoon over the sauce, garnish with a few sprigs of oregano and serve immediately with plenty of Parmesan shavings.

INGREDIENTS
Serves 4

1 carrot
2 celery stalks
1 onion
2 garlic cloves
450 g/1 lb lean minced beef steak
225 g/8 oz smoked streaky bacon, chopped
1 tbsp plain flour
150 ml/¼ pint red wine
379 g can chopped tomatoes
2 tbsp tomato purée
2 tsp dried mixed herbs
salt and freshly ground black pepper
pinch of sugar
350 g/12 oz spaghetti
sprigs of fresh oregano, to garnish
shavings of Parmesan cheese, to serve

Tasty Tip

This is an ideal sauce to use in a baked lasagne. Layer up the sauce with sheets of fresh or precooked lasagne and top with a ready-made bechamel sauce and Parmesan cheese. Bake for 30–40 minutes in a preheated oven 190°C/375°F/Gas Mark 5, or until bubbling and the top is golden.

Meatballs with Olives

1 Chop 2 of the shallots finely and place in a bowl with the garlic, beef, bread-crumbs, basil and seasoning to taste. With damp hands, bring the mixture together and shape into small balls about the size of an apricot.

2 Heat the olive oil in a frying pan and cook the meatballs for 8–10 minutes, turning occasionally, until browned and the beef is tender. Remove and drain on absorbent kitchen paper.

3 Slice the remaining shallots, add to the pan and cook for 5 minutes, until softened. Blend the pesto and mascarpone together, then stir into the pan

with the olives. Bring to the boil, reduce the heat and return the meatballs to the pan. Simmer for 5–8 minutes, or until the sauce has thickened and the meatballs are cooked thoroughly.

4 Meanwhile, bring a large saucepan of lightly salted water to the boil and cook the noodles for 8–10 minutes, or 'al dente'. Drain the noodles, reserving 2 tablespoons of the cooking liquor. Return the noodles to the pan with the cooking liquor and pour in the sauce. Stir the noodles, then sprinkle with chopped parsley. Garnish with a few sprigs of parsley and serve immediately with grated Parmesan cheese.

INGREDIENTS
Serves 4

250 g/9 oz shallots, peeled
2–3 garlic cloves, peeled
450 g/1 lb minced beef steak
2 tbsp fresh white or wholemeal
  breadcrumbs
3 tbsp freshly chopped basil
salt and freshly ground black
  pepper
2 tbsp olive oil
5 tbsp ready-made pesto sauce
5 tbsp mascarpone cheese
50 g/2 oz pitted black olives,
  halved
275 g/10 oz thick pasta noodles
freshly chopped flat-leaf parsley
sprigs of fresh flat-leaf parsley,
  to garnish
freshly grated Parmesan cheese,
  to serve

Helpful Hint

To stone olives, make a cut lengthways around the olive, then place on a chopping board with the cut facing upwards. Put the side of the knife (with the blade facing away from you) on top of the olive and tap sharply with the heel of your hand. The stone should come away leaving the olive in 2 pieces.

Traditional Lasagne

1 Preheat oven to 200°C/ 400°F/Gas Mark 6, 15 minutes before cooking. Cook the beef and pancetta in a large saucepan for 10 minutes, stirring to break up any lumps. Add the onion, celery and mushrooms and cook for 4 minutes, or until softened slightly.

2 Stir in the garlic and 1 tablespoon of the flour, then cook for 1 minute. Stir in the stock, herbs and tomato purée. Season to taste with salt and pepper. Bring to the boil, then cover, reduce the heat and simmer for 45 minutes.

3 Meanwhile, melt the butter in a small saucepan and stir in the remaining flour, mustard powder and nutmeg, until well blended. Cook for 2 minutes. Remove from the heat and gradually blend in the milk until smooth. Return to the heat and bring to the boil, stirring, until thickened. Gradually stir in half the Parmesan and Cheddar cheeses until melted. Season to taste.

4 Spoon half the meat mixture into the base of a large ovenproof dish. Top with a single layer of pasta. Spread over half the sauce and scatter with half the cheese. Repeat layers finishing with cheese. Bake in the preheated oven for 30 minutes, or until the pasta is cooked and the top is golden brown and bubbly. Serve immediately with crusty bread and a green salad.

Helpful Hint

This is a useful dish for entertaining. Assemble the lasagne ahead of time then either refrigerate or even freeze until needed. Allow to come to room temperature or to thaw completely and cook as above, adding an extra 5 minutes or so to the cooking time.

INGREDIENTS
Serves 4

450 g/1 lb lean minced beef steak
175 g/6 oz pancetta or smoked streaky bacon, chopped
1 large onion, peeled and chopped
2 celery stalks, trimmed and chopped
125 g/4 oz button mushrooms, wiped and chopped
2 garlic cloves, peeled and chopped
90 g/3½ oz plain flour
300 ml/½ pint beef stock
1 tbsp freeze-dried mixed herbs
5 tbsp tomato purée
salt and freshly ground black pepper
75 g/3 oz butter
1 tsp English mustard powder
pinch of freshly grated nutmeg
900 ml/1½ pints milk
125 g/4 oz Parmesan cheese, grated
125 g/4 oz Cheddar cheese, grated
8–12 precooked lasagne sheets

TO SERVE:
crusty bread
fresh green salad leaves

Fillet Steaks with Tomato & Garlic Sauce

1 Make a small cross on the top of each tomato and place in a large bowl. Cover with boiling water and leave for 2 minutes. Using a slotted spoon, remove the tomatoes and skin carefully. Repeat until all the tomatoes are skinned. Place on a chopping board, cut into quarters, remove the seeds and roughly chop, then reserve.

2 Peel and chop the garlic. Heat half the olive oil in a saucepan and cook the garlic for 30 seconds. Add the chopped tomatoes with the basil, oregano, red wine and season to taste with salt and pepper. Bring to the boil then reduce the heat, cover and simmer for 15 minutes, stirring occasionally, or until the sauce is reduced and thickened. Stir the olives into the sauce and keep warm while cooking the steaks.

3 Meanwhile, lightly oil a griddle pan or heavy-based frying pan with the remaining olive oil and cook the steaks for 2 minutes on each side to seal. Continue to cook the steaks for a further 2–4 minutes, depending on personal preference. Serve the steaks immediately with the garlic sauce and freshly cooked vegetables.

INGREDIENTS
Serves 4

700 g / 1½ lb ripe tomatoes
2 garlic cloves
2 tbsp olive oil
2 tbsp freshly chopped basil
2 tbsp freshly chopped oregano
2 tbsp red wine
salt and freshly ground black pepper
75 g / 3 oz pitted black olives, chopped
4 fillet steaks, about 175 g / 6 oz each in weight
freshly cooked vegetables, to serve

Helpful Hint

Fillet steak should be a deep mahogany colour with a good marbling of fat. If the meat is bright red or if the fat is bright white the meat has not been aged properly and will probably be quite tough.

Veal Escalopes with Marsala Sauce

1 Place the veal escalopes between sheets of non-pvc clingfilm and using a mallet or rolling pin, pound lightly to flatten out thinly to about 5 mm/¼ inch thickness. Remove the clingfilm and sprinkle the veal escalopes with lemon juice, salt and black pepper.

2 Place a sage leaf in the centre of each escalope. Top with a slice of prosciutto making sure it just fits, then roll up the escalopes enclosing the prosciutto and sage leaves. Secure each escalope with a cocktail stick.

3 Heat the olive oil and butter in a large non-stick frying pan and fry the onions for 5 minutes, or until softened. Add the garlic and rolled escalopes and cook for about 8 minutes, turning occasionally, until the escalopes are browned all over.

4 Add the Marsala wine and cream to the pan and bring to the boil, cover and simmer for 10 minutes, or until the veal is tender. Season to taste and then sprinkle with the parsley. Discard the cocktail sticks and serve immediately with a selection of freshly cooked vegetables.

INGREDIENTS
Serves 6

6 veal escalopes, about
    125 g/4 oz each
lemon juice
salt and freshly ground black
    pepper
6 sage leaves
6 slices prosciutto
2 tbsp olive oil
25 g/1 oz butter
1 onion, peeled and sliced
1 garlic clove, peeled and chopped
2 tbsp Marsala wine
4 tbsp double cream
2 tbsp freshly chopped parsley
sage leaves to garnish
selection of freshly cooked
    vegetables, to serve

Tasty Tip

If you prefer not to use veal, substitute with thinly sliced boneless pork loin or thin slices of turkey or chicken breast. You can substitute the sage leaves with basil sprigs and for a change add a little sliced cheese, such as Gruyère.

Cannelloni

1 Preheat oven to 190°C/ 375°F/Gas Mark 5, 10 minutes before cooking. Heat the olive oil in a frying pan and cook the mince and chicken livers for about 5 minutes, stirring occasionally, until browned all over. Break up any lumps if necessary with a wooden spoon.

2 Add the onion and garlic and cook for 4 minutes, until softened. Add the spinach, oregano, nutmeg and season to taste with salt and pepper. Cook until all the liquid has evaporated, then remove the pan from the heat and allow to cool. Stir in the ricotta cheese.

3 Meanwhile, melt the butter in a small saucepan and stir in the plain flour to form a roux.

Cook for 2 minutes, stirring occasionally. Remove from the heat and blend in the milk until smooth. Return to the heat and bring to the boil, stirring until the sauce has thickened. Reserve.

4 Spoon a thin layer of the tomato sauce on the base of a large ovenproof dish. Divide the pork filling between the cannelloni tubes. Arrange on top of the tomato sauce. Spoon over the remaining tomato sauce.

5 Pour over the white sauce and sprinkle with the Parmesan cheese. Bake in the preheated oven for 30–35 minutes, or until the cannelloni is tender and the top is golden brown. Serve immediately with a green salad.

INGREDIENTS
Serves 4

2 tbsp olive oil
175 g/6 oz fresh pork mince
75 g/3 oz chicken livers, chopped
1 small onion, peeled and chopped
1 garlic clove, peeled and chopped
175 g/6 oz frozen chopped
  spinach, thawed
1 tbsp freeze-dried oregano
pinch of freshly grated nutmeg
salt and freshly ground black
  pepper
175 g/6 oz ricotta cheese
25 g/1 oz butter
25 g/1 oz plain flour
600 ml/1 pint milk
600 ml/1 pint ready-made
  tomato sauce
16 precooked cannelloni tubes
50 g/2 oz Parmesan cheese,
  grated
green salad, to serve

Tasty Tip

To make chicken cannelloni, substitute 225 g/
8 oz boneless, skinless chicken breast that has been
finely chopped in a food processor. Minced chicken
is also available from large supermarkets.

Vitello Tonnato
(Veal in Tuna Sauce)

1 Place the veal in a large bowl and pour over the wine. Add the onion, carrot, celery, bay leaf, garlic cloves, parsley, salt and pepper. Cover tightly and chill overnight in the refrigerator. Transfer the contents of the bowl to a large saucepan, add just enough water to cover the meat. Bring to the boil, cover and simmer for 1–1¼ hours, or until the veal is tender.

2 Remove from the heat and allow the veal to cool in the juices. Using a slotted spoon, transfer the veal to a plate, pat dry with absorbent kitchen paper and reserve.

3 Place the tuna, capers, anchovy fillets, mayonnaise and lemon juice in a food processor or liquidiser and blend until smooth, adding a few spoonfuls of the pan juices to make the sauce of a coating consistency, if necessary. Season to taste with salt and pepper.

4 Using a sharp knife slice the veal thinly and arrange on a large serving platter.

5 Spoon the sauce over the veal. Cover with clingfilm and chill in the refrigerator overnight. Garnish with lemon wedges, capers and olives. Serve with salad and tomato wedges.

INGREDIENTS
Serves 6–8

900g/2 lb boned, rolled leg or
*   loin of veal*
300 ml/½ pint dry white wine
1 onion, peeled and chopped
1 carrot, peeled and chopped
2 celery stalks, trimmed and
*   chopped*
1 bay leaf
2 garlic cloves
few sprigs of parsley
salt and freshly ground black pepper
200 g can tuna in oil
2 tbsp capers, drained
6 anchovy fillets
200 ml/7 fl oz mayonnaise
juice of ½ lemon

TO GARNISH:
lemon wedges
capers
black olives

TO SERVE:
fresh green salad leaves
tomato wedges

Tasty Tip
Look for tuna steak that has been packed in olive oil – it has the best flavour for this dish. Drain well before using to remove any excess oil.

Italian Beef Pot Roast

1 Preheat oven to 150°C/ 300°F/Gas Mark 2, 10 minutes before cooking. Place the beef in a bowl. Add the onions, garlic, celery and carrots. Place the tomatoes in a bowl and cover with boiling water. Allow to stand for 2 minutes and drain. Peel away the skins, discard the seeds and chop, then add to the bowl with the red wine. Cover tightly and marinate in the refrigerator overnight.

2 Lift the marinated beef from the bowl and pat dry with absorbent kitchen paper. Heat the olive oil in a large casserole dish and cook the beef until it is browned all over, then remove from the dish. Drain the vegetables from the marinade, reserving the marinade. Add the vegetables to the casserole dish and fry gently for 5 minutes, stirring occasionally, until all the vegetables are browned.

3 Return the beef to the casserole dish with the marinade, beef stock, tomato purée, mixed herbs and season with salt and pepper. Bring to the boil, then cover and cook in the preheated oven for 3 hours.

4 Using a slotted spoon transfer the beef and any large vegetables to a plate and leave in a warm place. Blend the butter and flour to form a paste. Bring the casserole juices to the boil and then gradually stir in small spoonfuls of the paste. Cook until thickened. Serve with the sauce and a selection of vegetables.

INGREDIENTS
Serves 6

1.8 kg/4 lb brisket of beef
225 g/8 oz small onions, peeled
3 garlic cloves, peeled and chopped
2 celery sticks, trimmed and chopped
2 carrots, peeled and sliced
450 g/1 lb ripe tomatoes
300 ml/½ pint Italian red wine
2 tbsp olive oil
300 ml/½ pint beef stock
1 tbsp tomato purée
2 tsp freeze-dried mixed herbs
salt and freshly ground black pepper
25 g/1 oz butter
25 g/1 oz plain flour
freshly cooked vegetables, to serve

Helpful Hint

Most supermarkets do not sell brisket, but good butchers will be able to order it. Brisket is an excellent cut for all kinds of pot roasts, but make sure it is professionally trimmed as it can contain a lot of gristle and fat.

Italian Meatballs in Tomato Sauce

1 To make the tomato sauce, heat half the olive oil in a saucepan and cook half the chopped onion for 5 minutes, until softened.

2 Add the garlic, chopped tomatoes, tomato paste, mixed herbs and red wine to the pan and season to taste with salt and pepper. Stir well until blended. Bring to the boil, then cover and simmer for 15 minutes.

3 To make the meatballs, place the pork, bread-crumbs, remaining onion, egg yolk and half the Parmesan in a large bowl. Season well and mix together with your hands. Divide the mixture into 20 balls.

4 Flatten 1 ball out in the palm of your hands, place an olive in the centre, then squeeze the meat around the olive to enclose completely. Repeat with remaining mixture and olives.

5 Place the meatballs on a baking sheet and cover with clingfilm and chill in the refrigerator for 30 minutes.

6 Heat the remaining oil in a large frying pan and cook the meatballs for 8–10 minutes, turning occasionally, until golden brown. Pour in the sauce and heat through. Sprinkle with chives and the remaining Parmesan. Serve immediately with the freshly cooked pasta.

INGREDIENTS
Serves 4

FOR THE TOMATO SAUCE:
4 tbsp olive oil
1 large onion, peeled and finely chopped
2 garlic cloves, peeled and chopped
400 g can chopped tomatoes
1 tbsp sun-dried tomato paste
1 tbsp dried mixed herbs
150 ml/¼ pint red wine
salt and freshly ground black pepper

FOR THE MEATBALLS:
450 g/1 lb fresh pork mince
50 g/2 oz fresh breadcrumbs
1 medium egg yolk
75 g/3 oz Parmesan cheese, grated
20 small stuffed green olives
freshly snipped chives, to garnish
freshly cooked pasta, to serve

Tasty Tip

There are lots of different kinds of stuffed olives readily available – why not try pimento, almond or even anchovy stuffed olives in this recipe.

Italian Calf Liver

1 Cut the liver into very thin slices and place in a shallow dish. Sprinkle over the onion, bay leaves, parsley, sage and peppercorns. Blend the redcurrant jelly with 1 tablespoon of the oil and the vinegar. Pour over the liver, cover and leave to marinate for at least 30 minutes. Turn the liver occasionally or spoon over the marinade.

2 Remove the liver from the marinade, strain the liquor and reserve. Season the flour with salt and pepper, then use to coat the liver. Add the remaining oil to a heavy based frying pan,

then sauté the garlic and peppers for 5 minutes. Using a slotted spoon, remove from the pan.

3 Add the liver to the pan, turn the heat up to high and cook until the meat is browned on all sides. Return the garlic and peppers to the pan and add the reserved marinade, the sun-dried tomatoes and stock. Bring to the boil, then reduce the heat and simmer for 3–4 minutes, or until the liver is cooked. Add more seasoning, then garnish with a few sage leaves and serve immediately with diced sauté potatoes.

INGREDIENTS
Serves 4

450 g/1 lb calf liver, trimmed
1 onion, peeled and sliced
2 fresh bay leaves, coarsely torn
fresh parsley sprigs
fresh sage leaves
5 black peppercorns, lightly crushed
1 tbsp redcurrant jelly, warmed
4 tbsp walnut or olive oil
4 tbsp red wine vinegar
3 tbsp plain white flour
salt and freshly ground black pepper
2 garlic cloves, peeled and crushed
1 red pepper, deseeded and sliced
1 yellow pepper, deseeded and sliced
3 tbsp sun-dried tomatoes, chopped
150 ml/¼ pint chicken stock
fresh sage leaves, to garnish
diced sauté potatoes, to serve

Tasty Tip
Be careful not to overcook the liver in this recipe as it will become tough and dry, even though it is cooked in a sauce. Liver is best left a little pink in the centre.

Spaghetti Bolognese

1 Heat the olive oil in a large heavy-based pan, add the bacon and cook for 5 minutes or until slightly coloured. Add the onion, carrot, celery, garlic and bay leaf and cook, stirring, for 8 minutes, or until the vegetables are soft.

2 Add the minced beef to the pan and cook, stirring with a wooden spoon to break up any lumps in the meat, for 5-8 minutes, or until browned.

3 Stir the tomatoes and tomato paste into the mince and pour in the wine and stock. Bring to the boil, lower the heat and simmer for a least 40 minutes, stirring occasionally. The longer you leave the sauce to cook, the more intense the flavour. Season to taste with salt and pepper and remove the bay leaf.

4 Meanwhile, bring a large pan of lightly salted water to a rolling boil, add the spaghetti and cook for about 8 minutes or until 'al dente'. Drain and arrange on warmed serving plates. Top with the prepared Bolognese sauce and serve immediately sprinkled with grated Parmesan cheese.

INGREDIENTS
Serves 4

3 tbsp olive oil

50 g/2 oz unsmoked streaky bacon, rind removed and chopped

1 small onion, peeled and finely chopped

1 carrot, peeled and finely chopped

1 celery, trimmed and finely chopped

2 garlic cloves, peeled and crushed

1 bay leaf

500 g/1 lb 2 oz minced beef steak

400 g can chopped tomatoes

2 tbsp tomato paste

150 ml/¼ pint red wine

150 ml/¼ pint beef stock

salt and freshly gound black pepper

450 g/1 lb spaghetti

freshly grated Parmesan cheese, to serve

Food Fact

Bolognaise sauce or *ragù alla Bolognaise*, as it is known in Italy, is enjoyed throughout the world, especially in the United States and Britain. It originated in the city of Bologna in Emilia-Romagna, where it is always served with tagliatelle, rather than spaghetti.

Lasagne

1 Preheat the oven to 200°C/ 400°F/Gas Mark 6, 15 minutes before cooking. Melt the butter in a small heavy-based pan, add the flour and cook gently, stirring, for 2 minutes. Remove from the heat and gradually stir in the milk. Return to the heat and cook, stirring, for 2 minutes, or until the sauce thickens. Bring to the boil, remove from the heat and stir in the mustard. Season to taste with salt, pepper and nutmeg.

2 Butter a rectangular ovenproof dish and spread a thin layer of the white sauce over the base. Cover completely with 3 sheets of lasagne.

3 Spoon a quarter of the prepared Bolognese sauce over the lasagne. Spoon over a quarter of the remaining white sauce, then sprinkle with a quarter of the grated Parmesan cheese. Repeat the layers, finishing with Parmesan cheese.

4 Bake in the preheated oven for 30 minutes, or until golden-brown. Garnish with chopped parsley and serve immediately with warm garlic bread.

INGREDIENTS
Serves 4

75 g/3 oz butter
4 tbsp plain flour
750 ml/1¼ pints milk
1 tsp wholegrain mustard
salt and freshly ground black pepper
¼ tsp freshly grated nutmeg
9 sheets lasagne
1 quantity of prepared Bolognese sauce, see page 230
75g/3oz freshly grated Parmesan cheese
freshly chopped parsley, to garnish
garlic bread, to serve

Helpful Hint

For a change use lasagne verdi – it is green lasagne made with spinach. The shape varies according to the manufacturer and may be flat or wavy. Some have crimped edges, which help to trap the sauce and stop it running to the bottom of the dish. As brands come in slightly different sizes, it is worth trying several until you find the one that fits your lasagne dish perfectly!

Cannelloni with Spicy Bolognese Filling

1 Preheat the oven to 200°C/ 400°F/Gas Mark 6, 15 minutes before cooking the stuffed cannelloni. To make the Bolognese sauce, heat the oil in a large heavy-based pan, add the onion and garlic and cook for 8 minutes, or until soft. Add the minced beef and cook, stirring with a wooden spoon to break up lumps, for 5–8 minutes, or until the meat is browned.

2 Stir in the chilli flakes, fennel seeds, oregano, tomatoes and tomato paste and pour in the wine. Season well with salt and pepper. Bring to the boil, cover and lower the heat, then simmer for at least 30 minutes, stirring occasionally. Remove the lid and simmer for a further 10 minutes. Allow to cool slightly.

3 Using a teaspoon, fill the cannelloni tubes with the meat filling. Lay the stuffed cannelloni side by side in a lightly oiled ovenproof dish.

4 Mix the double cream with three-quarters of the Parmesan cheese and the nutmeg. Pour over the cannelloni and sprinkle with the remaining cheese. Bake in the preheated oven for 30 minutes, or until golden-brown and bubbling. Serve immediately with a green salad.

Helpful Hint

The bolognese filling can be made with all beef mince, as here, or more traditionally with a mixture of half beef and half lean minced pork. Minced chicken or turkey also work well in this recipe, although the colour is paler and the flavour less rich, but you can compensate for this by slightly increasing the quantity of herbs and spices.

INGREDIENTS
Serves 6

12 dried cannelloni tubes
300 ml/½ pint double cream
75 g/3 oz freshly grated
  Parmesan cheese
¼ tsp freshly grated nutmeg
crisp green salad, to serve

SPICY BOLOGNESE FILLING:
2 tbsp olive oil
1 small onion, peeled and finely
  chopped
2 garlic cloves, peeled and crushed
500 g/1 lb 2 oz minced
  beef steak
¼ tsp crushed chilli flakes
1 tsp fennel seeds
2 tbsp freshly chopped oregano
400 g can chopped tomatoes
1 tbsp sun-dried tomato paste
150 ml/¼ pint red wine
salt and freshly ground black
  pepper

Spaghetti & Meatballs

1 Preheat the oven to 200°C/ 400°F/Gas Mark 6, 15 minutes before using. Place the chopped tomatoes, tomato paste, chilli sauce and sugar in a saucepan. Season to taste with salt and pepper and bring to the boil. Cover and simmer for 15 minutes, then cook, uncovered, for a further 10 minutes, or until the sauce has reduced and thickened.

2 Meanwhile, make the meatballs. Place the meat, breadcrumbs and onion in a food processor. Blend until all the ingredients are well mixed. Add the beaten egg, tomato paste, parsley and oregano and season to taste. Blend again.

3 Shape the mixture into small balls, about the size of an apricot, and place on an oiled baking tray. Cook in the pre-heated oven for 25–30 minutes, or until browned and cooked.

4 Meanwhile, bring a large pan of lightly salted water to a rolling boil. Add the pasta and cook according to the packet instructions, or until 'al dente'.

5 Drain the pasta and return to the pan. Pour over the tomato sauce and toss gently to coat the spaghetti. Tip into a warmed serving dish and top with the meatballs. Garnish with chopped parsley and serve immediately with grated cheese.

INGREDIENTS
Serves 4

400 g can chopped tomatoes
1 tbsp tomato paste
1 tsp chilli sauce
¼ tsp brown sugar
salt and freshly ground black
 pepper
350 g/12 oz spaghetti
75g/3 oz Cheddar cheese, grated,
 plus extra to serve
freshly chopped parsley, to garnish

FOR THE MEATBALLS:
450 g/1 lb lean pork or beef
 mince
125 g/4 oz fresh breadcrumbs
1 large onion, peeled and finely
 chopped
1 medium egg, beaten
1 tbsp tomato paste
2 tbsp freshly chopped parsley
1 tbsp freshly chopped oregano

Tasty Tip

For a crisper outside to the meatballs, you can fry them instead of baking. Heat 2 tablespoons of olive oil in a very large frying pan and cook over a medium heat for about 15 minutes, turning occasionally, until well-browned.

Chorizo with Pasta in a Tomato Sauce

1 Melt the butter with the olive oil in a large heavy-based pan. Add the onions and sugar and cook over a very low heat, stirring occasionally, for 15 minutes, or until soft and starting to caramelize.

2 Add the garlic and chorizo to the pan and cook for 5 minutes. Stir in the chilli, chopped tomatoes and tomato paste, and pour in the wine. Season well with salt and pepper. Bring to the boil, cover, reduce the heat and simmer for 30 minutes, stirring occasionally. Remove the lid and simmer

for a further 10 minutes, or until the sauce starts to thicken.

3 Meanwhile, bring a large pan of lightly salted water to a rolling boil. Add the pasta and cook according to the packet instructions, or until 'al dente'.

4 Drain the pasta, reserving 2 tablespoons of the water, and return to the pan. Add the chorizo sauce with the reserved cooking water and toss gently until the pasta is evenly covered. Tip into a warmed serving dish, sprinkle with the parsley and serve immediately.

INGREDIENTS
Serves 4

25 g/1 oz butter
2 tbsp olive oil
2 large onions, peeled and finely sliced
1 tsp soft brown sugar
2 garlic cloves, peeled and crushed
225 g/8 oz chorizo, sliced
1 chilli, deseeded and finely sliced
400g can chopped tomatoes
1 tbsp sun-dried tomato paste
150 ml/¼ pint red wine
salt and freshly ground black pepper
450 g/1 lb rigatoni
freshly chopped parsley, to garnish

Helpful Hint

Although there are many different types of chilli, they all have a hot, spicy flavour. Take care when preparing chillies as the volatile oils in the seeds and the membrane can cause irritation – wash your hands thoroughly afterwards.

Moroccan Penne

1 Preheat the oven to 200°C/400°F/Gas Mark 6, 15 minutes before using. Heat the sunflower oil in a large flame-proof casserole. Add the chopped onion and fry for 5 minutes, or until softened.

2 Using a pestle and mortar, pound the garlic, coriander seeds, cumin seeds and grated nutmeg together into a paste. Add to the onion and cook for 3 minutes.

3 Add the lamb mince to the casserole and fry, stirring with a wooden spoon, for 4–5 minutes, or until the mince has broken up and browned.

4 Add the aubergine to the mince and fry for 5 minutes. Stir in the chopped tomatoes and vegetable stock and bring to the boil. Add the apricots and olives, then season well with salt and pepper. Return to the boil, lower the heat and simmer for 15 minutes.

5 Add the penne to the casserole, stir well, then cover and place in the preheated oven. Cook for 10 minutes then stir and return to the oven, uncovered, for a further 15–20 minutes, or until the pasta is 'al dente'. Remove from the oven, sprinkle with toasted pine nuts and serve immediately.

INGREDIENTS
Serves 4

1 tbsp sunflower oil
1 red onion, peeled and chopped
2 cloves garlic, peeled and crushed
1 tbsp coriander seeds
¼ tsp cumin seeds
¼ tsp freshly grated nutmeg
450 g / 1 lb lean lamb mince
1 aubergine, trimmed and diced
400 g can chopped tomatoes
300 ml / ½ pint vegetable stock
125 g / 4 oz ready-to-eat apricots, chopped
12 black olives, pitted
salt and freshly ground black pepper
350 g / 12 oz penne
1 tbsp toasted pine nuts, to garnish

Helpful Hint

You can sometimes buy pine nuts ready-toasted, but if you cannot find any they are easy to toast. Sprinkle them on a foil-lined grill pan and place under a medium grill for 3–4 minutes, turning frequently until they are golden-brown. Alternatively, dry-fry them in a non-stick frying pan, tossing the nuts every few seconds. Always watch nuts when cooking them as they can burn easily.

Spicy Chilli Beef

1 Heat the olive oil in a large heavy-based pan. Add the onion and red pepper and cook for 5 minutes, or until beginning to soften. Add the minced beef and cook over a high heat for 5–8 minutes, or until the meat is browned. Stir with a wooden spoon during cooking to break up any lumps in the meat. Add the garlic and chilli, fry for 1 minute then season to taste with salt and pepper.

2 Add the chopped tomatoes, tomato paste and the kidney beans to the pan. Bring to the boil, lower the heat, and simmer, covered, for at least 40 minutes,

stirring occasionally. Stir in the grated chocolate and cook for 3 minutes, or until melted.

3 Meanwhile, bring a large pan of lightly salted water to a rolling boil. Add the fusilli and cook according to the packet instructions, or until 'al dente'.

4 Drain the pasta, return to the pan and toss with the butter and parsley. Tip into a warmed serving dish or spoon on to individual plates. Spoon the sauce over the pasta. Sprinkle with paprika and serve immediately with spoonfuls of soured cream.

INGREDIENTS
Serves 4

2 tbsp olive oil
1 onion, peeled and finely chopped
1 red pepper, deseeded and sliced
450 g / 1 lb minced beef steak
2 garlic cloves, peeled and crushed
2 red chillies, deseeded and finely sliced
salt and freshly ground black pepper
400 g can chopped tomatoes
2 tbsp tomato paste
400 g can red kidney beans, drained
50 g / 2 oz good quality, plain dark chocolate, grated
350 g / 12 oz dried fusilli
knob of butter
2 tbsp freshly chopped flat-leaf parsley
paprika, to garnish
soured cream, to serve

Food Fact

The chocolate in this traditional spicy Mexican dish adds rich warm undertones, colour and a slight sweetness, but no-one will realise it is there unless you tell them. For maximum flavour, use a good quality, plain dark chocolate with a minimum sugar content and a high percentage of cocoa solids.

Pasta & Pork Ragù

1 Heat the sunflower oil in a large frying pan. Add the sliced leek and cook, stirring frequently, for 5 minutes, or until softened. Add the pork and cook, stirring, for 4 minutes, or until sealed.

2 Add the crushed garlic and the paprika and cayenne peppers to the pan and stir until all the pork is lightly coated in the garlic and pepper mixture.

3 Pour in the wine and 450 ml/¾ pint of the vegetable stock. Add the borlotti beans and carrots and season to taste with salt and pepper. Bring the sauce to the boil, then lower the heat and simmer for 5 minutes.

4 Meanwhile, place the egg tagliatelle in a large saucepan of lightly salted, boiling water, cover and simmer for 5 minutes, or until the pasta is cooked 'al dente'.

5 Drain the pasta, then add to the pork ragù; toss well. Adjust the seasoning, then tip into a warmed serving dish. Sprinkle with chopped parsley and serve with a little crème fraîche.

INGREDIENTS
Serves 4

1 tbsp sunflower oil
1 leek, trimmed and thinly sliced
225 g/8 oz pork fillet, diced
1 garlic clove, peeled and crushed
2 tsp paprika
¼ tsp cayenne pepper
150 ml/¼ pint white wine
600 ml/1 pint vegetable stock
400g can borlotti beans, drained and rinsed
2 carrots, peeled and diced
salt and freshly ground black pepper
225 g/8 oz fresh egg tagliatelle
1 tbsp freshly chopped parsley, to garnish
crème fraîche, to serve

Helpful Hint

Pork fillet, also known as tenderloin, is a very lean and tender cut of pork. It needs little cooking time, so is perfect for this quick and simple dish. Rump or sirloin steak or boneless skinned chicken breast, cut into thin strips, could be used instead, if preferred.

Sausage & Redcurrant Pasta Bake

1 Preheat the oven to 220°C/425°F/Gas Mark 7, 15 minutes before cooking. Prick the sausages, place in a shallow ovenproof dish and toss in the sunflower oil. Cook in the oven for 25–30 minutes, or until golden brown.

2 Meanwhile, melt the butter in a frying pan, add the sliced onion and fry for 5 minutes, or until golden-brown. Stir in the flour and cook for 2 minutes. Remove the pan from the heat and gradually stir in the chicken stock with the port or red wine.

3 Return the pan to the heat and bring to the boil, stirring continuously until the sauce starts to thicken. Add the thyme, bay leaf and redcurrant jelly and season well with salt and pepper. Simmer the sauce for 5 minutes.

4 Bring a large pan of salted water to a rolling boil, add the pasta and cook for about 4 minutes, or until 'al dente'. Drain thoroughly and reserve.

5 Lower the oven temperature to 200°C/400°F/Gas Mark 6. Remove the sausages from the oven, drain off any excess fat and return the sausages to the dish. Add the pasta. Pour over the sauce, removing the bay leaf, and toss together. Sprinkle with the Gruyère cheese and return to the oven for 15–20 minutes, or until bubbling and golden-brown. Serve immediately, garnished with thyme sprigs.

INGREDIENTS
Serves 4

450 g/1 lb good quality, thick pork sausages
2 tsp sunflower oil
25 g/1 oz butter
1 onion, peeled and sliced
2 tbsp plain white flour
450 ml/¾ pint chicken stock
150 ml/¼ pint port or good quality red wine
1 tbsp freshly chopped thyme leaves, plus sprigs to garnish
1 bay leaf
4 tbsp redcurrant jelly
salt and freshly ground black pepper
350 g/12 oz fresh penne
75 g/3 oz Gruyère cheese, grated

Tasty Tip

For a change, try speciality sausages for this recipe. Venison or wild boar sausages would work well with the rich sauce, as would Cumberland or spicy Cambridge pork sausages.

Pappardelle Pork with Brandy Sauce

1 Preheat the oven to 200°C/400°F/Gas Mark 6, 15 minutes before cooking. Using a sharp knife, cut two slits in each pork fillet then stuff each slit with chopped sage. Season well with salt and pepper and wrap each fillet with a slice of Parma ham.

2 Heat the olive oil in a large frying pan. Add the wrapped pork fillets and cook, turning once, for 1–2 minutes, or until the Parma ham is golden brown. Transfer to a roasting tin and cook in the preheated oven for 10–12 minutes.

3 Return the frying pan to the heat and add the brandy, scraping the bottom of the pan with a spoon to release all the flavours. Boil for 1 minute, then pour in the chicken stock. Boil for a further 2 minutes then pour in the cream and boil again for 2–3 minutes, or until the sauce has thickened slightly. Season the brandy sauce to taste.

4 Bring a large pan of lightly salted water to a rolling boil. Add the pasta and cook according to the packet instructions, or until 'al dente'. Drain the pasta thoroughly and return to the pan. Add the butter and chopped parsley and toss together. Keep the pasta warm.

5 Remove the pork from the oven and pour any juices into the brandy sauce. Pile the pasta on individual plates, season with pepper, spoon over the brandy sauce and serve immediately with the pork fillets.

INGREDIENTS
Serves 4

4 pork fillets, each weighing about 175 g/6 oz
1 tbsp freshly chopped sage, plus whole leaves to garnish
salt and freshly ground black pepper
4 slices Parma ham
1 tbsp olive oil
6 tbsp brandy
300 ml/½ pint chicken stock
200 ml/7 fl oz double cream
350 g/12 oz pappardelle
1–2 tsp butter
2 tbsp freshly chopped flat-leaf parsley

Tasty Tip

An inexpensive French cooking brandy can be used for this recipe, but for a special occasion use Calvados. Made from apples, it goes particularly well with pork.

Tagliatelle with Spicy Sausage Ragù

1 Preheat the oven to 200°C/ 400°F/Gas Mark 6, 15 minutes before cooking. Heat 1 tablespoon of the olive oil in a large frying pan. Prick the sausages, add to the pan and cook for 8–10 minutes, or until browned and cooked through. Remove and cut into thin diagonal slices. Reserve.

2 Return the pan to the heat and pour in the remaining olive oil. Add the onion and cook for 8 minutes, or until softened. Add the fennel seeds and minced pork and cook, stirring, for 5–8 minutes, or until the meat is sealed and browned.

3 Stir in the tomatoes, tomato paste and the wine or port. Season to taste with salt and pepper. Bring to the boil, cover and simmer for 30 minutes, stirring occasionally. Remove the lid and simmer for 10 minutes.

4 Bring a large pan of lightly salted water to a rolling boil. Add the pasta and cook according to the packet instructions, or until 'al dente'. Drain thoroughly and toss with the meat sauce.

5 Place half the pasta in an ovenproof dish, and cover with 4 tablespoons of the white sauce. Top with half the sausages and grated Parmesan cheese. Repeat the layering, finishing with white sauce and Parmesan cheese. Bake in the preheated oven for 20 minutes, until golden-brown. Serve immediately.

INGREDIENTS
Serves 4

3 tbsp olive oil

6 spicy sausages

1 small onion, peeled and finely chopped

1 tsp fennel seeds

175 g/6 oz fresh pork mince

225 g can chopped tomatoes with garlic

1 tbsp sun-dried tomato paste

2 tbsp red wine or port

salt and freshly ground black pepper

350 g/12 oz tagliatelle

300 ml/½ pint prepared white sauce, see page 232

50 g/2 oz freshly grated Parmesan cheese

Helpful Hint

Most supermarkets sell cans of chopped tomatoes with added flavouring; if you cannot find them, simply add a large crushed garlic clove to ordinary canned tomatoes.

Food Fact

The sweet aniseed flavour of fennel seeds has an affinity with the slight acidity of tomatoes.

Pasta with Beef, Capers & Olives

1 Heat the olive oil in a large frying pan over a high heat. Add the steak and cook, stirring, for 3–4 minutes, or until browned. Remove from the pan using a slotted spoon and reserve.

2 Lower the heat, add the spring onions and garlic to the pan and cook for 1 minute. Add the courgettes and pepper and cook for 3–4 minutes.

3 Add the oregano, capers and olives to the pan with the chopped tomatoes. Season to taste with salt and pepper, then simmer for 7 minutes, stirring

occasionally. Return the beef to the pan and simmer for 3–5 minutes, or until the sauce has thickened slightly.

4 Meanwhile, bring a large pan of lightly salted water to a rolling boil. Add the pasta and cook according to the packet instructions, or until 'al dente'.

5 Drain the pasta thoroughly. Return to the pan and add the beef sauce. Toss gently until the pasta is lightly coated. Tip into a warmed serving dish or on to individual plates. Sprinkle with chopped parsley and serve immediately.

INGREDIENTS
Serves 4

2 tbsp olive oil
300 g / 11 oz rump steak, trimmed and cut into strips
4 spring onions, trimmed and sliced
2 garlic cloves, peeled and chopped
2 courgettes, trimmed and cut into strips
1 red pepper, deseeded and cut into strips
2 tsp freshly chopped oregano
2 tbsp capers, drained and rinsed
4 tbsp pitted black olives, sliced
400 g can chopped tomatoes
salt and freshly ground black pepper
450 g / 1 lb fettuccine
1 tbsp freshly chopped parsley, to garnish

Tasty Tip

When cooking the beef, it is important that it fries rather than steams in the pan, giving a beautifully brown and caramelised outside while keeping the middle moist and tender. Make sure that the oil in the pan is hot so that the strips of beef sizzle when added. Pat the beef dry with absorbent kitchen paper and cook it in two batches, so there is plenty of room to move it around the pan. Tip the first batch on to a plate and reserve while cooking the second, then return to the pan with any juices.

Gnocchi & Parma Ham Bake

1 Heat the oven to 180° C /350°F/Gas Mark 4, 10 minutes before cooking. Heat 2 tablespoons of the olive oil in a large frying pan and cook the onion and garlic for 5 minutes, or until softened. Stir in the tomatoes, sun-dried tomato paste and mascarpone cheese. Season to taste with salt and pepper. Add half the tarragon. Bring to the boil, then lower the heat immediately and simmer for 5 minutes.

2 Meanwhile, bring 1.7 litres/3 pints water to the boil in a large pan. Add the remaining olive oil and a good pinch of salt. Add the gnocchi

and cook for 1–2 minutes, or until they rise to the surface.

3 Drain the gnocchi thoroughly and transfer to a large ovenproof dish. Add the tomato sauce and toss gently to coat the pasta. Combine the Cheddar or Parmesan cheese with the breadcrumbs and remaining tarragon and scatter over the pasta mixture. Top with the Parma ham and olives and season again.

4 Cook in the preheated oven for 20–25 minutes, or until golden and bubbling. Serve immediately, garnished with parsley sprigs.

INGREDIENTS
Serves 4

3 tbsp olive oil
1 red onion, peeled and sliced
2 garlic cloves, peeled
175 g/6 oz plum tomatoes, skinned and quartered
2 tbsp sun-dried tomato paste
250 g tub mascarpone cheese
salt and freshly ground black pepper
1 tbsp freshly chopped tarragon
300 g/11 oz fresh gnocchi
125 g/4 oz Cheddar or Parmesan cheese, grated
50 g/2 oz fresh white breadcrumbs
50 g/2 oz Parma ham, sliced
10 pitted green olives, halved
sprigs of flat-leaf parsley, to garnish

Helpful Hint

Make sure that you buy gnocchi potato dumplings for this recipe and not gnocchi sardi, a pasta of the same name. It is important to use a large pan of boiling water so that the gnocchi have plenty of room to move around, otherwise they would stick together during cooking. If you do not have a large enough pan, cook the gnocchi in two batches.

Chinese Beef
with Angel Hair Pasta

1 Crush the peppercorns, using a pestle and mortar. Transfer to a shallow bowl and combine with the chilli powder, Szechuan pepper, light soy sauce and sherry. Add the beef strips and stir until lightly coated. Cover and place in the refrigerator to marinate for 3 hours; stir occasionally during this time.

2 When ready to cook, bring a large pan of lightly salted water to a rolling boil. Add the pasta and cook according to the packet instructions, or until 'al dente'. Drain thoroughly and return to the pan. Add the sesame oil and toss lightly. Keep the pasta warm.

3 Heat a wok or large frying pan, add the sunflower oil and heat until very hot. Add the shredded spring onions with the sliced red and green peppers and stir-fry for 2 minutes.

4 Drain the beef, reserving the marinade, then add the beef to the wok or pan and stir-fry for 3 minutes. Pour the marinade and stir-fry for 1-2 minutes, until the steak is tender.

5 Pile the pasta on to 4 warmed plates. Top with the stir-fried beef and peppers and garnish with toasted sesame seeds and shredded spring onions. Serve immediately.

Food Fact

Szechuan pepper, which is also known as Sichuan pepper, anise pepper and *fagara*, is not related in any way to black and white pepper. It is the reddish-brown dried berry of the Chinese prickly ash tree and has a pronounced spicy, woody flavour. It is one of the essential ingredients of Chinese five-spice powder.

INGREDIENTS
Serves 4

1 tbsp pink peppercorns
1 tbsp chilli powder
1 tbsp Szechuan pepper
3 tbsp light soy sauce
3 tbsp dry sherry
450 g/1 lb sirloin steak, cut into strips
350 g/12 oz angel hair pasta
1 tbsp sesame oil
1 tbsp sunflower oil
1 bunch spring onions, trimmed and finely shredded, plus extra to garnish
1 red pepper, deseeded and thinly sliced
1 green pepper, deseeded and thinly sliced
1 tbsp toasted sesame seeds, to garnish

Lamb Arrabbiata

1 Heat 2 tablespoons of the olive oil in a large frying pan and cook the lamb for 5–7 minutes, or until sealed. Remove from the pan using a slotted spoon and reserve.

2 Heat the remaining oil in the pan, add the onion, garlic and chilli and cook until softened. Add the tomatoes, bring to the boil, then simmer for 10 minutes.

3 Return the browned lamb to the pan with the olives and pour in the wine. Bring the sauce back to the boil, reduce the heat then simmer, uncovered, for 15 minutes, until the lamb is tender. Season to taste with salt and pepper.

4 Meanwhile, bring a large pan of lightly salted water to a rolling boil. Add the pasta and cook according to the packet instructions, or until 'al dente'.

5 Drain the pasta, toss in the butter, then add to the sauce and mix lightly. Stir in 4 tablespoons of the chopped parsley, then tip into a warmed serving dish. Sprinkle with the remaining parsley and serve immediately.

INGREDIENTS
Serves 4

4 tbsp olive oil
450 g/1 lb lamb fillets, cubed
1 large onion, peeled and sliced
4 garlic cloves, peeled and finely chopped
1 red chilli, deseeded and finely chopped
400 g can chopped tomatoes
175 g/6 oz pitted black olives, halved
150 ml/¼ pint white wine
salt and freshly ground black pepper
275 g/10 oz farfalle pasta
1 tsp butter
4 tbsp freshly chopped parsley, plus 1 tbsp to garnish

Food Fact

When cooking pasta, remember to use a very large saucepan so that the pasta has plenty of time to move around freely. Once the water has come to the boil, add the pasta, stir, cover with a lid and return to the boil. The lid can then be removed so that the water does not boil over.

Helpful Hint

Lamb fillet can be quite fatty – cut off and discard as much fat as possible. If preferred leg of lamb can be used instead.

Creamed Lamb & Wild Mushroom Pasta

1 Place the porcini in a small bowl and cover with almost boiling water. Leave to soak for 30 minutes. Drain the porcini, reserving the soaking liquid. Chop the porcini finely.

2 Bring a large pan of lightly salted water to a rolling boil. Add the pasta and cook according to the packet instructions, or until 'al dente'.

3 Meanwhile, melt the butter with the olive oil in a large frying pan and fry the lamb to seal. Add the garlic, mushrooms and prepared porcini and cook for 5 minutes, or until just soft.

4 Add the wine and the reserved porcini soaking liquid, then simmer for 2 minutes. Stir in the cream with the seasoning and simmer for 1–2 minutes, or until just thickened.

5 Drain the pasta thoroughly, reserving about 4 tablespoons of the cooking water. Return the pasta to the pan. Pour over the mushroom sauce and toss lightly together, adding the pasta water if the sauce is too thick. Tip into a warmed serving dish or spoon on to individual plates. Garnish with the chopped parsley and serve immediately with grated Parmesan cheese.

INGREDIENTS
Serves 4
25 g/1 oz dried porcini
450 g/1 lb pasta shapes
25g/1 oz butter
1 tbsp olive oil
350 g/12 oz lamb neck fillet, thinly sliced
1 garlic clove, peeled and crushed
225 g/8 oz brown or wild mushrooms, wiped and sliced
4 tbsp white wine
125 ml/4 fl oz double cream
salt and freshly ground black pepper
1 tbsp freshly chopped parsley, to garnish
freshly grated Parmesan cheese, to serve

Helpful Hint

Dried porcini mushrooms have a rich, intense flavour. After soaking, they should be briefly rinsed to remove any grit or dirt. Strain the soaking liquid through muslin or a very fine sieve. If you do not have either of these, leave it to settle for about 10 minutes; grit will sink to the bottom and the liquid can be poured off, leaving any sediment behind.

Tagliatelle with Creamy Liver & Basil

1 Season the flour lightly with salt and pepper and place in a large plastic bag. Add the liver and toss gently to coat. Remove the liver from the bag and reserve.

2 Melt the butter with the olive oil in a large frying pan. Add the onion and garlic and fry for 6–8 minutes, or until the onions begin to colour. Add the liver and fry until brown on all sides.

3 Stir in the chicken stock, tomato paste and sun-dried tomatoes. Bring to the boil, reduce the heat and simmer very gently for 10 minutes.

4 Meanwhile, bring a large pan of lightly salted water to a rolling boil. Add the pasta and cook according to the packet instructions, or until 'al dente'.

5 Stir the chopped basil and cream into the liver sauce and season to taste.

6 Drain the pasta thoroughly, reserving 2 tablespoons of the cooking water. Tip the pasta into a warmed serving dish or pile on to individual plates. Stir the reserved cooking water into the liver sauce and pour over the pasta. Toss lightly to coat the pasta. Garnish with basil leaves and serve immediately.

INGREDIENTS
Serves 4

25 g / 1 oz plain flour
salt and freshly ground black pepper
450 g / 1 lb lamb's liver, thinly sliced and cut into bite-sized pieces
25 g / 1 oz butter
1 tbsp olive oil
2 red onions, peeled and sliced
1 garlic clove, peeled and sliced
150 ml / ¼ pint chicken stock
1 tbsp tomato paste
2 sun-dried tomatoes, finely chopped
1 tbsp freshly chopped basil
150 ml / ¼ pint double cream
350 g / 12 oz tagliatelle verdi
fresh basil leaves, to garnish

Helpful Hint

Although not as delicately flavoured as calves' liver, lamb's liver can be wonderfully tender and moist if gently simmered, as here. To tone down the flavour, it can be soaked in a little milk for 1 hour after preparation. Drain the liver and pat it dry on absorbent kitchen paper before cooking.

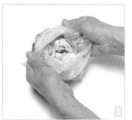

Gammon with Red Wine Sauce & Pasta

1 Preheat the grill to a medium heat before cooking. Heat the butter with the red wine in a large heavy-based pan. Add the onions, cover with a tight fitting lid and cook over a very low heat for 30 minutes, or until softened and transparent. Remove the lid from the pan, stir in the orange juice and sugar, then increase the heat and cook for about 10 minutes, until the onions are golden.

2 Meanwhile cook the gammon steak under the preheated grill, turning at least once, for 4–6 minutes, or until tender. Cut the cooked gammon into bite-sized pieces. Reserve and keep warm.

3 Meanwhile, bring a large pan of very lightly salted water to a rolling boil. Add the pasta and cook according to the packet instructions, or until 'al dente'. Drain the pasta thoroughly, return to the pan, season with a little pepper and keep warm.

4 Stir the wholegrain mustard and chopped parsley into the onion sauce then pour over the pasta. Add the gammon pieces to the pan and toss lightly to thoroughly coat the pasta with the sauce. Pile the pasta mixture on to 2 warmed serving plates. Garnish with sprigs of flat-leaf parsley and serve immediately.

INGREDIENTS
Serves 2

25 g/1 oz butter
150 ml/¼ pint red wine
4 red onions, peeled and sliced
4 tbsp orange juice
1 tsp soft brown sugar
225 g/8 oz gammon steak, trimmed
freshly ground black pepper
175 g/6 oz fusilli
3 tbsp wholegrain mustard
2 tbsp freshly chopped flat-leaf parsley, plus sprigs to garnish

Helpful Hint

Gammon can be slightly salty, so add only a little salt when cooking the pasta. Wholegrain mustard, sometimes labelled Meaux mustard, is made from mixed mustard seeds. This gives it a grainy texture and a fruity, spicy flavour that goes particularly well with gammon.

Prosciutto & Gruyère Carbonara

1 Place the egg yolks with 6 tablespoons of the Gruyère cheese in a bowl and mix lightly until well blended, then reserve.

2 Heat the olive oil in a large pan and cook the garlic and shallots for 5 minutes, or until golden-brown. Add the prosciutto ham, then cook for a further 1 minute. Pour in the dry vermouth and simmer for 2 minutes, then remove from the heat. Season to taste with salt and pepper and keep warm.

3 Meanwhile, bring a large pan of lightly salted water to a rolling boil. Add the pasta and cook according to the packet instructions, or until 'al dente'. Drain thoroughly, reserving 4 tablespoons of the water, and return the pasta to the pan.

4 Remove from the heat, then add the egg and cheese mixture with the butter to the pasta; toss lightly until coated. Add the prosciutto mixture and toss again, adding the reserved pasta water, if needed, to moisten. Season to taste and sprinkle with the remaining Gruyère cheese and the shredded basil leaves. Garnish with basil sprigs and serve immediately.

INGREDIENTS
Serves 4

3 medium egg yolks

50 g/2 oz Gruyère cheese, grated

2 tbsp olive oil

2 garlic cloves, peeled and crushed

2 shallots, peeled and finely chopped

200 g/7 oz prosciutto ham, cut into strips

4 tbsp dry vermouth

salt and freshly ground black pepper

450 g/1 lb spaghetti

15 g/½ oz butter

1 tbsp freshly shredded basil leaves

basil sprigs, to garnish

Food Fact

Gruyère cheese is now produced in many countries, including the United States and France. It is named after the Swiss mountain village where it originated and is still made. The pale yellow cheese is pitted with pea-sized holes and has a firm texture and a sweet, slightly nutty taste.

Gnocchi with Tuscan Beef Ragù

1 Preheat the oven to 200°C/ 400°F/Gas Mark 6, 15 minutes before cooking. Place the porcini in a small bowl and cover with almost boiling water. Leave to soak for 30 minutes. Drain, reserving the soaking liquid and straining it through a muslin-lined sieve. Chop the porcini.

2 Heat the olive oil in a large heavy-based pan. Add the onion, carrot, celery, fennel and garlic and cook for 8 minutes, stirring, or until soft. Add the minced steak and cook, stirring, for 5–8 minutes, or until sealed and any lumps are broken up.

3 Pour in the wine, then add the porcini with half the pine nuts, the rosemary and tomato paste. Stir in the porcini soaking liquid then simmer for 5 minutes. Add the chopped tomatoes and simmer gently for about 40 minutes, stirring occasionally.

4 Meanwhile, bring 1.7 litres/ 3 pints of lightly salted water to a rolling boil in a large pan. Add the gnocchi and cook for 1–2 minutes, until they rise to the surface.

5 Drain the gnocchi and place in an ovenproof dish. Stir in three-quarters of the mozzarella cheese with the beef sauce. Top with the remaining mozzarella and pine nuts, then bake in the preheated oven for 20 minutes, until golden-brown. Serve immediately.

INGREDIENTS
Serves 4

25 g/1 oz dried porcini
3 tbsp olive oil
1 small onion, peeled and finely chopped
1 carrot, peeled and finely chopped
1 celery, trimmed and finely chopped
1 fennel bulb, trimmed and sliced
2 garlic cloves, peeled and crushed
450 g/1 lb fresh beef steak mince
4 tbsp red wine
50 g/2 oz pine nuts
1 tbsp freshly chopped rosemary
2 tbsp tomato paste
400 g can chopped tomatoes
225 g/8 oz fresh gnocchi
salt and freshly ground black pepper
100 g/4 oz mozzarella cheese, cubed

Food Fact

Pine nuts are small, creamy-coloured, tear-shaped nuts from the base of the cone scales of the Mediterranean stone pine. They may become rancid if kept too long, due to their high oil content, so buy in small quantities and use within 1–2 months.

Saffron Roast Chicken with Crispy Onions

1 Preheat oven to 200°C/400°F/Gas Mark 6. Using your fingertips, gently loosen the skin from the chicken breast by sliding your hand between the skin and flesh. Cream together 50 g/2 oz of the butter with the saffron threads, the lemon rind and half the parsley, until smooth. Push the butter under the skin. Spread over the breast and the top of the thighs with your fingers. Pull the neck skin to tighten the skin over the breast and tuck under the bird, then secure with a skewer or cocktail stick.

2 Heat the olive oil and remaining butter in a large heavy-based frying pan and cook the onions and garlic cloves for 5 minutes, or until the onions are soft. Stir in the cumin seeds, cinnamon, pine nuts and sultanas and cook for 2 minutes. Season to taste with salt and pepper and place in a roasting tin.

3 Place the chicken, breast-side down, on the base of the onions and roast in the preheated oven for 45 minutes. Reduce the oven temperature to 170°C/325°F/Gas Mark 3. Turn the chicken breast-side up and stir the onions. Continue roasting until the chicken is a deep golden yellow and the onions are crisp. Allow to rest for 10 minutes, then sprinkle with the remaining parsley. Before serving, garnish with a sprig of parsley and serve immediately with the onions and garlic.

INGREDIENTS
Serves 4–6

1.6 kg/3½ lb oven-ready chicken, preferably free range
75 g/3 oz butter, softened
1 tsp saffron strands, lightly toasted
grated rind of 1 lemon
2 tbsp freshly chopped flat-leaf parsley
2 tbsp extra-virgin olive oil
450 g/1 lb onions, peeled and cut into thin wedges
8–12 garlic cloves, peeled
1 tsp cumin seeds
½ tsp ground cinnamon
50 g/2 oz pine nuts
50 g/2 oz sultanas
salt and freshly ground black pepper
sprig of fresh flat-leaf parsley, to garnish

Helpful Hint

Roasting the chicken breast-side down first helps to ensure that the white meat will be moist. Turning the chicken halfway through cooking will give a crisp, golden skin.

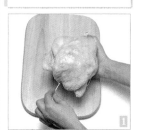

Pheasant with Portabella Mushrooms & Red Wine Gravy

1 Preheat oven to 180°C/ 350°F/Gas Mark 4. Heat the butter and oil in a large saucepan or frying pan. Add the pheasant halves and shallots working in batches, if necessary, and cook for 10 minutes, or until golden on all sides, shaking the pan to glaze the shallots. Transfer to a casserole dish large enough to hold the pieces in a single layer. Add the mushroom and thyme to the pan and cook for 2–3 minutes, or until beginning to colour. Transfer to the dish with the pheasant halves.

2 Add the wine to the saucepan, it will bubble and steam. Cook, stirring up any browned bits from the pan and allow to reduce by half. Pour in the stock and bring to the boil, then pour over the pheasant halves. Cover and braise in the preheated oven for 50 minutes, or until tender. Remove the pheasant halves and vegetables to a wide, shallow serving dish and set the casserole or roasting tin over a medium-high heat.

3 Skim off any surface fat and bring to the boil. Blend the cornflour with the vinegar and stir into the sauce with the redcurrant jelly. Boil until the sauce is reduced and thickened slightly. Stir in the parsley and season to taste with salt and pepper. Pour over the pheasant halves, garnish with sprigs of fresh thyme and serve immediately.

INGREDIENTS
Serves 4

25 g/1 oz butter
1 tbsp olive oil
2 small pheasants (preferably hens) rinsed, well dried and halved
8 shallots, peeled
300 g/11 oz portabella mushrooms, thickly sliced
2–3 sprigs of fresh thyme or rosemary, leaves stripped
300 ml/½ pint Valpolicella or fruity red wine
300 ml/½ pint hot chicken stock
1 tbsp cornflour
2 tbsp balsamic vinegar
2 tbsp redcurrant jelly, or to taste
2 tbsp freshly chopped flat-leaf parsley
salt and freshly ground black pepper
sprigs of fresh thyme, to garnish

Helpful Hint

To halve the pheasants, cut along one side of the breastbone, pulling the breast away from the ribcage in one piece. Cut through the thigh joint where it joins the back to give half a pheasant. Repeat along the other side of the breastbone.

Pheasant with Sage & Blueberries

1 Preheat oven to 180°C/ 350°F/Gas Mark 4, 10 minutes before cooking. Place the oil, shallots, sage and bay leaf in a bowl, with the juice from the lemon halves. Season with salt and pepper. Tuck each of the squeezed lemon halves into the birds with 75 g/3 oz of the blueberries, then rub the birds with the marinade and leave for 2–3 hours, basting occasionally.

2 Remove the birds from the marinade and cover each with 2 slices of Parma ham. Tie the legs of each bird with string and place in a roasting tin. Pour over the marinade and add the vermouth. Roast in the preheated oven for 1 hour, or until tender and golden and the juices run clear when a thigh is pierced with a sharp knife or skewer.

3 Transfer to a warm serving plate, cover with tinfoil and discard the string. Skim off any surface fat from the tin and set over a medium-high heat.

4 Add the stock to the tin and bring to the boil, scraping any browned bits from the bottom. Boil until slightly reduced. Whisk in the cream or butter, if using, and simmer until thickened, whisking constantly. Stir in the brandy and strain into a gravy jug. Add the remaining blueberries and keep warm.

5 Using a sharp carving knife, cut each of the birds in half and arrange on the plate with the crispy Parma ham. Serve immediately with roast potatoes and the gravy.

INGREDIENTS
Serves 4

3 tbsp olive oil
3 shallots, peeled and coarsely chopped
2 sprigs of fresh sage, coarsely chopped
1 bay leaf
1 lemon, halved
salt and freshly ground black pepper
2 pheasants or guinea fowl, rinsed and dried
125 g/4 oz blueberries
4 slices Parma ham or bacon
125 ml/4 fl oz vermouth or dry white wine
200 ml/⅓ pint chicken stock
3 tbsp double cream or butter (optional)
1 tbsp brandy
roast potatoes, to serve

Spatchcocked Poussins with Garlic Sage Butter

1 Preheat grill or light an outdoor charcoal grill and line the grill rack with tinfoil, just before cooking. Put the garlic cloves in a small saucepan and cover with cold water. Bring to the boil, then simmer for 5 minutes, or until softened. Drain and cool slightly. Cut off the root end of each clove and squeeze the softened garlic into a bowl.

2 Pound the garlic until smooth, then beat in the butter, chives, sage and lemon rind and juice. Season to taste with salt and pepper.

3 Using your fingertips, gently loosen the skin from each poussin breast by sliding your hand between the skin and the flesh. Push one-quarter of the herb butter under the skin, spreading evenly over the breast and the top of the thighs. Pull the neck skin gently to tighten the skin over the breast and tuck under the bird. Repeat with the remaining birds and herb butter.

4 Thread 2 wooden skewers crossways through each bird, from one wing through the opposite leg, to keep the poussin flat. Repeat with the remaining birds, brush with the olive oil and season with salt and pepper.

5 Arrange the poussins on the rack over the foil-lined rack and grill for 25 minutes, turning occasionally, until golden and crisp and the juices run clear when a thigh is pierced with a sharp knife or skewer. (Position the rack about 12.5 cm/5 inches from the heat source or the skin will brown before the birds are cooked through). Garnish with chives and sage leaves and serve immediately with grilled polenta and a few grilled tomatoes.

INGREDIENTS
Serves 4

FOR THE HERB BUTTER:
6 large garlic cloves
150 g/5 oz butter, softened
2 tbsp freshly snipped chives
2 tbsp freshly chopped sage
grated rind and juice of
   1 small lemon
salt and freshly ground black
   pepper

FOR THE POUSSINS:
4 spatchcocked poussins
2 tbsp extra-virgin olive oil

TO GARNISH:
chives
fresh sage leaves

TO SERVE:
grilled polenta (see recipe p. 358)
grilled tomatoes

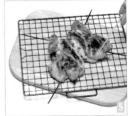

Chicken Cacciatore

1 Heat 1 tablespoon of the olive oil in a large, deep frying pan and add the diced pancetta or bacon and stir-fry for 2–3 minutes, or until crisp and golden brown. Using a slotted spoon, transfer the pancetta or bacon to a plate and reserve.

2 Season the flour with salt and pepper, then use to coat the chicken. Heat the remaining oil in the pan and brown the chicken pieces on all sides for about 15 minutes. Remove from the pan and add to the bacon.

3 Stir the garlic into the pan and cook for about 30 seconds. Add the red wine and cook, stirring and scraping any browned bits from the base of the pan. Allow the wine to boil until it is reduced by half. Add the tomatoes, stock, onions, bay leaf, brown sugar and oregano and stir well. Season to taste.

4 Return the chicken and bacon to the pan and bring to the boil. Cover and simmer for 30 minutes, then stir in the peppers and mushrooms and simmer for a further 15–20 minutes, or until the chicken and vegetables are tender and the sauce is reduced and slightly thickened. Stir in the chopped parsley and serve immediately with freshly cooked tagliatelle.

INGREDIENTS
Serves 4

2–3 tbsp olive oil
125 g/4 oz pancetta or streaky bacon, diced
25 g/1 oz plain flour
salt and freshly ground black pepper
1.4–1.6 kg/3–3½ lb chicken, cut into 8 pieces
2 garlic cloves, peeled and chopped
125 ml/4 fl oz red wine
400 g can chopped tomatoes
150 ml/¼ pint chicken stock
12 small onions, peeled
1 bay leaf
1 tsp brown sugar
1 tsp dried oregano
1 green pepper, deseeded and chopped
225 g/8 oz chestnut or field mushrooms, thickly sliced
2 tbsp freshly chopped parsley
freshly cooked tagliatelle, to serve

Tasty Tip
Use chestnut or field mushrooms in this recipe because they have a stronger flavour than button mushrooms and will also help to add colour to the sauce.

Lemon Chicken with Potatoes, Rosemary & Olives

1 Preheat oven to 200°C/400°F/Gas Mark 6, 15 minutes before cooking. Trim the chicken thighs and place in a shallow baking dish large enough to hold them in a single layer. Remove the rind from the lemon with a zester or if using a peeler cut into thin julienne strips. Reserve half and add the remainder to the chicken. Squeeze the lemon juice over the chicken, toss to coat well and leave to stand for 10 minutes.

2 Transfer the chicken to a roasting tin. Add the remaining lemon zest or julienne strips, olive oil, garlic, onions and half of the rosemary sprigs.

Toss gently and leave for about 20 minutes.

3 Cover the potatoes with lightly salted water and bring to the boil. Cook for 2 minutes, then drain well and add to the chicken. Season to taste with salt and pepper.

4 Roast the chicken in the preheated oven for 50 minutes, turning frequently and basting, or until the chicken is cooked. Just before the end of cooking time, discard the rosemary, and add fresh sprigs of rosemary. Add the olives and stir. Serve immediately with steamed carrots and courgettes.

INGREDIENTS
Serves 6

12 skinless boneless chicken thighs
1 large lemon
125 ml/4 fl oz extra-virgin olive oil
6 garlic cloves, peeled and sliced
2 onions, peeled and thinly sliced
bunch of fresh rosemary
1.1 kg/2 ½ lb potatoes, peeled and cut into 4 cm/1½ inch pieces
salt and freshly ground black pepper
18–24 black olives, pitted

TO SERVE:
steamed carrots
courgettes

Helpful Hint

It is worth seeking out unwaxed lemons for this recipe, or for any recipe in which the lemon zest is to be eaten. If unwaxed fruit are unavailable, pour hot water over them and scrub well before removing the zest.

Chicken with Porcini Mushrooms & Cream

1 Heat the olive oil in a large, heavy-based frying pan, then add the chicken breasts, skin-side down and cook for about 10 minutes, or until they are well browned. Remove the chicken breasts and reserve. Add the garlic, stir into the juices and cook for 1 minute.

2 Pour the vermouth or white wine into the pan and season to taste with salt and pepper. Return the chicken to the pan. Bring to the boil, reduce the heat to low and simmer for about 20 minutes, or until tender.

3 In another large frying pan, heat the butter and add the sliced porcini or wild mushrooms. Stir-fry for about 5 minutes, or until the mushrooms are golden and tender.

4 Add the porcini or wild mushrooms and any juices to the chicken. Season to taste, then add the chopped oregano. Stir together gently and cook for 1 minute longer. Transfer to a large serving plate and garnish with sprigs of fresh basil, if desired. Serve immediately with rice.

INGREDIENTS
Serves 4

2 tbsp olive oil
4 boneless chicken breasts,
*   preferably free range*
2 garlic cloves, peeled and crushed
150 ml/¼ pint dry vermouth or
*   dry white wine*
salt and freshly ground black
*   pepper*
25 g/1 oz butter
450 g/1 lb porcini or wild
*   mushrooms, thickly sliced*
1 tbsp freshly chopped oregano
sprigs of fresh basil, to garnish
*   (optional)*
freshly cooked rice, to serve

Tasty Tip

Porcini or cep mushrooms grow wild and are relatively easy to find, if you know where to look. They can, however, be very expensive to buy fresh. If they are unavailable, substitute with fresh button or chestnut mushrooms and 15 g/½oz reconstituted dried porcini instead.

Helpful Hint

If using dried mushrooms, cover with almost boiling water, leave for 20 minutes, then drain, straining soaking liquor to use.

Turkey Escalopes Marsala with Wilted Watercress

1 Place each turkey escalope between 2 sheets of non-stick baking parchment and using a meat mallet or rolling pin pound to make an escalope about 3 mm/⅛ inch thick. Put the flour in a shallow dish, add the thyme, season to taste with salt and pepper and stir to blend. Coat each escalope lightly on both sides with the flour mixture, then reserve.

2 Heat the olive oil in a large frying pan, then add the watercress and stir-fry for about 2 minutes, until just wilted and brightly coloured. Season with salt and pepper. Using a slotted spoon, transfer the watercress to a plate and keep warm.

3 Add half the butter to the frying pan and when melted, add the mushrooms. Stir-fry for 4 minutes, or until golden and tender. Remove from the pan and reserve.

4 Add the remaining butter to the pan and, working in batches if necessary, cook the flour-coated escalopes for 2–3 minutes on each side, or until golden and cooked thoroughly, adding the remaining oil, if necessary. Remove from the pan and keep warm.

5 Add the Marsala wine to the pan and stir, scraping up any browned bits from the bottom of the pan. Add the stock or water and bring to the boil over a high heat. Season lightly.

6 Return the escalopes and mushrooms to the pan and reheat gently until piping hot. Divide the warm watercress between 4 serving plates.

7 Arrange 1 escalope over each serving of wilted watercress and spoon over the mushrooms and Marsala sauce. Serve immediately.

INGREDIENTS
Serves 4

4 turkey escalopes, each about 150 g/5 oz
25 g/1 oz plain flour
½ tsp dried thyme
salt and freshly ground black pepper
1–2 tbsp olive oil
125 g/4 oz watercress
40 g/1½ oz butter
225 g/8 oz mushrooms, wiped and quartered
50 ml/2 fl oz dry Marsala wine
50 ml/2 fl oz chicken stock or water

Helpful Hint

Turkey escalopes are simply thin slices of turkey breast fillets which have been flattened. If they are unavailable, substitute chicken breasts that have been halved horizontally and flattened between pieces of clingfilm.

Lemon Chicken with Basil & Linguine

1 Blend the lemon rind and juice, garlic, half the oil, half the basil and salt and pepper in a large bowl. Add the chicken pieces and toss well to coat. Allow to stand for about 1 hour, stirring occasionally.

2 Heat the remaining oil in a large non-stick frying pan, then add the sliced onion and cook for 3–4 minutes, or until slightly softened. Using a slotted spoon, drain the chicken pieces and add to the frying pan, reserving the marinade. Cook the chicken for 2–3 minutes, or until golden brown, then add the sliced celery and mushroom halves and cook for a further 2–3 minutes.

3 Sprinkle in the flour and stir until the chicken and vegetables are coated. Gradually stir the wine into the pan until a thick sauce forms, then stir in the stock and reserved marinade. Bring to the boil, stirring constantly. Cover and simmer for about 10 minutes, then stir in the remaining basil.

4 Meanwhile, bring a large saucepan of lightly salted water to the boil. Slowly add the linguine and simmer for 7–10 minutes, or until 'al dente'. Drain well and turn into a large serving bowl, pour over the sauce and garnish with the lemon zest and fresh basil leaves. Serve immediately.

INGREDIENTS
Serves 4

grated rind and juice of 1 large lemon
2 garlic cloves, peeled and crushed
2 tbsp basil-flavoured extra-virgin olive oil
4 tbsp freshly chopped basil
salt and freshly ground black pepper
450 g / 1 lb skinless, boneless chicken breast, cut into bite-sized pieces
1 onion, peeled and finely chopped
3 celery stalks, trimmed and thinly sliced
175 g / 6 oz mushrooms, wiped and halved
2 tbsp plain flour
150 ml / ¼ pint white wine
150 ml / ¼ pint chicken stock
350–450 g / 12 oz–1 lb linguine

TO GARNISH:
lemon zest
fresh basil leaves

Tasty Tip

Make basil-flavoured olive oil for this recipe by putting a large handful of chopped basil leaves into the bowl of a small food processor or blender. Add 3–4 tablespoons good-quality olive oil and blend to a purée. Pass the oil through a fine sieve. This oil will not keep and should be used immediately.

Chicken Liver &
Tomato Sauce with Tagliolini

1 Heat half the olive oil in a large, deep, heavy-based frying pan and add the onion. Cook, stirring frequently, for 4–5 minutes, or until soft and translucent. Stir in the garlic and cook for a further minute.

2 Add the red wine and cook, stirring until the wine is reduced by half, then add the tomatoes, tomato purée and half the sage or thyme. Bring to the boil, stirring to break up the tomatoes. Simmer for 30 minutes, stirring occasionally, or until the sauce has reduced and thickened. Season to taste with salt and pepper.

3 Bring a large saucepan of lightly salted water to the boil. Add the pasta and cook for 7–10 minutes, or until 'al dente'.

4 Meanwhile, in a large heavy-based frying pan, melt the remaining oil and the butter and heat until very hot. Pat the chicken livers dry and dust lightly with a little flour. Add to the pan, a few at a time, and cook for 5 minutes, or until crisp and browned, turning carefully – the livers should still be pink inside.

5 Drain the pasta well and turn into a large, warmed serving bowl. Stir the livers carefully into the tomato sauce, then pour the sauce over the drained pasta and toss gently to coat. Garnish with a sprig of fresh sage and serve immediately.

Helpful Hint

Many recipes using wine call for it to be simmered until reduced by half. This is to eliminate the alcohol from the wine and to concentrate the flavour. Without this reduction the sauce would taste of raw wine which can be quite sour.

INGREDIENTS
Serves 4

50 ml/2 fl oz extra-virgin olive oil

1 onion, peeled and finely chopped

2 garlic cloves, peeled and finely chopped

125 ml/4 fl oz dry red wine

2 x 400 g cans Italian peeled plum tomatoes with juice

1 tbsp tomato purée

1 tbsp freshly chopped sage or thyme leaves

salt and freshly ground black pepper

350 g/12 oz fresh or dried tagliolini, papardelle or tagliatelle

25 g/1 oz butter

225 g/8 oz fresh chicken livers, trimmed and cut in half

plain flour for dusting

sprigs of fresh sage, to garnish (optional)

Creamy Chicken Cannelloni

1 Preheat oven to 190°C/
375°F/Gas Mark 5, 10
minutes before cooking. Lightly
butter a 28 x 23 cm/11 x 9 inch
ovenproof baking dish. Heat half
the butter in a large heavy-based
frying pan, then add the garlic
and mushrooms and cook gently
for 5 minutes. Stir in the basil and
the spinach and cook, covered,
until the spinach is wilted and
just tender, stirring frequently.
Season to taste with salt and
pepper, then spoon into the dish
and reserve.

2 Melt the remaining butter
in a small saucepan, then stir
in the flour and cook for about
2 minutes, stirring constantly.
Remove from the heat, stir in
the stock, then the wine and the
cream. Return to the heat, bring

to the boil and simmer, until the
sauce is thick and smooth, then
season to taste.

3 Measure 125 ml/4 fl oz of
the cream sauce into a bowl.
Add the chopped chicken, Parma
ham and the dried thyme. Season
to taste, then spoon the chicken
mixture into the cannelloni tubes,
arranging them in 2 long rows
on top of the spinach layer.

4 Add half the Gruyère cheese
to the cream sauce and heat,
stirring, until the cheese melts.
Pour over the sauce and top
with the remaining Gruyère and
the Parmesan cheeses. Bake in the
preheated oven for 35 minutes, or
until golden and bubbling.
Garnish with a sprig of fresh
basil and serve immediately.

INGREDIENTS
Serves 6

50 g/2 oz butter
*2 garlic cloves, peeled and finely
crushed*
*225 g/8 oz button mushrooms,
thinly sliced*
2 tbsp freshly chopped basil
*450 g/1 lb fresh spinach,
blanched*
*salt and freshly ground black
pepper*
2 tbsp plain flour
300 ml/½ pint chicken stock
150 ml/¼ pint dry white wine
150 ml/¼ pint double cream
*350 g/12 oz skinless, boneless,
cooked chicken, chopped*
*175 g/6 oz Parma ham, finely
chopped*
½ tsp dried thyme
*225 g/8 oz precooked cannelloni
tubes*
*175 g/6 oz Gruyère cheese,
grated*
*40 g/1 ½ oz Parmesan cheese,
grated*
sprig of fresh basil, to garnish

Tasty Tip

This rich sauce demands a salad to accompany it. Whisk
together 1 teaspoon Dijon mustard, 2 teaspoons lemon juice,
a pinch of sugar and salt and pepper to taste. When blended,
whisk in 3–4 tablespoons good-quality olive oil. Add
175 g/6 oz of mixed salad leaves and toss to coat.

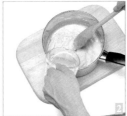

Duck Lasagna with Porcini & Basil

1 Preheat oven to 180°C/ 350°F/Gas Mark 4, 10 minutes before cooking. Put the duck with the vegetables, garlic, peppercorns, bay leaves and thyme into a large stock pot and cover with cold water. Bring to the boil, skimming off any fat, then reduce the heat and simmer for 1 hour. Transfer the duck to a bowl and cool slightly.

2 When cool enough to handle, remove the meat from the duck and dice. Return all the bones and trimmings to the simmering stock and continue to simmer for 1 hour. Strain the stock into a large bowl and leave until cold. Remove and discard the fat that has risen to the top of the stock.

3 Put the porcini in a colander and rinse under cold running water. Leave for 1 minute to dry off, then turn out on to a chopping board and chop finely. Place in a small bowl, then pour over

the sherry and leave for about 1 hour, or until the porcini are plump and all the sherry is absorbed.

4 Heat 25 g/1 oz of the butter in a frying pan. Shred the basil leaves and add to the hot butter, stirring until wilted. Add the soaked porcini and any liquid, mix well and reserve.

5 Oil a 30.5 x 23 cm/12 x 9 inch deep baking dish and pour a little stock into the base. Cover with 6–8 lasagna sheets, making sure that sheets slightly overlap. Continue to layer the pasta with a little stock, duck meat, the mushroom-basil mixture and Parmesan. Add a little butter every other layer.

6 Cover with tinfoil and bake in the preheated oven for 40–45 minutes, or until cooked. Stand for 10 minutes before serving. Garnish with a sprig of parsley and serve with salad.

INGREDIENTS
Serves 6

1.4–1.8 kg/3–4 lb duck, quartered
1 onion, unpeeled and quartered
2 carrots, peeled and cut into pieces
1 celery stalk, cut into pieces
1 leek, trimmed and cut into pieces
2 garlic cloves, unpeeled and smashed
1 tbsp black peppercorns
2 bay leaves
6–8 sprigs of fresh thyme
50 g/2 oz dried porcini mushrooms
125 ml/4 oz dry sherry
75 g/3 oz butter, diced
1 bunch of fresh basil leaves, stripped from stems
24 precooked lasagna sheets
75 g/3 oz Parmesan cheese, grated
sprig of parsley, to garnish
mixed salad, to serve

Turkey Tetrazzini

1 Preheat oven to 180°C/ 350°F/Gas Mark 4. Lightly oil a large ovenproof dish. Bring a large saucepan of lightly salted water to the boil. Add the tagliatelle and cook for 7–9 minutes, or until 'al dente'. Drain well and reserve.

2 In a heavy-based saucepan, heat the butter and add the bacon. Cook for 2–3 minutes, or until crisp and golden. Add the onion and mushrooms and cook for 3–4 minutes, or until the vegetables are tender.

3 Stir in the flour and cook for 2 minutes. Remove from the heat and slowly stir in the stock. Return to the heat and cook, stirring until a smooth, thick sauce has formed. Add the tagliatelle, then pour in the cream and sherry. Add the turkey and parsley. Season to taste with the nutmeg and salt and pepper. Toss well to coat.

4 Turn the mixture into the prepared dish, spreading evenly. Sprinkle the top with the Parmesan cheese and bake in the preheated oven for 30–35 minutes, or until crisp, golden and bubbling. Garnish with chopped parsley and Parmesan cheese. Serve straight from the dish.

INGREDIENTS
Serves 4

275 g/10 oz green and white tagliatelle
50 g/2 oz butter
4 slices streaky bacon, diced
1 onion, peeled and finely chopped
175 g/6 oz mushrooms, thinly sliced
40 g/1 ½ oz plain flour
450 ml/¾ pint chicken stock
150 ml/¼ pint double cream
2 tbsp sherry
450 g/1 lb cooked turkey meat, cut into bite-sized pieces
1 tbsp freshly chopped parsley
freshly grated nutmeg
salt and freshly ground black pepper
25 g/1 oz Parmesan cheese, grated

TO GARNISH:
freshly chopped parsley
Parmesan cheese, grated

Tasty Tip

This is a great way to use Christmas leftovers – it is worth putting extra meat in the freezer. Use frozen leftovers within 1 month.

Poached Chicken with Salsa Verde Herb Sauce

1 Place the chicken breasts with the stock in a large frying pan and bring to the boil. Reduce the heat and simmer for 10–15 minutes, or until cooked. Leave to cool in the stock.

2 To make the salsa verde, switch the motor on a food processor, then drop in the garlic cloves and chop finely. Add the parsley and mint and, using the pulse button, pulse 2–3 times. Add the capers and, if using, add the gherkins, anchovies and rocket. Pulse 2–3 times until the sauce is evenly textured.

3 With the machine still running, pour in the lemon juice or red wine vinegar, then add the olive oil in a slow, steady stream until the sauce is smooth. Season to taste with salt and pepper, then transfer to a large serving bowl and reserve.

4 Carve each chicken breast into thick slices and arrange on serving plates, fanning out the slices slightly. Spoon over a little of the salsa verde on to each chicken breast, garnish with sprigs of mint and serve immediately with freshly cooked vegetables.

INGREDIENTS
Serves 6

*6 boneless chicken breasts, each
    about 175 g /6 oz*
*600 ml/1 pint chicken stock,
    preferably homemade*

FOR THE SALSA VERDE:

2 garlic cloves, peeled and chopped
4 tbsp freshly chopped parsley
3 tbsp freshly chopped mint
2 tsp capers
2 tbsp chopped gherkins (optional)
*2–3 anchovy fillets in olive oil,
    drained and finely chopped
    (optional)*
*1 handful wild rocket leaves,
    chopped (optional)*
*2 tbsp lemon juice or red wine
    vinegar*
*125 ml/4 fl oz extra-virgin
    olive oil*
*salt and freshly ground black
    pepper*
sprigs of mint, to garnish
freshly cooked vegetables, to serve

Helpful Hint

The salsa verde can be made ahead and
stored in an airtight container for 1 day. Be sure to bring
to room temperature and stir well before serving.

Chicken Parcels with Courgettes & Pasta

1 Preheat oven to 200°C/400°F/Gas Mark 6, 15 minutes before cooking. Lightly brush 4 large sheets of non-stick baking parchment with half the oil. Bring a saucepan of lightly salted water to the boil and cook the pasta for 10 minutes, or until 'al dente'. Drain and reserve.

2 Heat the remaining oil in a frying pan and cook the onion for 2–3 minutes. Add the garlic and cook for 1 minute. Add the courgettes and cook for 1 minute, then remove from the heat, season to taste with salt and pepper and add half the oregano.

3 Divide the cooked pasta equally between the 4 sheets

of baking parchment, positioning the pasta in the centre. Top the pasta with equal amounts of the vegetable mixture, and sprinkle a quarter of the chopped tomatoes over each.

4 Score the surface of each chicken breast about 1 cm/½ inch deep. Place a chicken breast on top of the pasta and sprinkle each with the remaining oregano and the white wine. Fold the edges of the paper along the top, then along each side, creating a sealed envelope.

5 Bake in the preheated oven for 30–35 minutes, or until cooked. Serve immediately.

INGREDIENTS
Serves 4

2 tbsp olive oil
125 g/4 oz farfalle pasta
1 onion, peeled and thinly sliced
1 garlic clove, peeled and finely chopped
2 medium courgettes, trimmed and thinly sliced
salt and freshly ground black pepper
2 tbsp freshly chopped oregano
4 plum tomatoes, deseeded and coarsely chopped
4 x 175 g/6 oz boneless, skinless chicken breasts
150 ml/¼ pint Italian white wine

Helpful Hint

This is a great recipe for entertaining. The parcels can be prepared ahead and baked when needed. For a dramatic presentation, serve in the paper.

Chicken Under a Brick

1 Rinse the chicken and dry well, inside and out. Using poultry shears or kitchen scissors, cut along each side of the backbone of the chicken and discard or use for stock. Place the chicken skin-side up on a work surface and, using the palm of your hand, press down firmly to break the breast bone and flatten the bird.

2 Turn the chicken breast-side up and use a sharp knife to slit the skin between the breast and thigh on each side. Fold the legs in and push the drumstick bones through the slits. Tuck the wing under, the chicken should be as flat as possible.

3 Heat the olive oil in a large, heavy-based frying pan until very hot, but not smoking. Place the chicken in the pan, skin-side down, and place a flat lid or plate directly on top of the chicken. Top with a brick (hence the name) or 2 kg/5 lb weight. Cook for 12–15 minutes, or until golden brown.

4 Remove the weights and lid and, using a pair of tongs, turn the chicken carefully, then season to taste with salt and pepper. Cover and weight the lid again, then cook for 12–15 minutes longer, until the chicken is tender and the juices run clear when a thigh is pierced with a sharp knife or skewer.

5 Transfer the chicken to a serving plate and cover loosely with tinfoil to keep warm. Allow to rest for at least 10 minutes before carving. Garnish with sprigs of basil and chives and serve with salad leaves.

INGREDIENTS
Serves 4–6

1.8 kg/4 lb free range corn-fed, oven-ready chicken
50 ml/2 fl oz olive oil
sea salt and freshly ground black pepper

TO GARNISH:
sprigs of fresh basil
chives
tossed bitter salad leaves, to serve

Tasty Tip

In a large bowl, whisk together 1 teaspoon of whole-grain mustard, 1 crushed garlic clove, 2 teaspoons of balsamic vinegar and seasoning. When combined thoroughly, whisk in 3–4 tablespoons of good-quality olive oil to taste. Toss with a mixture of bitter leaves such as frisée, radicchio, and chicory and serve with the chicken.

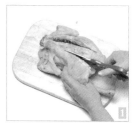

Chicken & Asparagus with Tagliatelle

1 Using a swivel-bladed vegetable peeler, lightly peel the asparagus stalks and then cook in lightly salted, boiling water for 2–3 minutes, or until just tender. Drain and refresh in cold water, then cut into 4 cm/1½ inch pieces and reserve.

2 Melt the butter in a large frying pan then add the spring onions and the chicken and fry for 4 minutes. Add the vermouth and allow to reduce until the liquid has evaporated. Pour in the cream and half the chives. Cook gently for 5–7 minutes, until the sauce has

thickened and slightly reduced and the chicken is tender.

3 Bring a large saucepan of lightly salted water to the boil and cook the tagliatelle for 4–5 minutes, or until 'al dente'. Drain and immediately add to the chicken and cream sauce.

4 Using a pair of spaghetti tongs or kitchen forks, lightly toss the sauce and pasta until it is mixed thoroughly. Add the remaining chives and the Parmesan cheese and toss gently. Garnish with snipped chives and serve immediately, with extra Parmesan cheese, if you like.

INGREDIENTS
Serves 4

275 g/10 oz fresh asparagus
50 g/2 oz butter
4 spring onions, trimmed and
 coarsely chopped
350 g/12 oz boneless, skinless
 chicken breast, thinly sliced
2 tbsp white vermouth
300 ml/½ pint double cream
2 tbsp freshly chopped chives
400 g/14 oz fresh tagliatelle
50 g/2 oz Parmesan or pecorino
 cheese, grated
snipped chives, to garnish
extra Parmesan cheese (optional),
 to serve

Tasty Tip

Freshly made pasta will cook in 30–60 seconds.
It is cooked when it rises to the surface. Bought fresh
pasta will take between 2–3 minutes. Dried pasta takes
longer to cook (between 4–10 minutes) depending
on the variety – check the packet instructions.

Marinated Pheasant Breasts with Grilled Polenta

1 Preheat grill just before cooking. Blend 2 tablespoons of the olive oil with the chopped rosemary or sage, cinnamon and orange zest and season to taste with salt and pepper.

2 Place the pheasant breasts in a large, shallow dish, pour over the oil and marinate until required, turning occasionally.

3 Bring the water and 1 teaspoon of salt to the boil in a large, heavy-based saucepan. Slowly whisk in the polenta in a thin, steady stream. Reduce the heat and simmer for 5–10 minutes, or until very thick, stirring constantly.

4 Stir the butter and cheese into the polenta, the parsley and a little black pepper.

5 Turn the polenta out on to a lightly oiled, non-stick baking tray and spread into an even layer about 2 cm/¾ inch thick. Leave to cool, then chill in the refrigerator for about 1 hour, or until the polenta is chilled.

6 Turn the cold polenta on to a work surface. Cut into 10 cm/4 inch squares. Brush with olive oil and arrange on a grill rack. Grill for 2–3 minutes on each side until crisp and golden, then cut each square into triangles and keep warm.

7 Transfer the marinated pheasant breasts to the grill rack and grill for 5 minutes, or until crisp and beginning to colour, turning once. Serve the pheasants immediately with the polenta triangles and salad leaves.

INGREDIENTS
Serves 4

3 tbsp extra-virgin olive oil
1 tbsp freshly chopped rosemary or sage leaves
½ tsp ground cinnamon
grated zest of 1 orange
salt and freshly ground black pepper
8 pheasant or wood pigeon breasts
600 ml/1 pint water
125 g/4 oz quick-cook polenta
2 tbsp butter, diced
40 g/1½ oz Parmesan cheese, grated
1–2 tbsp freshly chopped parsley
assorted salad leaves, to serve

Tasty Tip

Heat a griddle pan and griddle the pigeon breasts, skin-side down for 2–3 minutes. Turn and griddle 2 minutes longer for rare, 3–4 minutes longer if you prefer them well done.

Braised Rabbit with Red Peppers

1 Place the rabbit pieces in a shallow dish with half the olive oil, the lemon zest and juice, thyme, and some black pepper. Turn until well coated, then cover and leave to marinate for about 1 hour.

2 Heat half the remaining oil in a large, heavy-based casserole dish, add the onion and cook for 5 minutes, then add the peppers and cook for a further 12–15 minutes, or until softened, stirring occasionally. Stir in the garlic, crushed tomatoes and brown sugar and cook, covered, until soft, stirring occasionally.

3 Heat the remaining oil in a large frying pan, drain the rabbit, reserving the marinade, and pat the rabbit dry with absorbent kitchen paper. Add the rabbit to the pan and cook on all sides until golden. Transfer the rabbit to the casserole dish and mix to cover with the tomato sauce.

4 Add the reserved marinade to the frying pan, cook stirring to loosen any browned bits from the pan, add to the rabbit and stir gently.

5 Cover the pan and simmer for 30 minutes or until the rabbit is tender. Serve the rabbit and the vegetable mixture on a bed of polenta or creamy mashed potatoes.

INGREDIENTS
Serves 4

1.1 kg/2½ lb rabbit pieces
125 ml/4 fl oz olive oil
grated zest and juice of 1 lemon
2–3 tbsp freshly chopped thyme
salt and freshly ground black pepper
1 onion, peeled and thinly sliced
4 red peppers, deseeded and cut into 2.5 cm/1 inch pieces
2 garlic cloves, peeled and crushed
400 g can strained, crushed tomatoes
1 tsp brown sugar
freshly cooked polenta or creamy mashed potatoes, to serve

Helpful Hint

Casseroling is an excellent way to cook rabbit as it has a tendency to be dry. Buy from a good-quality butcher, who will also be able to joint it for you.

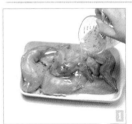

Chicken & Pasta Salad

1 Bring a large saucepan of lightly salted water to the boil. Add the pasta and cook for 10 minutes, or until 'al dente'.

2 Drain the pasta and rinse under cold running water, then drain again. Place in a large serving bowl and toss with the olive oil.

3 Add the chicken, diced red and yellow peppers, sliced sun-dried tomatoes, capers, olives, spring onions and mozzarella to the pasta and toss gently until mixed. Season to taste with salt and pepper.

4 To make the dressing, put the vinegar, mustard and sugar into a small bowl or jug and whisk until well blended and the sugar is dissolved. Season with some pepper, then gradually whisk in the olive oil in a slow, steady stream until a thickened vinaigrette forms.

5 Put the mayonnaise in a bowl and gradually whisk in the dressing until smooth. Pour over the pasta mixture and mix gently until all the ingredients are coated. Turn into a large, shallow serving bowl and serve at room temperature.

INGREDIENTS
Serves 6

450 g/1 lb short pasta
2–3 tbsp extra-virgin olive oil
300 g/11 oz cold cooked chicken,
    cut into bite-sized pieces
    (preferably roasted)
1 red pepper, deseeded and diced
1 yellow pepper, deseeded and
    diced
4–5 sun-dried tomatoes, sliced
2 tbsp capers, rinsed and drained
125 g/4 oz pitted Italian black
    olives
4 spring onions, chopped
225 g/8 oz mozzarella cheese,
    preferably buffalo, diced
salt and freshly ground black
    pepper

FOR THE DRESSING:
50 ml/2 fl oz red or white wine
    vinegar
1 tbsp mild mustard
1 tsp sugar
75–125 ml/ 3–4 fl oz extra-
    virgin olive oil
125 ml/4 fl oz mayonnaise

Tasty Tip

In the bowl of a food processor or blender, whisk together 1 egg yolk, 1 teaspoon Dijon mustard and the juice of half a lemon with some seasoning, until it is foaming. Add 225 ml/8 fl oz light olive oil in a steady but slow stream until the mayonnaise is thick and all the oil has been added. Season to taste and use to dress the salad. Keep the remainder in the refrigerator for other uses.

Hot Duck Pasta Salad

1 Preheat the oven to 200°C/ 400°F/Gas Mark 6. Place the duck breasts on a baking tray lined with tinfoil. Mix together the wholegrain mustard and honey, season lightly with salt and pepper then spread over the duck breasts. Roast in the pre-heated oven for 20–30 minutes, or until tender. Remove from the oven and keep warm.

2 Meanwhile, place the eggs in a small saucepan, cover with water and bring to the boil. Simmer for 8 minutes, then drain. Bring a large pan of lightly salted water to a rolling boil. Add the beans and pasta, return to the boil and cook according to the packet instructions, or until 'al dente'. Drain the pasta and beans and refresh under cold running water.

3 Place the pasta and beans in a bowl, add the carrot, sweetcorn and spinach leaves and toss lightly. Shell the eggs, cut into wedges and arrange on top of the pasta. Slice the duck breasts then place them on top of the salad. Beat the dressing ingredients together in a bowl until well blended, then drizzle over the salad. Serve immediately.

INGREDIENTS
Serves 6

3 boneless and skinless duck breasts
1 tbsp wholegrain mustard
1 tbsp clear honey
salt and freshly ground black pepper
4 medium eggs
450 g / 1 lb fusilli
125 g / 4 oz French beans, trimmed
1 large carrot, peeled and cut into thin batons
125 g / 4 oz sweetcorn kernels, cooked if frozen
75 g / 3 oz fresh baby spinach leaves, shredded

FOR THE DRESSING:
8 tbsp French dressing
1 tsp horseradish sauce
4 tbsp crème fraîche

Helpful Hint

Eggs should never be boiled rapidly as this may cause the shells to crack and make the egg white rubbery. When cooking hard-boiled eggs for salads, turn the eggs gently once or twice in the first few minutes of cooking, so that the yolks stay in the middle. As soon as the eggs are cooked, remove them from the pan and place in a bowl of very cold water to prevent dark rings forming around the yolk.

Chicken Tagliatelle

1 Bring a large pan of lightly salted water to a rolling boil. Add the pasta and cook according to the packet instructions, or until 'al dente'. Add the peas to the pan 5 minutes before the end of cooking time and cook until tender. Drain the pasta and peas, return to the pan and keep warm.

2 Trim the chicken if necessary, then cut into bite-sized pieces. Heat the olive oil in a large frying pan, add the chicken and cook for 8 minutes, or until golden, stirring occasionally.

3 Add the cucumber and cook for 2 minutes, or until slightly softened, stirring occasionally. Stir in the vermouth, bring to the boil, then lower the heat and simmer for 3 minutes, or until reduced slightly.

4 Add the cream to the pan, bring to the boil, stirring constantly, then stir in the Stilton cheese and snipped chives. Season to taste with salt and pepper. Heat through thoroughly, stirring occasionally, until the cheese is just beginning to melt.

5 Toss the chicken mixture into the pasta. Tip into a warmed serving dish or on to individual plates. Garnish and serve immediately.

INGREDIENTS
Serves 4

350 g/12 oz tagliatelle
125 g/4 oz frozen peas
4 boneless and skinless chicken breasts
2 tbsp olive oil
¼ cucumber, cut into strips
150 ml/¼ pint dry vermouth
150 ml/¼ pint double cream
125 g/4 oz Stilton cheese, crumbled
3 tbsp freshly snipped chives, plus extra to garnish
salt and freshly ground black pepper
fresh herbs, to garnish

Helpful Hint

Chives add a mild onion flavour and attractive colour to this dish. If you do not have any, finely shred the green tops of spring onions and use them instead. If preferred, a mixture of dry white wine and 1–2 tablespoons of dry sherry can be substituted for the vermouth.

Mixed Vegetable & Chicken Pasta

1 Preheat the grill just before using. Cut the chicken into thin strips. Trim the leeks, leaving some of the dark green tops, then shred and wash thoroughly in plenty of cold water. Peel the onion and cut into thin wedges.

2 Bring a large pan of lightly salted water to a rolling boil. Add the pasta and cook according to the packet instructions, or until 'al dente'.

3 Meanwhile, melt butter with the olive oil in a large heavy-based pan, add the chicken and cook, stirring occasionally, for 8 minutes, or until browned all over. Add the leeks and onion and cook for 5 minutes, or until softened. Add the garlic and cherry tomatoes and cook for a further 2 minutes.

4 Stir the cream and asparagus tips into the chicken and vegetable mixture, bring to the boil slowly, then remove from the heat. Drain the pasta thoroughly and return to the pan. Pour the sauce over the pasta, season to taste with salt and pepper, then toss lightly.

5 Tip the pasta mixture into a gratin dish and sprinkle with the cheese. Cook under the preheated grill for 5 minutes, or until bubbling and golden, turning the dish occasionally. Serve immediately with a green salad.

INGREDIENTS
Serves 4

3 boneless and skinless chicken
  breasts
2 leeks
1 red onion
350 g/12 oz pasta shells
25 g/1 oz butter
2 tbsp olive oil
1 garlic clove, peeled and chopped
175 g/6 oz cherry tomatoes,
  halved
200 ml/7 fl oz double cream
425 g can asparagus tips, drained
salt and freshly ground black
  pepper
125 g/4 oz double Gloucester
  cheese with chives, crumbled
green salad, to serve

Tasty Tip

Fresh asparagus is in season during May and June and can be used in place of canned. Tie in small bundles and cook in lightly salted, boiling water for 5–8 minutes.

Herb-baked Chicken with Tagliatelle

1 Preheat the oven to 200°C/ 400°F/Gas Mark 6, 15 minute before cooking. Mix together the breadcrumbs, 1 tablespoon of the olive oil, the oregano and tomato paste. Season to taste with salt and pepper. Place the chicken breasts well apart in a roasting tin and coat with the breadcrumb mixture.

2 Mix the plum tomatoes with the chopped basil and white wine. Season to taste, then spoon evenly round the chicken.

3 Drizzle the remaining olive oil over the chicken breasts and cook in the preheated oven for 20–30 minutes, or until the chicken is golden and the juices run clear when a skewer is inserted into the flesh.

4 Meanwhile, bring a large pan of lightly salted water to a rolling boil. Add the pasta and cook according to the packet instructions, or until 'al dente'.

5 Drain the pasta thoroughly and transfer to warmed serving plates. Arrange the chicken breasts on top of the pasta and spoon over the sauce. Garnish with sprigs of basil and serve immediately.

INGREDIENTS
Serves 4

75 g/3 oz fresh white breadcrumbs
3 tbsp olive oil
1 tsp dried oregano
2 tbsp sun-dried tomato paste
salt and freshly ground black pepper
4 boneless and skinless chicken breasts, each about 150 g/5 oz
2 x 400 g cans plum tomatoes
4 tbsp freshly chopped basil
2 tbsp dry white wine
350 g/12 oz tagliatelle
fresh basil sprigs, to garnish

Food Fact

Sun-dried tomatoes are ripened on the vine, then split open and dried in the sun to give a deep, concentrated caramelised flavour. Sun-dried tomato paste usually comes in glass jars, but can also be found in tubes. Once opened, store in the refrigerator and, if in a jar, cover the surface with a teaspoonful of olive oil to keep fresh.

Creamy Chicken & Sausage Penne

1 Heat the olive oil in a large frying pan, add the shallots and cook for 3 minutes, or until golden. Remove and drain on absorbent kitchen paper. Add the chicken thighs to the pan and cook for 5 minutes, turning frequently until browned. Drain on absorbent kitchen paper.

2 Add the smoked sausage and chestnut mushrooms to the pan and cook for 3 minutes, or until browned. Drain separately on absorbent kitchen paper.

3 Return the shallots, chicken and sausage to the pan, then add the garlic, paprika and thyme and cook for 1 minute, stirring. Pour in the wine and stock and season to taste with black pepper. Bring to the boil, lower the heat and simmer, covered, for 15 minutes.

4 Add the mushrooms to the pan and simmer, covered, for 15 minutes, or until the chicken is tender.

5 Meanwhile, bring a large pan of lightly salted water to a rolling boil. Add the penne and cook according to the packet instructions, or until 'al dente'. Drain thoroughly.

6 Stir the mascarpone cheese into the chicken sauce and heat through, stirring gently. Spoon the pasta on to a warmed serving dish, top with the sauce, garnish and serve immediately.

INGREDIENTS
Serves 4

2 tbsp olive oil
225 g/8 oz shallots, peeled
8 chicken thighs
175 g/6 oz smoked sausage,
 thickly sliced
125 g/4 oz chestnut mushrooms,
 wiped and halved
2 garlic cloves, peeled and chopped
1 tbsp paprika
1 small bunch fresh thyme,
 chopped, plus leaves to garnish
150 ml/¼ pint red wine
300 ml/½ pint chicken stock
freshly ground black pepper
350 g/12 oz penne
250 g carton mascarpone cheese

Food Fact

Mascarpone is a rich, soft white cheese, more like cream than cheese. Its slightly sweet flavour means that it is frequently used in desserts, but it also makes a wonderfully smooth quick sauce for cooked pasta as it simply melts in the heat.

Creamy Turkey & Tomato Pasta

1 Preheat the oven to 200°C/ 400°F/Gas Mark 6. Heat 2 tablespoons of the olive oil in a large frying pan. Add the turkey and cook for 5 minutes, or until sealed, turning occasionally. Transfer to a roasting tin and add the remaining olive oil, the vine tomatoes, garlic and balsamic vinegar. Stir well and season to taste with salt and pepper. Cook in the preheated oven for 30 minutes, or until the turkey is tender, turning the tomatoes and turkey once.

2 Meanwhile, bring a large pan of lightly salted water to a rolling boil. Add the pasta and cook according to the packet instructions, or until 'al dente'. Drain, return to the pan and keep warm. Stir the basil and seasoning into the crème fraîche.

3 Remove the roasting tin from the oven and discard the vines. Stir the crème fraîche and basil mix into the turkey and tomato mixture and return to the oven for 1–2 minutes, or until thoroughly heated through.

4 Stir the turkey and tomato mixture into the pasta and toss lightly together. Tip into a warmed serving dish. Garnish with Parmesan cheese shavings and serve immediately.

INGREDIENTS
Serves 4

4 tbsp olive oil
450 g / 1 lb turkey breasts, cut into bite-sized pieces
550 g / 1¼ lb cherry tomatoes, on the vine
2 garlic cloves, peeled and chopped
4 tbsp balsamic vinegar
4 tbsp freshly chopped basil
salt and freshly ground black pepper
200 ml tub crème fraîche
350 g / 12 oz tagliatelle
shaved Parmesan cheese, to garnish

Helpful Hint

Balsamic vinegar is dark in colour with a mellow sweet and sour flavour. It is made from concentrated grape juice and fermented in wooden barrels. Like good wine, the vinegar improves and becomes darker and more syrupy the longer it is aged. Less expensive vinegars bought from supermarkets have been matured for three or four years only. The flavour is nonetheless wonderful and perfect for this recipe.

Parma Ham-wrapped Chicken with Ribbon Pasta

1 Cut each chicken breast into 3 pieces and season well with salt and pepper. Wrap each chicken piece in a slice of Parma ham to enclose completely, securing if necessary with either fine twine or cocktail sticks.

2 Heat the oil in a large frying pan and cook the chicken, turning occasionally, for 12–15 minutes, or until thoroughly cooked. Remove from the pan with a slotted spoon and reserve.

3 Meanwhile, bring a large pan of lightly salted water to a rolling boil. Add the pasta and cook according to the packet instructions, or until 'al dente'.

4 Add the garlic and spring onions to the frying pan and cook, stirring occasionally, for 2 minutes, or until softened. Stir in the tomatoes, lemon juice and crème fraîche. Bring to the boil, lower the heat and simmer, covered, for 3 minutes. Stir in the parsley and sugar, season to taste, then return the chicken to the pan and heat for 2–3 minutes, or until piping hot.

5 Drain the pasta thoroughly and mix in the chopped parsley, then spoon on to a warmed serving dish or individual plates. Arrange the chicken and sauce over the pasta. Garnish and serve immediately.

INGREDIENTS
Serves 4

4 boneless and skinless chicken breasts
salt and freshly ground black pepper
12 slices Parma ham
2 tbsp olive oil
350 g/12 oz ribbon pasta
1 garlic clove, peeled and chopped
1 bunch spring onions, trimmed and diagonally sliced
400 g can chopped tomatoes
juice of 1 lemon
150 ml/¼ pint crème fraîche
3 tbsp freshly chopped parsley
pinch of sugar
freshly grated Parmesan cheese, to garnish

Food Fact

Crème fraîche has a slightly sour taste and a thick, spoonable texture. It is made in a similar way to yogurt, by introducing a bacterial culture to cream. This produces lactic acid, which makes the cream curdle and thicken. The half-fat version is best avoided for cooking; it sometimes separates when boiled.

Baked Aubergines
with Tomato & Mozzarella

1 Preheat the oven to 200° C/400°F/Gas Mark 6, 15 minutes before cooking. Place the aubergine slices in a colander and sprinkle with salt. Leave for 1 hour or until the juices run clear. Rinse and dry on absorbent kitchen paper.

2 Heat 3–5 tablespoons of the olive oil in a large frying pan and cook the prepared aubergines in batches for 2 minutes on each side, or until softened. Remove and drain on absorbent kitchen paper.

3 Heat 1 tablespoon of olive oil in a saucepan, add the turkey mince and cook for 5 minutes, or until browned and sealed.

4 Add the onion to the pan and cook for 5 minutes, or until softened. Add the chopped garlic, the tomatoes and mixed herbs. Pour in the wine and season to taste with salt and pepper. Bring to the boil, lower the heat then simmer for 15 minutes, or until thickened.

5 Meanwhile, bring a large pan of lightly salted water to a rolling boil. Add the macaroni and cook according to the packet instructions, or until 'al dente'. Drain thoroughly.

6 Spoon half the tomato mixture into a lightly oiled ovenproof dish. Top with half the aubergine, pasta and chopped basil, then season lightly. Repeat the layers, finishing with a layer of aubergine. Sprinkle with the mozzarella and Parmesan cheeses, then bake in the preheated oven for 30 minutes, or until golden and bubbling. Serve immediately.

INGREDIENTS
Serves 4

3 medium aubergines, trimmed and sliced
salt and freshly ground black pepper
4–6 tbsp olive oil
450 g/1 lb fresh turkey mince
1 onion, peeled and chopped
2 garlic cloves, peeled and chopped
2 x 400 g cans cherry tomatoes
1 tbsp fresh mixed herbs
200 ml/7 fl oz red wine
350 g/12 oz macaroni
5 tbsp freshly chopped basil
125 g/4 oz mozzarella cheese, drained and chopped
50 g/2 oz freshly grated Parmesan cheese

Helpful Hint

Aubergines are salted to remove bitterness, although they are now less bitter. Salting also removes moisture so they absorb less oil when fried.

Mini Chicken
Balls with Tagliatelle

1 Mix the chicken and tomatoes together and season to taste with salt and pepper. Divide the mixture into 32 pieces and roll into balls. Transfer to a baking sheet, cover and leave in the refrigerator for 1 hour.

2 Melt the butter in a large frying pan, add the chicken balls and cook for 5 minutes, or until golden, turning occasionally. Remove, drain on absorbent kitchen paper and keep warm.

3 Add the leeks and broad beans to the frying pan and cook, stirring, for 10 minutes or until cooked and tender. Return the chicken balls to the pan, then stir in the cream and Parmesan cheese and heat through.

4 Meanwhile, bring a large pan of lightly salted water to a rolling boil. Add the pasta and cook according to the packet instructions, or until 'al dente'.

5 Bring a separate frying pan full of water to the boil, crack in the eggs and simmer for 2–4 minutes, or until poached to personal preference.

6 Meanwhile, drain the pasta thoroughly and return to the pan. Pour the chicken ball and vegetable sauce over the pasta, toss lightly and heat through for 1–2 minutes. Arrange on warmed individual plates and top with the poached eggs. Garnish with fresh herbs and serve immediately.

INGREDIENTS
Serves 4

450 g/1 lb fresh chicken mince
50 g/2 oz sun-dried tomatoes, drained and finely chopped
salt and freshly ground black pepper
25 g/1 oz butter
1 tbsp oil
350 g/12 oz leeks, trimmed and diagonally sliced
125 g/4 oz frozen broad beans
300 ml/½ pint single cream
50 g/2 oz freshly grated Parmesan cheese
350 g/12 oz tagliatelle
4 medium eggs
fresh herbs, to garnish

Helpful Hint

Chilling the chicken balls firms them, so that they retain their shape when cooked. They need plenty of room for turning; if necessary cook in two batches, halving the butter for each. The butter must be sizzling before the meatballs are added.

Pasta & Pepper Salad

1 Preheat the oven to 200°C/ 400°F/Gas Mark 6. Spoon the olive oil into a roasting tin and heat in the oven for 2 minutes, or until almost smoking. Remove from the oven, add the peppers, courgette and aubergine and stir until coated. Bake for 30 minutes, or until charred, stirring occasionally.

2 Bring a large pan of lightly salted water to a rolling boil. Add the pasta and cook according to the packet instructions, or until 'al dente'. Drain and refresh under cold running water. Drain thoroughly, place in a large salad bowl and reserve.

3 Remove the cooked vegetables from the oven and allow to cool. Add to the cooled pasta, together with the quartered tomatoes, chopped basil leaves, pesto, garlic and lemon juice. Toss lightly to mix.

4 Shred the chicken roughly into small pieces and stir into the pasta and vegetable mixture. Season to taste with salt and pepper, then sprinkle the crumbled feta cheese over the pasta and stir gently. Cover the dish and leave to marinate for 30 minutes, stirring occasionally. Serve the salad with fresh crusty bread.

INGREDIENTS
Serves 4

4 tbsp olive oil
1 each red, orange and yellow pepper, deseeded and cut into chunks
1 large courgette, trimmed and cut into chunks
1 medium aubergine, trimmed and diced
275 g/10 oz fusilli
4 plum tomatoes, quartered
1 bunch fresh basil leaves, roughly chopped
2 tbsp pesto
2 garlic cloves, peeled and roughly chopped
1 tbsp lemon juice
225 g/8 oz boneless and skinless roasted chicken breast
salt and freshly ground black pepper
125 g/4 oz feta cheese, crumbled
crusty bread, to serve

Helpful Hint

Use a large non-stick roasting tin for cooking the vegetables if you have one, and check and move them around frequently, so that they brown evenly. For extra flavour, use a garlic or chilli-flavoured olive oil and tuck a sprig or two of fresh herbs, such as rosemary or thyme, under the vegetables.

Chicken Marengo

1 Season the flour with salt and pepper and toss the chicken in the flour to coat. Heat 2 tablespoons of the olive oil in a large frying pan and cook the chicken for 7 minutes, or until browned all over, turning occasionally. Remove from the pan using a slotted spoon and keep warm.

2 Add the remaining oil to the pan, add the onion and cook, stirring occasionally, for 5 minutes, or until softened and starting to brown. Add the garlic, tomatoes, tomato paste, basil and thyme. Pour in the wine or chicken stock and season well. Bring to the boil.

Stir in the chicken pieces and simmer for 15 minutes, or until the chicken is tender and the sauce has thickened.

3 Meanwhile, bring a large pan of lightly salted water to a rolling boil. Add the rigatoni and cook according to the packet instructions, or until 'al dente'.

4 Drain the rigatoni thoroughly, return to the pan and stir in the chopped parsley. Tip the pasta into a warmed large serving dish or spoon on to individual plates. Spoon over the chicken sauce and serve immediately.

INGREDIENTS
Serves 4

2 tbsp plain flour
salt and freshly ground black pepper
4 boneless and skinless chicken breasts, cut into bite-sized pieces
4 tbsp olive oil
1 Spanish onion, peeled and chopped
1 garlic clove, peeled and chopped
400 g can chopped tomatoes
2 tbsp sun-dried tomato paste
3 tbsp freshly chopped basil
3 tbsp freshly chopped thyme
125 ml/4 fl oz dry white wine or chicken stock
350 g/12 oz rigatoni
3 tbsp freshly chopped flat-leaf parsley

Helpful Hint

Spanish onions have a milder flavour and tend to be larger than English ones. Cook the onion over a fairly low heat until really soft, stirring frequently towards the end to stop it sticking. Let it caramelise and brown very slightly as this adds a richer flavour and golden colour to the final dish.

Turkey & Oven-roasted Vegetable Salad

1 Preheat the oven to 200°C/ 400°F/Gas Mark 6, 15 minutes before cooking. Line a large roasting tin with tinfoil, pour in half the olive oil and place in the oven for 3 minutes, or until very hot. Remove from the oven, add the courgettes and peppers and stir until evenly coated. Bake for 30–35 minutes, or until slightly charred, turning occasionally.

2 Add the pine nuts to the tin. Return to the oven and bake for 10 minutes, or until the pine nuts are toasted. Remove from the oven and allow the vegetables to cool completely.

3 Bring a large pan of lightly salted water to a rolling boil. Add the macaroni and cook according to the packet instructions, or until 'al dente'. Drain and refresh under cold running water then drain thoroughly and place in a large salad bowl.

4 Cut the turkey into bite-sized pieces and add to the macaroni. Add the artichokes and tomatoes with the cooled vegetables and pan juices to the pan. Blend together the coriander, garlic, remaining oil, vinegar and seasoning. Pour over the salad, toss lightly and serve.

INGREDIENTS
Serves 4

6 tbsp olive oil
3 medium courgettes, trimmed and sliced
2 yellow peppers, deseeded and sliced
125 g/4 oz pine nuts
275 g/10 oz macaroni
350 g/12 oz cooked turkey
280 g jar or can chargrilled artichokes, drained and sliced
225 g/8 oz baby plum tomatoes, quartered
4 tbsp freshly chopped coriander
1 garlic clove, peeled and chopped
3 tbsp balsamic vinegar
salt and freshly ground black pepper

Helpful Hint

Other vegetables would be equally delicious. Try baby aubergines, trimmed and quartered lengthwise, or scrubbed new potatoes. If you cannot find chargrilled artichokes, use ordinary ones: drain and pat dry, then add to 1 tablespoon of hot olive oil in a frying pan and cook for 2–3 minutes, or until lightly charred.

Spicy Chicken & Pasta Salad

1 Bring a large pan of lightly salted water to a rolling boil. Add the pasta shells and cook according to the packet instructions, or until 'al dente'. Drain and refresh under cold running water then drain thoroughly and place in a large serving bowl.

2 Meanwhile, melt the butter in a heavy-based pan, add the onion and cook for 5 minutes, or until softened. Add the curry paste and cook, stirring, for 2 minutes. Stir in the apricots and tomato paste, then cook for 1 minute. Remove from the heat and allow to cool.

3 Blend the mango chutney and mayonnaise together in a small bowl. Drain the pineapple slices, adding 2 tablespoons of the pineapple juice to the mayonnaise mixture; reserve the pineapple slices. Season the mayonnaise to taste with salt and pepper.

4 Cut the pineapple slices into chunks and stir into the pasta together with the mayonnaise mixture, curry paste and cooked chicken pieces. Toss lightly together to coat the pasta. Sprinkle with the almond slivers, garnish with coriander sprigs and serve.

INGREDIENTS
Serves 6

450 g / 1 lb pasta shells
25 g / 1 oz butter
1 onion, peeled and chopped
2 tbsp mild curry paste
125 g / 4 oz ready-to-eat dried
   apricots, chopped
2 tbsp tomato paste
3 tbsp mango chutney
300 ml / ½ pint mayonnaise
425 g can pineapple slices in
   fruit juice
salt and freshly ground black
   pepper
450 g / 1 lb skinned and boned
   cooked chicken, cut into bite-
   sized pieces
25 g / 1 oz flaked toasted almond
   slivers
coriander sprigs, to garnish

Helpful Hint

If you cannot buy almonds slivers, you can prepare your own. Place whole or half blanched almonds in a small bowl and pour over plenty of boiling water. Leave to soak for 20 minutes, then drain the almonds and cut into slivers using a sharp knife. Spread on a foil-lined grill pan and toast under a low grill for 1–2 minutes to make them dry and crunchy again.

Chicken Gorgonzola & Mushroom Macaroni

1 Bring a large pan of lightly salted water to a rolling boil. Add the macaroni and cook according to the packet instructions, or until 'al dente'.

2 Meanwhile, melt the butter in a large frying pan, add the chestnut and button mushrooms and cook for 5 minutes, or until golden, stirring occasionally. Add the chicken to the pan and cook for 4 minutes, or until heated through thoroughly and slightly golden, stirring occasionally.

3 Blend the cornflour with a little of the milk in a jug to form a smooth paste, then gradually blend in the remaining milk and pour into the frying pan. Bring to the boil slowly, stirring constantly. Add cheese and cook for 1 minute, stirring frequently until melted.

4 Stir the sage and chives into the frying pan. Season to taste with salt and pepper then heat through. Drain the macaroni thoroughly and return to the pan. Pour the chicken and mushroom sauce over the macaroni and toss lightly to coat. Tip into a warmed serving dish, and serve immediately with extra Gorgonzola cheese.

INGREDIENTS
Serves 4

450 g/1 lb macaroni
75 g/3 oz butter
225 g/8 oz chestnut mushrooms, wiped and sliced
225 g/8 oz baby button mushrooms, wiped and halved
350 g/12 oz cooked chicken, skinned and chopped
2 tsp cornflour
300 ml/½ pint semi-skimmed milk
50 g/2 oz Gorgonzola cheese, chopped, plus extra to serve
2 tbsp freshly chopped sage
1 tbsp freshly chopped chives, plus extra chive leaves to garnish
salt and freshly ground black pepper

Food Fact

First mentioned in AD 879, Gorgonzola is the oldest named cheese in the world. It was named after the Italian town where cattle rested on their annual return from their summer pastures to their winter stalls. The original *piccante* is firm and heavily blue-veined with a strong flavour, while *dolce*, often simply labelled extra creamy, has a milder taste and a softer texture.

Spaghetti with Turkey & Bacon Sauce

1 Bring a large pan of lightly salted water to a rolling boil. Add the spaghetti and cook according to the packet instructions, or until 'al dente'.

2 Meanwhile, melt the butter in a large frying pan. Using a sharp knife, cut the streaky bacon into small dice. Add the bacon to the pan with the turkey strips and cook for 8 minutes, or until browned, stirring occasionally to prevent sticking. Add the onion and garlic and cook for 5 minutes, or until softened, stirring occasionally.

3 Place the eggs and cream in a bowl and season to taste with salt and pepper. Beat together then pour into the frying pan and cook, stirring, for 2 minutes or until the mixture begins to thicken but does not scramble.

4 Drain the spaghetti thoroughly and return to the pan. Pour over the sauce, add the grated Parmesan cheese and toss lightly. Heat through for 2 minutes, or until piping hot. Tip into a warmed serving dish and sprinkle with freshly chopped coriander. Serve immediately.

INGREDIENTS
Serves 4

450 g/1 lb spaghetti
25 g /1 oz butter
225 g/8 oz smoked streaky bacon, rind removed
350 g/12 oz fresh turkey strips
1 onion, peeled and chopped
1 garlic clove, peeled and chopped
3 medium eggs, beaten
300 ml/½ pint double cream
salt and freshly ground black pepper
50 g/2 oz freshly grated Parmesan cheese
2–3 tbsp freshly chopped coriander, to garnish

Helpful Hint

It is a good idea to remove the pan from the heat before adding the beaten eggs to the pan, as there should be enough residual heat in the sauce to cook them. If the sauce does not start to thicken after 2 minutes, return to a very low heat and continue cooking gently until it does.

Cheesy Baked Chicken Macaroni

1 Preheat the grill just before cooking. Heat the oil in large frying pan and cook the chicken for 8 minutes, or until browned, stirring occasionally. Drain on absorbent kitchen paper and reserve. Add the pancetta slices to the pan and fry on both sides until crispy. Remove from the pan and reserve.

2 Add the onion and garlic to the frying pan and cook for 5 minutes, or until softened. Stir in the tomato sauce, chopped tomatoes and basil and season to taste with salt and pepper. Bring to the boil, lower the heat and simmer the sauce for 5 minutes.

3 Meanwhile, bring a large pan of lightly salted water to a rolling boil. Add the macaroni and cook according to the packet instructions, or until 'al dente'.

4 Drain the macaroni thoroughly, return to the pan and stir in the sauce, chicken and mozzarella cheese. Spoon into a shallow ovenproof dish.

5 Sprinkle the pancetta over the macaroni. Sprinkle over the Gruyère and Parmesan cheeses. Place under the preheated grill and cook for 5–10 minutes, or until golden-brown; turn the dish occasionally. Garnish and serve immediately.

INGREDIENTS
Serves 4

1 tbsp olive oil
350 g/12 oz boneless and
  skinless chicken breasts, diced
75 g/3 oz pancetta, diced
1 onion, peeled and chopped
1 garlic clove, peeled and chopped
350 g packet fresh tomato sauce
400 g can chopped tomatoes
2 tbsp freshly chopped basil, plus
  leaves to garnish
salt and freshly ground black
  pepper
350 g/12 oz macaroni
150 g/5oz mozzarella cheese,
  drained and chopped
50 g/2 oz Gruyère cheese, grated
50 g/2 oz freshly grated
  Parmesan cheese

Tasty Tip

This dish can be made with any pasta shape or flavour; try green spinach pasta for a change. Check the contents of the packet of fresh tomato sauce carefully; it may already contain herbs and spices, so you may need to cut out or reduce the garlic and fresh basil accordingly.

Food Fact

Pancetta (cured dried belly of pork) imparts a wonderful flavour to a dish; it is available from Italian delicatessens.

Spicy Mexican Chicken

1 Heat the oil in a large frying pan, add the chicken mince and cook for 5 minutes, stirring frequently with a wooden spoon to break up any lumps. Add the onion, garlic and pepper and cook for 3 minutes, stirring occasionally. Stir in the chilli powder and cook for a further 2 minutes.

2 Stir in the tomato paste, pour in the chicken stock and season to taste with salt and pepper. Bring to the boil, reduce the heat, and simmer, covered, for 20 minutes.

3 Add the kidney and chilli beans and cook, stirring occasionally, for 10 minutes, or until the chicken is tender.

4 Meanwhile, bring a large pan of lightly salted water to a rolling boil. Add the spaghetti and cook according to the packet instructions, or until 'al dente'.

5 Drain the spaghetti thoroughly, arrange on warmed plates and spoon over the chicken and bean mixture. Serve with the grated cheese, guacamole and salsa.

INGREDIENTS
Serves 4

2 tbsp olive oil

450 g / 1 lb chicken mince

1 red onion, peeled and chopped

2 garlic cloves, peeled and chopped

1 red pepper, deseeded and chopped

1–2 tsp hot chilli powder

2 tbsp tomato paste

225 ml / 8 fl oz chicken stock

salt and freshly ground black pepper

420 g can red kidney beans, drained

420 g can chilli beans, drained

350 g / 12 oz spaghetti

TO SERVE:
Monterey Jack or Cheddar cheese, grated
guacamole
hot chilli salsa

Helpful Hint

A variety of chilli powders are available. The most usual is the red powder made from dried red chillies, which may be mild or hot. A darker powder, which contains a mixture of ground chilli and herbs, is specifically for use in Mexican and southwest American dishes.

Pesto Chicken Tagliatelle

1 Heat the oil in a large frying pan, add the chicken and cook for 8 minutes, or until golden-brown, stirring occasionally. Using a slotted spoon, remove the chicken from the pan, drain on absorbent kitchen paper and reserve.

2 Melt the butter in the pan. Add the leeks and cook for 3–5 minutes, or until slightly softened, stirring occasionally. Add the oyster and chestnut mushrooms and cook for 5 minutes, or until browned, stirring occasionally.

3 Bring a large pan of lightly salted water to the boil, add the tagliatelle, return to the boil and cook for 4 minutes, or until 'al dente'.

4 Add the chicken, pesto and crème fraîche to the mushroom mixture. Stir, then heat through thoroughly. Stir in the grated Parmesan cheese and season to taste with salt and pepper.

5 Drain the tagliatelle thoroughly and pile on to warmed plates. Spoon over the sauce and serve immediately.

INGREDIENTS
Serves 4

2 tbsp olive oil

350 g/12 oz boneless and skinless chicken breasts, cut into chunks

75 g/3 oz butter

2 medium leeks, trimmed and sliced thinly

125 g/4 oz oyster mushrooms, trimmed and halved

200 g/7 oz small open chestnut mushrooms, wiped and halved

450 g/1lb fresh tagliatelle

4–6 tbsp red pesto

200 ml/7 fl oz crème fraîche

50 g/2 oz freshly grated Parmesan cheese

salt and freshly ground black pepper

Food Fact

Classic pesto is green because it is made from basil. Red pesto is made from a purée of sun-dried tomatoes. Both types of pesto make great store-cupboard standbys as they can be simply tossed with cooked pasta for the speediest of meals. They are even more wonderful livened up with a little crème fraîche, as here, or mascarpone cheese.

Chicken & Prawn-stacked Ravioli

1 Heat the olive oil in a large frying pan, add the onion and garlic and cook for 5 minutes, or until softened, stirring occasionally. Add the chicken pieces and fry for 4 minutes, or until heated through, turning occasionally.

2 Stir in the chopped tomato, wine and cream and bring to the boil. Lower the heat and simmer for about 5 minutes, or until reduced and thickened. Stir in the prawns and tarragon and season to taste with salt and pepper. Heat the sauce through gently.

3 Meanwhile, bring a large pan of lightly salted water

to the boil and add 2 lasagne sheets. Return to the boil and cook for 2 minutes, stirring gently to avoid sticking. Remove from the pan using a slotted spoon and keep warm. Repeat with the remaining sheets.

4 Cut each sheet of lasagne in half. Place two pieces on each of the warmed plates and divide half of the chicken mixture among them. Top each serving with a second sheet of lasagne and divide the remainder of the chicken mixture among them. Top with a final layer of lasagne. Garnish with tarragon sprigs and serve immediately.

INGREDIENTS
Serves 4

1 tbsp olive oil

1 onion, peeled and chopped

1 garlic clove, peeled and chopped

450 g / 1 lb boned and skinned cooked chicken, cut into large pieces

1 beefsteak tomato, deseeded and chopped

150 ml/¼ pint dry white wine

150 ml/¼ pint double cream

250 g/9 oz peeled cooked prawns, thawed if frozen

2 tbsp freshly chopped tarragon, plus sprigs to garnish

salt and freshly ground black pepper

8 sheets fresh lasagne

Helpful Hint

Always check the packet instructions when cooking lasagne; some brands may need longer cooking than others. It should be cooked until 'al dente' – tender, but firm to the bite. Dried lasagne – either plain or verde – may be used instead of fresh if preferred, but it will take longer to cook.

Penne with Pan-fried Chicken & Capers

1 Trim the chicken and cut into bite-sized pieces. Season the flour with salt and pepper then toss the chicken in the seasoned flour and reserve.

2 Bring a large saucepan of lightly salted water to a rolling boil. Add the penne and cook according to the packet instructions, or until 'al dente'.

3 Meanwhile, heat the olive oil in a large frying pan. Add the chicken to the pan and cook for 8 minutes, or until golden on all sides, stirring frequently. Transfer the chicken to a plate and reserve.

4 Add the onion and garlic to the oil remaining in the frying pan and cook for 5 minutes, or until softened, stirring frequently.

5 Return the chicken to the frying pan. Stir in the pesto and mascarpone cheese and heat through, stirring gently, until smooth. Stir in the wholegrain mustard, lemon juice, basil and capers. Season to taste, then continue to heat through until piping hot.

6 Drain the penne thoroughly and return to the saucepan. Pour over the sauce and toss well to coat. Arrange the pasta on individual warmed plates. Scatter with the cheese and serve immediately.

INGREDIENTS
Serves 4

4 boneless and skinless chicken
  breasts
25 g/1 oz plain flour
salt and freshly ground black
  pepper
350 g/12 oz penne
2 tbsp olive oil
25 g/1 oz butter
1 red onion, peeled and sliced
1 garlic clove, peeled and chopped
4–6 tbsp pesto
250 g carton mascarpone cheese
1 tsp wholegrain mustard
1 tbsp lemon juice
2 tbsp freshly chopped basil
3 tbsp capers in brine, rinsed and
  drained
freshly shaved Pecorino Romano
  cheese

Food Fact

Pecorino Romano is a cooked, pressed cheese made in dairies in and around Rome. It is similar to Parmesan (which may be used instead, if preferred) with a dense texture, pale yellow colour and almost smoky aroma. Its flavour is very salty, so take care when seasoning the pasta and chicken when cooking.

Risi e Bisi

1 Shell the peas, if using fresh ones. Melt the butter and olive oil together in a large, heavy-based saucepan. Add the chopped pancetta or bacon, the chopped onion and garlic and gently fry for about 10 minutes, or until the onion is softened and is just beginning to colour.

2 Pour in the vegetable stock, then add the caster sugar, lemon juice and bay leaf. Add the fresh peas if using. Bring the mixture to a fast boil.

3 Add the rice, stir and simmer, uncovered, for about 20 minutes, or until the rice is tender. Occasionally, stir the mixture gently while it cooks. If using frozen petits pois, stir them into the rice about 2 minutes before the end of the cooking time.

4 When the rice is cooked, remove the bay leaf and discard. Stir in 2½ tablespoons of the chopped parsley and the grated Parmesan cheese. Season to taste with salt and pepper.

5 Transfer the rice to a large serving dish. Garnish with the remaining chopped parsley, a sprig of fresh parsley and julienne strips of orange rind. Serve immediately while piping hot.

INGREDIENTS
Serves 4

700 g / 1½ lb young peas in pods
  or 175 g / 6 oz frozen petits
  pois, thawed
25 g / 1 oz unsalted butter
1 tsp olive oil
3 rashers pancetta or unsmoked
  back bacon, chopped
1 small onion, peeled and finely
  chopped
1 garlic clove, peeled and finely
  chopped
1.3 litres / 2¼ pints vegetable stock
pinch of caster sugar
1 tsp lemon juice
1 bay leaf
200 g / 7 oz Arborio rice
3 tbsp freshly chopped parsley
50 g / 2 oz Parmesan cheese,
  finely grated
salt and freshly ground black
  pepper

TO GARNISH:
sprig of fresh parsley
julienne strips of orange rind

Food Fact

This dish of rice with peas comes from Venice. It's much moister than a risotto and should be like a very thick soup.

Rice & Vegetable Timbale

1 Preheat oven to 190°C/ 375°F/Gas Mark 5, 10 minutes before cooking. Sprinkle the breadcrumbs over the base and sides of a thickly buttered 20.5 cm/8 inch round loose-bottomed tin.

2 Heat the olive oil in a large frying pan and gently fry the courgettes, aubergine, mushrooms and garlic for 5 minutes, or until beginning to soften. Stir in the vinegar. Tip the vegetables into a large sieve placed over a bowl to catch the juices.

3 Fry the onion gently in the butter for 10 minutes, until soft. Add the rice and stir for a minute to coat. Add a ladleful of stock and any juices from the vegetables and simmer, stirring, until the rice has absorbed all of the liquid.

4 Continue adding the stock in this way, until the rice

is just tender. This should take about 20 minutes. Remove from the heat and leave to cool for 5 minutes. Stir in the eggs, cheese and basil. Season to taste with salt and pepper.

5 Spoon a quarter of the rice into the prepared tin. Top with one-third of the vegetable mixture. Continue layering up in this way, finishing with a layer of rice.

6 Level the top of the layer of rice, gently pressing down the mixture. Cover with a piece of tinfoil. Put on a baking sheet and bake in the preheated oven for 50 minutes, or until firm.

7 Leave the timbale to stand in the tin for 10 minutes, still covered with tinfoil, then turn out on to a warmed serving platter. Garnish with a sprig of fresh basil and slices of radish and serve immediately.

INGREDIENTS
Serves 6

25 g/1 oz dried white
  breadcrumbs
3 tbsp olive oil
2 courgettes, sliced
1 small aubergine, cut into
  1 cm/½ inch dice
175 g/6 oz mushrooms, sliced
1 garlic clove, peeled and crushed
1 tsp balsamic vinegar
1 onion, peeled and finely
  chopped
25 g/1 oz unsalted butter
400 g/14 oz Arborio rice
about 1.3 litres/2¼ pints boiling
  vegetable stock
2 medium eggs, lightly beaten
25 g/1 oz Parmesan cheese,
  finely grated
2 tbsp freshly chopped basil
salt and freshly ground black
  pepper

TO GARNISH:

sprig of fresh basil
1 radish, thinly sliced

Vegetables Braised in Olive Oil & Lemon

1 Put the pared lemon rind and juice into a large saucepan. Add the olive oil, bay leaf, thyme and the water. Bring to the boil. Add the spring onions and mushrooms. Top with the broccoli and cauliflower, trying to add them so that the stalks are submerged in the water and the tops are just above it. Cover and simmer for 3 minutes.

2 Scatter the courgettes on top, so that they are steamed rather than boiled. Cook, covered, for a further 3–4 minutes, until all the vegetables are tender. Using a slotted spoon, transfer the vegetables from the liquid into a warmed serving dish. Increase the heat and boil rapidly for 3–4 minutes, or until the liquid is reduced to about 8 tablespoons. Remove the lemon rind, bay leaf and thyme sprig and discard.

3 Stir the chives into the reduced liquid, season to taste with salt and pepper and pour over the vegetables. Sprinkle with lemon zest and serve immediately.

INGREDIENTS
Serves 4

small strip of pared rind and juice of ½ lemon
4 tbsp olive oil
1 bay leaf
large sprig of thyme
150 ml/¼ pint water
4 spring onions, trimmed and finely chopped
175 g/6 oz baby button mushrooms
175 g/6 oz broccoli, cut into small florets
175 g/6 oz cauliflower, cut into small florets
1 medium courgette, sliced on the diagonal
2 tbsp freshly snipped chives
salt and freshly ground black pepper
lemon zest, to garnish

Tasty Tip

Serve these vegetables as an accompaniment to roasted or grilled chicken, fish or turkey. Alternatively, toast some crusty bread, rub with a garlic clove and drizzle with a little olive oil and top with a spoonful of vegetables.

Melanzane Parmigiana

1 Preheat oven to 200°C/ 400°F/Gas Mark 6, 15 minutes before cooking. Cut the aubergines lengthways into thin slices. Sprinkle with salt and leave to drain in a colander over a bowl for 30 minutes.

2 Meanwhile, heat 1 tablespoon of the olive oil in a saucepan and fry the onion for 10 minutes, until softened. Add the paprika and cook for 1 minute. Stir in the wine, stock, tomatoes and tomato purée. Simmer, uncovered, for 25 minutes, or until fairly thick. Stir in the oregano and season to taste with salt and pepper. Remove from the heat.

3 Rinse the aubergine slices thoroughly under cold water and pat dry on absorbent

kitchen paper. Heat 2 tablespoons of the oil in a griddle pan and cook the aubergines in batches, for 3 minutes on each side, until golden. Drain well on absorbent kitchen paper.

4 Pour half of the tomato sauce into the base of a large ovenproof dish. Cover with half the aubergine slices, then top with the mozzarella. Cover with the remaining aubergine slices and pour over the remaining tomato sauce. Sprinkle with the grated Parmesan cheese.

5 Bake in the preheated oven for 30 minutes, or until the aubergines are tender and the sauce is bubbling. Garnish with a sprig of fresh basil and cool for a few minutes before serving.

INGREDIENTS
Serves 4

900 g/2 lb aubergines
salt and freshly ground black pepper
5 tbsp olive oil
1 red onion, peeled and chopped
½ tsp mild paprika pepper
150 ml/¼ pint dry red wine
150 ml/¼ pint vegetable stock
400 g can chopped tomatoes
1 tsp tomato purée
1 tbsp freshly chopped oregano
175 g/6 oz mozzarella cheese, thinly sliced
40 g/1½ oz Parmesan cheese, coarsely grated
sprig of fresh basil, to garnish

Helpful Hint

Salting the aubergine draws out some of the moisture, so you'll need less oil when frying.

Stuffed Tomatoes with Grilled Polenta

1 Preheat grill just before cooking. To make the polenta, pour the stock into a saucepan. Add a pinch of salt and bring to the boil. Pour in the polenta in a fine stream, stirring all the time. Simmer for about 15 minutes, or until very thick. Stir in the butter and add a little pepper. Turn the polenta out on to a chopping board and spread to a thickness of just over 1 cm/½ inch. Cool, cover with clingfilm and chill in the refrigerator for 30 minutes.

2 To make the stuffed tomatoes, cut the tomatoes in half then scoop out the seeds and press through a fine sieve to extract the juices. Season the insides of the tomatoes with salt and pepper and reserve.

3 Heat the olive oil in a saucepan and gently fry the garlic and spring onions for 3 minutes. Add the tomatoes' juices, bubble for 3–4 minutes, until most of the liquid has evaporated. Stir in the herbs, Parma ham and a little black pepper with half the breadcrumbs. Spoon into the hollowed out tomatoes and reserve.

4 Cut the polenta into 5 cm/ 2 inch squares, then cut each in half diagonally to make triangles. Put the triangles on a piece of tinfoil on the grill rack and grill for 4–5 minutes on each side, until golden. Cover and keep warm.

5 Grill the tomatoes under a medium-hot grill for about 4 minutes – any exposed Parma ham will become crisp. Sprinkle with the remaining breadcrumbs and grill for 1–2 minutes, or until the breadcrumbs are golden brown. Garnish with snipped chives and serve immediately with the grilled polenta.

INGREDIENTS
Serves 4

FOR THE POLENTA:
300 ml/½ pint vegetable stock
salt and freshly ground black
  pepper
50 g/2 oz quick-cook polenta
15 g/½ oz butter

FOR THE STUFFED
  TOMATOES:
4 large tomatoes
1 tbsp olive oil
1 garlic clove, peeled and crushed
1 bunch spring onions, trimmed
  and finely chopped
2 tbsp freshly chopped parsley
2 tbsp freshly chopped basil
2 slices Parma ham, cut into thin
  slivers
50 g/2 oz fresh white
  breadcrumbs
snipped chives, to garnish

Rigatoni with Roasted Beetroot & Rocket

1 Preheat oven to 150°C/ 300°F/Gas Mark 2, 10 minutes before cooking. Wrap the beetroot individually in tinfoil and bake for 1–1½ hours, or until tender. (Test by opening one of the parcels and scraping the skin away from the stem end – it should come off very easily.)

2 Leave the beetroot until cool enough to handle, then peel and cut each beetroot into 6–8 wedges, depending on the size. Mix the garlic, orange rind and juice, lemon juice, walnut oil

and salt and pepper together, then drizzle over the beetroot and toss to coat well.

3 Meanwhile, bring a large saucepan of lightly salted water to the boil. Cook the pasta for 10 minutes, or until 'al dente'.

4 Drain the pasta thoroughly, then add the warm beetroot, rocket leaves and Dolcelatte cheese. Quickly and gently toss together, then divide between serving bowls and serve immediately before the rocket wilts.

INGREDIENTS
Serves 4

350 g/12 oz raw baby beetroot, unpeeled
1 garlic clove, peeled and crushed
½ tsp finely grated orange rind
1 tbsp orange juice
1 tsp lemon juice
2 tbsp walnut oil
salt and freshly ground black pepper
350 g/12 oz dried fettucini
75 g/3 oz rocket leaves
125 g/4 oz Dolcelatte cheese, cut into small cubes

Helpful Hint

Many large supermarkets sell raw beetroot, but baby beetroot may be more readily available from specialist or ethnic greengrocers. Look for beetroot with the leaves attached. The bulbs should be firm without any soft spots and the leaves should not be wilted.

Mixed Salad with Anchovy Dressing & Ciabatta Croûtons

1 Divide the endive and chicory into leaves and reserve some of the larger ones. Arrange the smaller leaves in a wide salad bowl.

2 Cut the fennel bulb in half from the stalk to the root end, then cut across in fine slices. Quarter the artichokes, then quarter and slice the cucumber and halve the tomatoes. Add to the salad bowl with the olives.

3 To make the dressing, drain the anchovies and put in a blender with the mustard, garlic, olive oil, lemon juice, 2 table-spoons of hot water and black

pepper. Whiz together until smooth and thickened.

4 To make the croûtons, cut the bread into 1 cm/½ inch cubes. Heat the oil in a frying pan, add the bread cubes and fry for 3 minutes, turning frequently until golden. Remove and drain on absorbent kitchen paper.

5 Drizzle half the anchovy dressing over the prepared salad and toss to coat. Arrange the reserved endive and chicory leaves around the edge, then drizzle over the remaining dress-ing. Scatter over the croûtons and serve immediately.

INGREDIENTS
Serves 4

1 small head endive
1 small head chicory
1 fennel bulb
400 g can artichokes, drained and rinsed
½ cucumber
125 g/4 oz cherry tomatoes
75 g/3 oz black olives

FOR THE ANCHOVY DRESSING:

50 g can anchovy fillets
1 tsp Dijon mustard
1 small garlic clove, peeled and crushed
4 tbsp olive oil
1 tbsp lemon juice
freshly ground black pepper

FOR THE CIABATTA CROÛTONS:

2 thick slices ciabatta bread
2 tbsp olive oil

Helpful Hint

To reduce the fat in the croûtons, cut the bread into cubes as above and toss in a large bowl with 2–3 teaspoons of olive oil. Bake in a preheated oven 180°C/350°F/Gas Mark 4 for 15–20 minutes, or until just golden and crisp. Serve as above.

Rice-filled Peppers

1 Preheat oven to 200°C/ 400°F/Gas Mark 6. Put the tomatoes in a small bowl and pour over boiling water to cover. Leave for 1 minute, then drain. Plunge the tomatoes into cold water to cool, then peel off the skins. Quarter, remove the seeds and chop.

2 Heat the olive oil in a frying pan, and cook the onion gently for 10 minutes, until softened. Add the garlic, chopped tomatoes and sugar.

3 Gently cook the tomato mixture for 10 minutes until thickened. Remove from the heat and stir the rice, pine nuts and oregano into the sauce. Season to taste with salt and pepper.

4 Halve the peppers lengthways, cutting through and leaving the stem on. Remove the seeds and cores, then put the peppers in a lightly oiled roasting tin, cut-side down and cook in the preheated oven for about 10 minutes.

5 Turn the peppers so they are cut side up. Spoon in the filling, then cover with tinfoil. Return to the oven for 15 minutes, or until the peppers are very tender, removing the tinfoil for the last 5 minutes to allow the tops to brown a little.

6 Serve 1 red pepper half and 1 yellow pepper half per person with a mixed salad and plenty of warmed, crusty bread.

INGREDIENTS
Serves 4

8 ripe tomatoes
2 tbsp olive oil
1 onion, peeled and chopped
1 garlic clove, peeled and crushed
½ tsp dark muscovado sugar
125 g/4 oz cooked long-grain rice
50 g/2 oz pine nuts, toasted
1 tbsp freshly chopped oregano
salt and freshly ground black
  pepper
2 large red peppers
2 large yellow peppers

TO SERVE:
mixed salad
crusty bread

Helpful Hint

It may be necessary to take a very thin slice from the bottom of the peppers to enable them to stand on the baking sheet. Be careful not to cut right through.

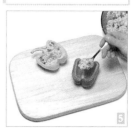

Pasta with Spicy Red Pepper Sauce

1 Preheat grill. Set the whole peppers on the grill rack about 10 cm/4 inches away from the heat, then grill, turning frequently, for 10 minutes, until the skins are blackened and blistered.

2 Put the peppers in a plastic bag, and leave until cool enough to handle. Peel off the skin, then halve the peppers and scrape away the seeds. Chop the pepper flesh roughly and put in a food processor or blender.

3 Heat the olive oil in a large saucepan and gently fry the onion for 5 minutes. Stir in the garlic, anchovy fillets and chilli and cook for a further 5 minutes, stirring. Add to the food processor and blend until fairly smooth.

4 Return the mixture to the saucepan with the tomatoes and stir in the lemon rind and juice. Season to taste with salt and pepper. Add 2–3 tablespoons of vegetable stock if the sauce is a little thick. Bring to the boil and bubble for 1–2 minutes.

5 Meanwhile, bring a large saucepan of lightly salted water to the boil and cook the pasta for 10 minutes, or until 'al dente'. Drain thoroughly. Add the sauce and toss well to coat.

6 Tip into a warmed serving dish or on to individual plates. Scatter with shavings of Parmesan cheese and a few basil leaves before serving.

INGREDIENTS
Serves 4

2 red peppers
2 tbsp olive oil
1 onion, peeled and chopped
2 garlic cloves, peeled and crushed
4 anchovy fillets
1 red chilli, seeded and finely chopped
200 g/7 oz can chopped tomatoes
finely grated rind and juice of ½ lemon
salt and freshly ground black pepper
2–3 tbsp vegetable stock (optional)
400 g/14 oz dried pasta, such as tagliatelle, linguine or shells

TO GARNISH:
shaved Parmesan cheese
fresh basil leaves

Tasty Tip

If you prefer a chunkier sauce, do not put the peppers through the food processor but finely chop instead. Add to the saucepan with the onion mixture and carry on from step 4.

Rigatoni with Oven-dried Cherry Tomatoes & Mascarpone

1 Preheat oven to 140°C/ 275°F/Gas Mark 1. Halve the cherry tomatoes and place close together on a non-stick baking tray, cut-side up. Sprinkle lightly with the sugar, then with a little salt and pepper. Bake in the preheated oven for 1¼ hours, or until dry, but not beginning to colour. Leave to cool on the baking tray. Put in a bowl, drizzle over the olive oil and toss to coat.

2 Bring a large saucepan of lightly salted water to the boil and cook the pasta for

about 10 minutes or until 'al dente'. Add the petits pois, 2–3 minutes before the end of the cooking time. Drain thoroughly and return the pasta and the petits pois to the saucepan.

3 Add the mascarpone to the saucepan. When melted, add the tomatoes, mint, parsley and a little black pepper. Toss gently together, then transfer to a warmed serving dish or individual plates and garnish with sprigs of fresh mint. Serve immediately.

INGREDIENTS
Serves 4

350 g/12 oz red cherry tomatoes
1 tsp caster sugar
salt and freshly ground black
  pepper
2 tbsp olive oil
400 g/14 oz dried rigatoni
125 g/4 oz petits pois
2 tbsp mascarpone cheese
1 tbsp freshly chopped mint
1 tbsp freshly chopped parsley
sprigs of fresh mint, to garnish

Tasty Tip

Double the quantity of tomatoes. When cooked, pack tightly into a sterilised jar layered up with fresh herbs and garlic. Cover with olive oil and leave in the refrigerator for a few days. Use as above or serve as an antipasto with bread, cold meats and olives. Do not keep for longer than 2 weeks.

Red Pepper & Basil Tart

1 Preheat oven to 200°C/ 400°F/Gas Mark 6, 15 minutes before cooking. Sift the flour and salt into a bowl. Make a well in the centre. Stir together the egg, oil and 1 tablespoon of tepid water. Add to the dry ingredients, drop in the olives and mix to a dough. Knead on a lightly floured surface for a few seconds until smooth, then wrap in clingfilm and chill in the refrigerator for 30 minutes.

2 Roll out the pastry and use to line a 23 cm/9 inch loose-bottomed fluted flan tin. Lightly prick the base with a fork. Cover and chill in the refrigerator for 20 minutes.

3 Cook the peppers under a hot grill for 10 minutes, or until the skins are blackened and

blistered. Put the peppers in a plastic bag, cool for 10 minutes, then remove the skin and slice.

4 Line the pastry case with tinfoil or greaseproof paper weighed down with baking beans and bake in the preheated oven for 10 minutes. Remove the tinfoil and beans and bake for a further 5 minutes. Reduce the oven temperature to 180°C/ 350°F/Gas Mark 4.

5 Beat the mascarpone cheese until smooth. Gradually add the milk and eggs. Stir in the peppers, basil and season to taste with salt and pepper. Spoon into the flan case and bake for 25–30 minutes, or until lightly set. Garnish with a sprig of fresh basil and serve immediately with a mixed salad.

INGREDIENTS
Serves 4–6

FOR THE OLIVE PASTRY:
225 g/8 oz plain flour
pinch of salt
50 g/2 oz pitted black olives,
  finely chopped
1 medium egg, lightly beaten, plus
  1 egg yolk
3 tbsp olive oil

FOR THE FILLING:
2 large red peppers, quartered and
  deseeded
175 g/6 oz mascarpone cheese
4 tbsp milk
2 medium eggs
3 tbsp freshly chopped basil
salt and freshly ground black
  pepper
sprig of fresh basil, to garnish
mixed salad, to serve

Helpful Hint

Pre-baking (or baking blind) the pastry shell before filling is an important step in making any kind of quiche or tart with a moist filling. It ensures that the pastry will not become soggy and that it will be cooked through.

Spinach Dumplings with Rich Tomato Sauce

1 To make the tomato sauce, heat the olive oil in a large saucepan and fry the onion gently for 5 minutes. Add the garlic and chilli and cook for a further 5 minutes, until softened.

2 Stir in the wine, chopped tomatoes and lemon rind. Bring to the boil, cover and simmer for 20 minutes, then uncover and simmer for 15 minutes, or until the sauce has thickened. Remove the lemon rind and season to taste with salt and pepper.

3 To make the spinach dumplings, wash the spinach thoroughly and remove any tough stalks. Cover and cook in a large saucepan over a low heat with just the water clinging to the leaves. Drain, then squeeze out all the excess water. Finely chop and put in a large bowl.

4 Add the ricotta, breadcrumbs, Parmesan cheese and egg yolk to the spinach. Season with nutmeg and salt and pepper. Mix together and shape into 20 walnut-sized balls.

5 Toss the spinach balls in the flour. Heat the olive oil in a large non-stick frying pan and fry the balls gently for 5–6 minutes, carefully turning occasionally. Garnish with fresh basil leaves and serve immediately with the tomato sauce and tagliatelle.

INGREDIENTS
Serves 4

FOR THE SAUCE:
2 tbsp olive oil
1 onion, peeled and chopped
1 garlic clove, peeled and crushed
1 red chilli, deseeded and chopped
150 ml/¼ pint dry white wine
400 g can chopped tomatoes
pared strip of lemon rind

FOR THE DUMPLINGS:
450 g/1 lb fresh spinach
50 g/2 oz ricotta cheese
25 g/1 oz fresh white
    breadcrumbs
25 g/1 oz Parmesan cheese,
    grated
1 medium egg yolk
¼ tsp freshly grated nutmeg
salt and freshly ground black
    pepper
5 tbsp plain flour
2 tbsp olive oil, for frying
fresh basil leaves, to garnish
freshly cooked tagliatelle, to serve

Helpful Hint

It is very important to squeeze out all the excess water from the cooked spinach, otherwise the dumplings will fall apart when they are fried.

Venetian-style Vegetables & Beans

1 Put the beans in a bowl, cover with plenty of cold water and leave to soak for at least 8 hours, or overnight.

2 Drain and rinse the beans. Put in a large saucepan with 1.1 litres/2 pints cold water. Tie the parsley and rosemary in muslin and add to the beans with the olive oil. Boil rapidly for 10 minutes, then lower the heat and simmer for 20 minutes with the saucepan half-covered. Stir in the tomatoes and shallots and simmer for a further 10–15 minutes, or until the beans are cooked.

3 Meanwhile, slice the red and white onion into rings and then finely dice the carrot and celery. Heat the olive oil in a saucepan and cook the onions over a very low heat for about 10 minutes. Add the carrot, celery and bay leaves to the saucepan and cook for a further 10 minutes, stirring frequently, until the vegetables are tender. Sprinkle with sugar, stir and cook for 1 minute.

4 Stir in the vinegar. Cook for 1 minute, then remove the saucepan from the heat. Drain the beans through a fine sieve, discarding all the herbs, then add the beans to the onion mixture and season well with salt and pepper. Mix gently, then tip the beans into a large serving bowl. Leave to cool, then serve at room temperature.

INGREDIENTS
Serves 4

250 g/9 oz dried pinto beans
3 sprigs of fresh parsley
1 sprig of fresh rosemary
2 tbsp olive oil
200 g can chopped tomatoes
2 shallots, peeled

FOR THE VEGETABLE MIXTURE:
1 large red onion, peeled
1 large white onion, peeled
1 medium carrot, peeled
2 sticks celery, trimmed
3 tbsp olive oil
3 bay leaves
1 tsp caster sugar
3 tbsp red wine vinegar
salt and freshly ground black pepper

Helpful Hint

If time is short, put the beans into a large saucepan and cover with cold water. Bring to the boil and boil rapidly for 10 minutes. Turn off the heat and leave to stand for 2 hours. Drain well and cover with fresh water. Cook as above.

Roast Butternut Squash Risotto

1 Preheat oven to 190°C/375°F/Gas Mark 5. Cut the butternut squash in half, thickly peel, then scoop out the seeds and discard. Cut the flesh into 2 cm/¾ inch cubes.

2 Pour the oil into a large roasting tin and heat in the preheated oven for 5 minutes. Add the butternut squash and garlic cloves. Turn in the oil to coat, then roast in the oven for about 25–30 minutes, or until golden brown and very tender, turning the vegetables halfway through cooking time.

3 Melt the butter in a large saucepan. Add the rice and stir over a high heat for a few seconds. Add the saffron and the wine and bubble fiercely until almost totally reduced, stirring frequently. At the same time heat the stock in a separate saucepan and keep at a steady simmer.

4 Reduce the heat under the rice to low. Add a ladleful of stock to the saucepan and simmer, stirring, until absorbed. Continue adding the stock in this way until the rice is tender. This will take about 20 minutes and it may not be necessary to add all the stock.

5 Turn off the heat, stir in the herbs, Parmesan cheese and seasoning. Cover and leave to stand for 2–3 minutes. Quickly remove the skins from the roasted garlic. Add to the risotto with the butternut squash and mix gently. Garnish with sprigs of oregano and serve immediately with Parmesan cheese.

INGREDIENTS
Serves 4

1 medium butternut squash
2 tbsp olive oil
1 garlic bulb, cloves separated, but unpeeled
15 g/½ oz unsalted butter
275 g/10 oz Arborio rice
large pinch of saffron strands
150 ml/¼ pint dry white wine
1 litre/1¾ pints vegetable stock
1 tbsp freshly chopped parsley
1 tbsp freshly chopped oregano
50 g/2 oz Parmesan cheese, finely grated
salt and freshly ground black pepper
sprigs of fresh oregano, to garnish
extra Parmesan cheese, to serve

Helpful Hint

It is important to keep the stock simmering alongside the risotto because this ensures that the cooking process is not interrupted.

Hot Grilled Chicory & Pears

1 Preheat grill. Spread the chopped almonds in a single layer on the grill pan. Cook under a hot grill for about 3 minutes, moving the almonds around occasionally, until lightly browned. Reserve.

2 Halve the chicory length-ways and cut out the cores. Mix together the olive and walnut oils. Brush about 2 tablespoons all over the chicory.

3 Put the chicory in a grill pan, cut-side up and cook under a hot grill for 2–3 min-utes, or until beginning to char. Turn and cook for a further 1–2 minutes, then turn again.

4 Peel, core and thickly slice the pears. Brush with 1 tablespoon of the oils, then place the pears on top of the chicory. Grill for a further 3–4 minutes, or until both the chicory and pears are soft.

5 Transfer the chicory and pears to 4 warmed serving plates. Whisk together the remaining oil, lemon juice and oregano and season to taste with salt and pepper.

6 Drizzle the dressing over the chicory and pears and scatter with the toasted almonds. Garnish with fresh oregano and serve with ciabatta bread.

INGREDIENTS
Serves 4

50 g/2 oz unblanched almonds, roughly chopped
4 small heads of chicory
2 tbsp olive oil
1 tbsp walnut oil
2 firm ripe dessert pears
2 tsp lemon juice
1 tsp freshly chopped oregano.
salt and freshly ground black pepper
freshly chopped oregano, to garnish
warmed ciabatta bread, to serve

Helpful Hint
If preparing the pears ahead of time for this recipe, dip or brush them with some lemon juice to ensure that they do not discolour before cooking.

Aubergine Cannelloni with Watercress Sauce

1 Preheat oven to 190°C/375°F/Gas Mark 5, 10 minutes before cooking. Cut the aubergines lengthways into thin slices, discarding the side pieces. Heat 2 tablespoons of oil in a frying pan and cook the aubergine slices in a single layer in several batches, turning once, until golden on both sides.

2 Mix the cheeses, basil and seasoning together. Lay the aubergine slices on a clean surface and spread the cheese mixture evenly between them.

3 Roll up the slices from one of the short ends to enclose the filling. Place, seam-side down in a single layer in an ovenproof dish. Bake in the preheated oven for 15 minutes, or until golden.

4 To make the watercress sauce, blanch the watercress leaves in boiling water for about 30 seconds. Drain well, then rinse in a sieve under cold running water and squeeze dry. Put the stock, shallot, lemon rind and thyme in a small saucepan. Boil rapidly until reduced by half, then remove from the heat and strain.

5 Put the watercress and strained stock in a food processor and blend until fairly smooth. Return to the saucepan, stir in the crème fraîche, lemon juice and season to taste with salt and pepper. Heat gently until the sauce is piping hot.

6 Serve a little of the sauce drizzled over the aubergines and the rest separately in a jug. Garnish the cannelloni with sprigs of watercress and lemon zest. Serve immediately.

INGREDIENTS
Serves 4

4 large aubergines, about 250 g/9 oz each
5–6 tbsp olive oil
350 g/12 oz ricotta cheese
75 g/3 oz Parmesan cheese, grated
3 tbsp freshly chopped basil
salt and freshly ground black pepper

FOR THE WATERCRESS SAUCE:

75 g/3 oz watercress, trimmed
200 ml/⅓ pint vegetable stock
1 shallot, peeled and sliced
pared strip of lemon rind
1 large sprig of thyme
3 tbsp crème fraîche
1 tsp lemon juice

TO GARNISH:

sprigs of watercress
lemon zest

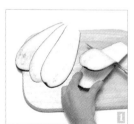

Panzanella

1 Cut the bread into thick slices, leaving the crusts on. Add 1 teaspoon of red wine vinegar to a jug of iced water, put the slices of bread in a bowl and pour over the water. Make sure the bread is covered completely. Leave to soak for 3–4 minutes until just soft.

2 Remove the soaked bread from the water and squeeze it gently, first with your hands and then in a clean tea towel to remove any excess water. Put the bread on a plate, cover with clingfilm and chill in the refrigerator for about 1 hour.

3 Meanwhile, whisk together the olive oil, the remaining red wine vinegar and lemon juice in a large serving bowl. Add the garlic and onion and stir to coat well.

4 Halve the cucumber and remove the seeds. Chop both the cucumber and tomatoes into 1 cm/½ inch dice. Add to the garlic and onions with the olives. Tear the bread into bite-sized chunks and add to the bowl with the fresh basil leaves. Toss together to mix and serve immediately, with a grinding of sea salt and black pepper.

INGREDIENTS
Serves 4

250 g/9 oz day-old Italian-style bread

1 tbsp red wine vinegar

4 tbsp olive oil

1 tsp lemon juice

1 small garlic clove, peeled and finely chopped

1 red onion, peeled and finely sliced

1 cucumber, peeled if preferred

225 g/8 oz ripe tomatoes, deseeded

150 g/5 oz pitted black olives

about 20 basil leaves, coarsely torn or left whole if small

sea salt and freshly ground black pepper

Tasty Tip

Choose an open-textured Italian-style bread such as ciabatta for this classic Tuscany salad. Look in your local delicatessen for different flavoured marinated olives. Try chilli and garlic, or basil, garlic and orange.

Vegetable Frittata

1 Preheat grill just before cooking. Lightly beat the eggs with the parsley, tarragon and half the cheese. Season to taste with black pepper and reserve. (Salt is not needed as the pecorino is very salty.)

2 Bring a large saucepan of lightly salted water to the boil. Add the new potatoes and cook for 8 minutes. Add the carrots and cook for 4 minutes, then add the broccoli florets and the courgettes and cook for a further 3–4 minutes, or until all the vegetables are barely tender. Drain well.

3 Heat the oil in a 20.5 cm/ 8 inch heavy-based frying pan. Add the spring onions and cook for 3–4 minutes, or until

softened. Add all the vegetables and cook for a few seconds, then pour in the beaten egg mixture.

4 Stir gently for about a minute, then cook for a further 1–2 minutes, or until the bottom of the frittata is set and golden brown.

5 Place the pan under a hot grill for 1 minute, or until almost set and just beginning to brown. Sprinkle with the remaining cheese and grill for a further 1 minute, or until it is lightly browned.

6 Loosen the edges and slide out of the pan. Cut into wedges and serve hot or warm with a mixed green salad and crusty Italian bread.

INGREDIENTS
Serves 2

6 medium eggs
2 tbsp freshly chopped parsley
1 tbsp freshly chopped tarragon
25 g/1 oz pecorino or Parmesan cheese, finely grated
freshly ground black pepper
175 g/6 oz tiny new potatoes
2 small carrots, peeled and sliced
125 g/4 oz broccoli, cut into small florets
1 courgette, about 125 g/4 oz, sliced
2 tbsp olive oil
4 spring onions, trimmed and thinly sliced

TO SERVE:
mixed green salad
crusty Italian bread

Food Fact

A frittata is a heavy omelette, usually with a vegetable, meat or cheese filling that is cooked slowly and often finished in the oven or under the grill. It is closer to a Spanish tortilla than to a classic French omelette.

Panzerotti

1 Sift the flour and salt into a bowl. Stir in the yeast. Make a well in the centre. Add the oil and the warm water and mix to a soft dough. Knead on a lightly floured surface until smooth and elastic. Put in an oiled bowl, cover and leave in a warm place to rise while making the filling.

2 To make the filling, heat the oil in a frying pan and cook the onion for 5 minutes. Add the garlic, yellow pepper and courgette. Cook for about 5 minutes, or until the vegetables are tender. Tip into a bowl and leave to cool slightly. Stir in the olives, mozzarella cheese and season to taste with salt and pepper.

3 Briefly reknead the dough. Divide into 16 equal pieces.

Roll out each to a circle about 10 cm/4 inches. Mix together the tomato purée and dried herbs, then spread about 1 teaspoon on each circle, leaving a 2 cm/¾ inch border around the edge.

4 Divide the filling equally between the circles, it will seem a small amount, but if you overfill, they will leak during cooking. Brush the edges with water, then fold in half to enclose the filling. Press to seal, then crimp the edges.

5 Heat the oil in a deep-fat fryer to 180°C/350°F. Deep-fry the panzerotti in batches for 3 minutes, or until golden. Drain on absorbent kitchen paper and keep warm in a low oven until ready to serve with fresh rocket.

INGREDIENTS
Serves 16

450 g/1 lb strong white flour
pinch of salt
1 tsp easy-blend dried yeast
2 tbsp olive oil
300 ml/½ pint warm water
fresh rocket leaves, to serve

FOR THE FILLING:

1 tbsp olive oil
1 small red onion, peeled and finely chopped
2 garlic cloves, peeled and crushed
½ yellow pepper, deseeded and chopped
1 small courgette, about 75 g/3 oz, trimmed and chopped
50 g/2 oz black olives, pitted and quartered
125 g/4 oz mozzarella cheese, cut into tiny cubes
salt and freshly ground black pepper
5–6 tbsp tomato purée
1 tsp dried mixed herbs
oil for deep-frying

Helpful Hint

Make sure that the panzerotti are left to rest before serving. The filling will be very hot when they are freshly cooked.

Pasta Primavera

1 Trim and halve the French beans. Bring a large saucepan of lightly salted water to the boil and cook the beans for 4–5 minutes, adding the sugar snap peas after 2 minutes, so that both are tender at the same time. Drain the beans and sugar snap peas and briefly rinse under cold running water.

2 Heat the butter and oil in a large non-stick frying pan. Add the baby carrots and cook for 2 minutes, then stir in the courgettes and leeks and cook for 10 minutes, stirring, until the vegetables are almost tender.

3 Stir the cream and lemon rind into the vegetables and bubble over a gentle heat until

the sauce is slightly reduced and the vegetables are cooked.

4 Meanwhile, bring a large saucepan of lightly salted water to the boil and cook the tagliatelle for 10 minutes, or until 'al dente'.

5 Add the beans, sugar snaps, Parmesan cheese and herbs to the sauce. Stir for 30 seconds, or until the cheese has melted and the vegetables are hot.

6 Drain the tagliatelle, add the vegetables and sauce, then toss gently to mix and season to taste with salt and pepper. Spoon into a warmed serving bowl and garnish with a few sprigs of dill and serve immediately.

INGREDIENTS
Serves 4

150 g/5 oz French beans
150 g/5 oz sugar snap peas
40 g/1½ oz butter
1 tsp olive oil
225 g/8 oz baby carrots, scrubbed
2 courgettes, trimmed and
   thinly sliced
175 g/6 oz baby leeks, trimmed
   and cut into 2.5 cm/1 inch
   lengths
200 ml/7 fl oz double cream
1 tsp finely grated lemon rind
350 g/12 oz dried tagliatelle
25 g/1 oz Parmesan cheese,
   grated
1 tbsp freshly snipped chives
1 tbsp freshly chopped dill
salt and freshly ground black
   pepper
sprigs of fresh dill, to garnish

Food Fact

Primavera means 'spring' and this dish is classically made with spring vegetables. At other times, use available baby vegetables.

Spaghetti with Pesto

1 To make the pesto, place the Parmesan cheese in a food processor with the basil leaves, pine nuts and garlic and process until well blended.

2 With the motor running, gradually pour in the extra virgin olive oil, until a thick sauce forms. Add a little more oil if the sauce seems too thick. Season to taste with salt and pepper. Transfer to a bowl, cover and store in the refrigerator until required.

3 Bring a large pan of lightly salted water to a rolling boil. Add the spaghetti and cook according to the packet instructions, or until 'al dente'.

4 Drain the spaghetti thoroughly and return to the pan. Stir in the pesto and toss lightly. Heat through gently, then tip the pasta into a warmed serving dish or spoon on to individual plates. Garnish with basil leaves and serve immediately with extra Parmesan cheese.

INGREDIENTS
Serves 4

200 g/7 oz freshly grated
  Parmesan cheese, plus extra
  to serve
25 g/1 oz fresh basil leaves, plus
  extra to garnish
6 tbsp pine nuts
3 large garlic cloves, peeled
200 ml/7 fl oz extra virgin olive
  oil, plus more if necessary
salt and freshly ground pepper
400 g/14 oz spaghetti

Helpful Hint
You can still make pesto if you do not have a food processor. Tear the basil leaves and place them in a mortar with the garlic, pine nuts and a tablespoonful of the oil. Pound to a paste using a pestle, gradually working in the rest of the oil. Transfer to a bowl and stir in the cheese. Season to taste with salt and pepper. Pesto will keep for 2–3 days if stored in the refrigerator.

Pasta Shells with Broccoli & Capers

1 Bring a large pan of lightly salted water to a rolling boil. Add the orecchiette, return to the boil and cook for 2 minutes. Add the broccoli to the pan. Return to the boil and continue cooking for 8–10 minutes, or until the conchiglie is 'al dente'.

2 Meanwhile, heat the olive oil in a large frying pan, add the onion and cook for 5 minutes, or until softened, stirring frequently. Stir in the capers and chilli flakes, if using, and cook for a further 2 minutes.

3 Drain the pasta and broccoli and add to the frying pan. Toss the ingredients to mix thoroughly. Sprinkle over the cheeses, then stir until the cheeses have just melted. Season to taste with salt and pepper, then tip into a warmed serving dish. Garnish with chopped parsley and serve immediately with extra Parmesan cheese.

INGREDIENTS
Serves 4

400 g / 14 oz conchiglie (shells)

450 g / 1 lb broccoli florets, cut into small pieces

5 tbsp olive oil

1 large onion, peeled and finely chopped

4 tbsp capers in brine, rinsed and drained

½ tsp dried chilli flakes (optional)

75 g / 3 oz freshly grated Parmesan cheese, plus extra to serve

25 g / 1 oz pecorino cheese, grated

salt and freshly ground black pepper

2 tbsp freshly chopped flat-leaf parsley, to garnish

Helpful Hint

Chilli flakes are made from dried, crushed chillies and add a pungent hot spiciness to this dish. There are lots of other chilli products that you could use instead. For instance, substitute a tablespoonful of chilli oil for one of the tablespoons of olive oil or add a dash of Tabasco sauce at the end of cooking.

Venetian Herb Orzo

1 Rinse the spinach leaves in several changes of cold water and reserve. Finely chop the rocket leaves with the parsley and mint. Thinly slice the green of the spring onions.

2 Bring a large saucepan of water to the boil, add the spinach leaves, herbs and spring onions and cook for about 10 seconds. Remove and rinse under cold running water. Drain well and, using your hands, squeeze out all the excess moisture.

3 Place the spinach, herbs and spring onions in a food processor. Blend for 1 minute then, with the motor running,

gradually pour in the olive oil until the sauce is well blended.

4 Meanwhile, bring a large pan of lightly salted water to a rolling boil. Add the pasta and cook according to the packet instructions, or until 'al dente'. Drain thoroughly and place in a large warmed bowl.

5 Add the spinach sauce to the orzo and stir lightly until the orzo is well coated. Stir in an extra tablespoon of olive oil if the mixture seems too thick. Season well with salt and pepper. Serve immediately on warmed plates or allow to cool to room temperature.

INGREDIENTS
Serves 4-6

200 g/7 oz baby spinach leaves
150 g/5 oz rocket leaves
50 g/2 oz flat-leaf parsley
6 spring onions, trimmed
few leaves of fresh mint
3 tbsp extra virgin olive oil, plus
* more if required*
450 g/11 oz orzo
salt and freshly ground black
* pepper*

Food Fact

Rocket was first introduced to Britain in the late sixteenth century, but went out of fashion during Victorian times. It adds a peppery flavour to many dishes. The tender tiny leaves have the most delicate flavour and as they grow in size the flavour becomes more pronounced.

Cheesy Pasta with Tomatoes & Cream

1 Place the ricotta cheese in a bowl and beat until smooth, then add the remaining cheeses with the eggs, herbs and seasoning to taste. Beat well until creamy and smooth.

2 Cut the prepared pasta dough into quarters. Working with one-quarter at a time, and covering the remaining quarters with a clean, damp tea towel, roll out the pasta very thinly. Using a 10 cm/4 inch pastry cutter or small saucer, cut out as many rounds as possible.

3 Place a small tablespoonful of the filling mixture slightly below the centre of each round. Lightly moisten the edge of the round with water and fold in half to form a filled half-moon shape. Using a dinner fork, press the edges together firmly.

4 Transfer to a lightly floured baking sheet and continue filling the remaining pasta. Leave to dry for 15 minutes.

5 Heat the oil in a large saucepan, add the onions and cook for 3–4 minutes, or until beginning to soften. Add the garlic and cook for 1–2 minutes, then add the tomatoes, vermouth and cream and bring to the boil. Simmer for 10–15 minutes, or until thickened and reduced.

6 Bring a large saucepan of salted water to the boil. Add the filled pasta and return to the boil. Cook, stirring frequently to prevent sticking, for 5 minutes, or until 'al dente'. Drain and return to the pan. Pour over the tomato and cream sauce, garnish with basil leaves and serve immediately.

INGREDIENTS
Serves 4

225 g/8 oz fresh ricotta cheese
225 g/8 oz smoked mozzarella, grated, (use normal if smoked is unavailable)
5 g/4 oz freshly grated pecorino or Parmesan cheese
2 medium eggs, lightly beated
2–3 tbsp finely chopped mint, basil or parsley
salt and freshly ground black pepper

FOR THE SAUCE:

2 tbsp olive oil
1 small onion, peeled and finely chopped
2 garlic cloves, peeled and finely chopped
450g/1 lb ripe plum tomatoes, peeled, deseeded and finely chopped
50 ml/2 fl oz white vermouth
225 ml/8 fl oz double cream
fresh basil leaves, to garnish

Pastini-stuffed Peppers

1 Preheat the oven to 190°C/ 375°F/Gas Mark 5, 10 minutes before cooking. Bring a pan of water to the boil. Trim the bottom of each pepper so it sits straight. Blanch the peppers for 2–3 minutes, then drain on absorbent kitchen paper.

2 Return the water to the boil, add ½ teaspoon of salt and the pastini and cook for 3–4 minutes, or until 'al dente'. Drain thoroughly, reserving the water. Rinse under cold running water, drain again and reserve.

3 Heat 2 tablespoons of the olive oil in a large frying pan, add the onion and cook for 3–4 minutes. Add the garlic and cook for 1 minute. Stir in the

tomatoes and wine and cook for 5 minutes, stirring frequently. Add the olives, herbs, mozzarella cheese and half the Parmesan cheese. Season to taste with salt and pepper. Remove from the heat and stir in the pastini.

4 Dry the insides of the peppers with absorbent kitchen paper, then season lightly. Arrange the peppers in a lightly oiled shallow baking dish and fill with the pastini mixture. Sprinkle with the remaining Parmesan cheese and drizzle over the remaining oil. Pour in boiling water to come 1 cm/½ inch up the sides of the dish. Cook in the preheated oven for 25 minutes, or until cooked. Serve immediately with freshly made tomato sauce.

INGREDIENTS
Serves 6

6 red, yellow or orange peppers, tops cut off and deseeded
salt and freshly ground black pepper
175 g/6 oz pastini
4 tbsp olive oil
1 onion, peeled and finely chopped
2 garlic cloves, peeled and finely chopped
3 ripe plum tomatoes, skinned, deseeded and chopped
50 ml/2 fl oz dry white wine
8 pitted black olives, chopped
4 tbsp freshly chopped mixed herbs, such as parsley, basil, oregano or marjoram
125 g/4 oz mozzarella cheese, diced
4 tbsp grated Parmesan cheese
fresh tomato sauce, preferably home-made, to serve

Tasty Tip

For a rich tomato sauce, roughly chop 900 g/2 lb ripe tomatoes, then place in a saucepan with 1 crushed garlic clove, 1 tablespoon olive oil and 2 tablespoons Worcestershire sauce. Cook until soft, sieve or purèe and serve with the peppers.

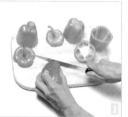

Fusilli with Courgettes & Sun-dried Tomatoes

1 Heat 2 tablespoons of the olive oil in a large frying pan, add the onion and cook for 5-7 minutes, or until softened. Add the chopped garlic and courgette slices and cook for a further 5 minutes, stirring occasionally.

2 Stir the chopped tomatoes and the sun-dried tomatoes into the frying pan and season to taste with salt and pepper. Cook until the courgettes are just tender and the sauce is slightly thickened.

3 Bring a large pan of lightly salted water to a rolling boil. Add the fusilli and cook according to the packet instructions, or until 'al dente'.

4 Drain the fusilli thoroughly and return to the pan. Add the butter and remaining oil and toss to coat. Stir the chopped basil or parsley into the courgette mixture and pour over the fusilli. Toss and tip into a warmed serving dish. Serve with grated Parmesan or pecorino cheese.

INGREDIENTS
Serves 6

5 tbsp olive oil

1 large onion, peeled and thinly sliced

2 garlic cloves, peeled and finely chopped

700 g / 1½ lb courgettes, trimmed and sliced

400 g can chopped plum tomatoes

12 sun-dried tomatoes, cut into thin strips

salt and freshly ground black pepper

450 g / 1 lb fusilli

25 g / 1 oz butter, diced

2 tbsp freshly chopped basil or flat-leaf parsley

grated Parmesan or pecorino cheese, for serving

Food Fact

Sun-dried tomatoes come in jars with olive oil or simply dried in packets, in which case they will need re-hydrating. The latter are better for this recipe as they will soak up the juices from the chopped tomatoes and courgettes and help to thicken the sauce.

Linguine with Walnut Pesto

1 Bring a saucepan of water to the boil. Add the walnut halves and simmer for about 1 minute. Drain and turn on to a clean tea towel. Using the towel, rub the nuts gently to loosen the skins, turn into a coarse sieve or colander and shake to separate the skins. Discard the skins and coarsely chop the nuts.

2 With the the food processor motor running, drop in the garlic cloves and chop finely. Remove the lid, then add the walnuts, breadcrumbs, olive and walnut oils and the parsley. Blend to a paste with a crumbly texture.

3 Scrape the nut mixture into a bowl, add the softened butter and, using a wooden spoon, cream them together.

Gradually beat in the cream and the Parmesan cheese. Season the walnut pesto to taste with salt and pepper.

4 Bring a large pan of lightly salted water to a rolling boil. Add the linguine and cook according to the packet instructions, or until 'al dente'.

5 Drain the linguine thoroughly, reserving 1–2 tablespoons of the cooking water. Return the linguine and reserved water to the pan. Add the walnut pesto, 1 tablespoon at a time, tossing and stirring until well coated. Tip into a warmed serving dish or spoon on to individual plates. Serve immediately with the extra grated Parmesan cheese.

INGREDIENTS
Serves 4

125 g/4 oz walnut halves
1–2 garlic cloves, peeled and
    coarsely chopped
40 g/1 ½ oz dried breadcrumbs
3 tbsp extra virgin olive oil
1 tbsp walnut oil
3–4 tbsp freshly chopped parsley
50 g/2 oz butter, softened
2 tbsp double cream
25 g/1 oz Parmesan cheese,
    grated, plus extra to serve
salt and freshly ground black
    pepper
450 g/1 lb linguine

Helpful Hint

It is important to use dried breadcrumbs for this recipe. Avoid the bright orange variety, which are unsuitable. Spread about 50 g/2 oz fresh breadcrumbs (they will weigh less when dried) on a baking sheet and bake in a very low oven for about 20–25 minutes, stirring occasionally, until dry but not coloured.

Four-cheese Tagliatelle

1 Place the whipping cream with the garlic cloves in a medium pan and heat gently until small bubbles begin to form around the edge of the pan. Using a slotted spoon, remove and discard the garlic cloves.

2 Add all the cheeses to the pan and stir until melted. Season with a little salt and a lot of black pepper. Keep the sauce warm over a low heat, but do not allow to boil.

3 Meanwhile, bring a large pan of lightly salted water to the boil. Add the taglietelle, return to the boil and cook for 2–3 minutes, or until 'al dente'.

4 Drain the pasta thoroughly and return to the pan. Pour the sauce over the pasta, add the chives then toss lightly until well coated. Tip into a warmed serving dish or spoon on to individual plates. Garnish with a few basil leaves and serve immediately with extra Parmesan cheese.

INGREDIENTS
Serves 4

300 ml / ½ pint whipping cream
4 garlic cloves, peeled and lightly bruised
75 g / 3 oz fontina cheese, diced
75 g / 3 oz Gruyère cheese, grated
75 g / 3 oz mozzarella cheese, preferably, diced
50 g / 2 oz Parmesan cheese, grated, plus extra to serve
salt and freshly ground black pepper
275 g / 10 oz fresh green tagliatelle
1–2 tbsp freshly snipped chives
fresh basil leaves, to garnish

Helpful Hint

Fresh pasta takes much less time to cook than dried pasta and 2–3 minutes is usually long enough for it to be 'al dente', but check the packet for cooking instructions. Tagliatelle comes from Bologna, where it is usually served with a meat sauce. Green tagliatelle is generally flavoured with spinach, but it is also available flavoured with fresh herbs, which would go particularly well with the rich cheese sauce in this recipe.

Spaghetti alla Puttanesca

1 Heat the olive oil in a large frying pan, add the anchovies and cook, stirring with a wooden spoon and crushing the anchovies, until they disintegrate. Add the garlic and dried chillies and cook for 1 minute, stirring frequently.

2 Add the tomatoes, olives, capers, oregano and tomato paste and cook, stirring occasionally, for 15 minutes, or until the liquid has evaporated and the sauce is thickened. Season the tomato sauce to taste with salt and pepper.

3 Meanwhile, bring a large pan of lightly salted water to a rolling boil. Add the spaghetti and cook according to the packet instructions, or until 'al dente'.

4 Drain the spaghetti thoroughly, reserving 1–2 tablespoons of the the cooking water. Return the spaghetti with the reserved water to the pan. Pour the tomato sauce over the spaghetti, add the chopped parsley and toss to coat. Tip into a warmed serving dish or spoon on to individual plates and serve immediately.

INGREDIENTS
Serves 4

4 tbsp olive oil
50 g/2 oz anchovy fillets in olive oil, drained and coarsely chopped
2 garlic cloves, peeled and finely chopped
½ tsp crushed dried chillies
400 g can chopped plum tomatoes
125 g/4 oz pitted black olives, cut in half
2 tbsp capers, rinsed and drained
1 tsp freshly chopped oregano
1 tbsp tomato paste
salt and freshly ground black pepper
400 g/14 oz spaghetti
2 tbsp freshly chopped parsley

Helpful Hint

Anchovies are mature sardines. They are heavily salted after filleting to preserve them, so should only be used in small quantities. For a less salty dish, drain them and soak in a little milk for about 20 minutes before using. You can, of course, omit the anchovies to make a vegetarian version of this recipe.

Tagliatelle Primavera

1 Bring a medium saucepan of salted water to the boil. Add the asparagus and blanch for 1–2 minutes, or until just beginning to soften. Using a slotted spoon, transfer to a colander and rinse under cold running water. Repeat with the carrots and courgettes. Add the mangetout, return to the boil, drain, rinse immediately and drain again. Reserve the blanched vegetables.

2 Heat the butter in a large frying pan, add the onion and red pepper and cook for 5 minutes, or until they begin to soften and colour. Pour in the dry vermouth; it will bubble and steam and evaporate almost immediately. Stir in the cream and simmer over a medium-low heat until reduced by about half. Add the blanched vegetables with the leeks, peas and seasoning and heat through for 2 minutes.

3 Meanwhile, bring a large saucepan of lightly salted water to the boil, add the tagliatelle and return to the boil. Cook for 2-3 minutes, or until 'al dente'. Drain thoroughly and return to the pan.

4 Stir the chopped parsley into the cream and vegetable sauce then pour over the pasta and toss to coat. Sprinkle with the grated Parmesan cheese and toss lightly. Tip into a warmed serving bowl or spoon on to individual plates and serve immediately.

INGREDIENTS
Serves 4

125 g/4 oz asparagus, lightly peeled and cut into 6.5 cm/2½ inch lengths

125 g/4 oz carrots, peeled and cut into julienne strips

125 g/4 oz courgettes, trimmed and cut into julienne strips

50 g/2 oz small mangetout

50 g/2 oz butter

1 small onion, peeled and finely chopped

1 small red pepper, deseeded and finely chopped

50 ml/2 fl oz dry vermouth

225 ml/8 fl oz double cream

1 small leek, trimmed and cut into julienne strips

75 g/3 oz fresh green peas (or frozen, thawed)

salt and freshly ground black pepper

400 g/14 oz fresh tagliatelle

2 tbsp freshly chopped flat-leaf parsley

25 g/1 oz Parmesan cheese, grated

Helpful Hint

If using baby asparagus spears – readily available in most major supermarkets – there is no need to peel the stems. This is only necessary on the long spears which can have a woody stalk as the season progresses.

Aubergine & Ravioli Parmigiana

1 Preheat the oven to 180°C/
350°F/Gas Mark 4, about 15
minutes before cooking. Heat 2
tablespoons of the olive oil in a
large, heavy-based pan, add the
onion and cook for 6–7 minutes,
or until softened. Add the garlic,
cook for 1 minute then stir in the
tomatoes, sugar, bay leaf, dried
oregano and basil, then bring
to the boil, stirring frequently.
Simmer for 30–35 minutes, or
until thickened and reduced, stirring occasionally. Stir in the fresh
basil and season to taste with salt
and pepper. Remove the tomato
sauce from the heat and reserve.

2 Heat the remaining olive oil
in a large, heavy-based frying pan over a high heat. Dip the
aubergine slices in the egg mixture then in the breadcrumbs.

Cook in batches until golden on
both sides. Drain on absorbent
kitchen paper. Add more oil
between batches if necessary.

3 Spoon a little tomato sauce
into the base of a lightly oiled
large baking dish. Cover with a
layer of aubergine slices, a sprinkling of Parmesan cheese, a layer
of mozzarella cheese, then more
sauce. Repeat the layers then cover
the sauce with a layer of cooked
ravioli. Continue to layer in this
way, ending with a layer of mozzarella cheese. Sprinkle the top
with Parmesan cheese.

4 Drizzle with a little extra
olive oil if liked, then bake
in the preheated oven for 30
minutes, or until golden-brown
and bubbling. Serve immediately.

INGREDIENTS
Serves 6

4 tbsp olive oil
1 large onion, peeled and finely
chopped
2–3 garlic cloves, peeled and
crushed
2 x 400 g cans chopped tomatoes
2 tsp brown sugar
1 dried bay leaf
1 tsp dried oregano
1 tsp dried basil
2 tbsp freshly shredded basil
salt and freshly ground black
pepper
2–3 medium aubergines, sliced
crosswise 1 cm/½ inch thick
2 medium eggs, beaten with
1 tbsp water
125 g/4 oz dried breadcrumbs
75 g/3 oz freshly grated
Parmesan cheese
400 g/14 oz mozzarella cheese,
thinly sliced
250 g/9 oz cheese-filled ravioli,
cooked and drained

Helpful Hint

Aubergines absorb a huge amount of oil during
cooking, so use a good non-stick frying pan and gradually
add oil as required. You can use baby aubergines for this
recipe if you prefer. Trim off the stalk ends, then
cut them lengthwise into 1 cm/½ inch strips.

Courgette Lasagne

1 Preheat the oven to 200°C/ 400°F/Gas Mark 6, 15 minutes before cooking. Heat the oil in a large frying pan, add the onion and cook for 3–5 minutes. Add the mushrooms, cook for 2 minutes then add the courgettes and cook for a further 3–4 minutes, or until tender. Stir in the garlic, thyme and basil or parsley and season to taste with salt and pepper. Remove from the heat and reserve.

2 Spoon one-third of the white sauce on to the base of a lightly oiled large baking dish. Arrange a layer of lasagne over the sauce. Spread half the courgette mixture over the pasta, then sprinkle with some of the mozzarella and some of the Parmesan cheese. Repeat with more white sauce and another layer of lasagne, then cover with half the drained tomatoes.

3 Cover the tomatoes with lasagne, the remaining courgette mixture, and some mozzarella and Parmesan cheese. Repeat the layers ending with a layer of lasagne sheets, white sauce and the remaining Parmesan cheese. Bake in the preheated oven for 35 minutes, or until golden. Serve immediately.

INGREDIENTS
Serves 8

2 tbsp olive oil

1 medium onion, peeled and
finely chopped

225 g/8 oz mushrooms, wiped
and thinly sliced

3–4 courgettes, trimmed and
thinly sliced

2 garlic cloves, peeled and finely
chopped

½ tsp dried thyme

1–2 tbsp freshly chopped basil or
flat-leaf parsley

salt and freshly ground black
pepper

1 quantity prepared white sauce
see page 232

350 g/12 oz lasagne sheets,
cooked

225 g/8 oz mozzarella cheese,
grated

50 g/2 oz Parmesan cheese,
grated

400 g can chopped tomatoes,
drained

Helpful Hint

There is now a huge range of canned tomatoes available. Look out for canned cherry tomatoes, which have a much sweeter flavour, or those with added ingredients and flavourings. Tomatoes with chopped peppers, garlic or fresh herbs would all work well here and would add extra flavour.

Baked Macaroni Cheese

1 Preheat the oven to 190°C/ 375°F/Gas Mark 5, 10 minutes before cooking. Bring a large pan of lightly salted water to a rolling boil. Add the macaroni and cook according to the packet instructions, or until 'al dente'. Drain thoroughly and reserve.

2 Meanwhile, melt 50 g/ 2 oz of the butter in a large, heavy-based saucepan, add the onion and cook, stirring frequently, for 5–7 minutes, or until softened. Sprinkle in the flour and cook, stirring constantly, for 2 minutes. Remove the pan from the heat, stir in the milk, return to the heat and cook, stirring, until a smooth sauce has formed.

3 Add the bay leaf and thyme to the sauce and season to taste with salt, pepper, cayenne pepper and freshly grated nutmeg. Simmer for about 15 minutes, stirring frequently, until thickened and smooth.

4 Remove the sauce from the heat. Add the cooked leeks, mustard and Cheddar cheese and stir until the cheese has melted. Stir in the macaroni then tip into a lightly oiled baking dish.

5 Sprinkle the breadcrumbs and Parmesan cheese over the macaroni. Dot with the remaining butter, then bake in the preheated oven for 1 hour, or until golden. Garnish with a basil sprig and serve immediately.

INGREDIENTS
Serves 8

450 g/1 lb macaroni
75 g/3 oz butter
1 onion, peeled and finely
    chopped
40 g/1½ oz plain flour
1 litre/1¾ pints milk
1–2 dried bay leaves
½ tsp dried thyme
salt and freshly ground black
    pepper
cayenne pepper
freshly grated nutmeg
2 small leeks, trimmed, finely
    chopped, cooked and drained
1 tbsp Dijon mustard
400 g/14 oz mature Cheddar
    cheese, grated
2 tbsp dried breadcrumbs
2 tbsp freshly grated Parmesan
    cheese
basil sprig, to garnish

Helpful Hint

Make sure that you only simmer the macaroni until just 'al dente' and drain straight away, as it will be further cooked in the oven where it needs to soak up the flavoursome sauce. For a more substantial dish, chopped, lean smoked bacon can be stirred into the macaroni before baking.

Penne with Vodka & Caviar

1 Bring a large pan of lightly salted water to a rolling boil. Add the penne and cook according to the packet instructions, or until 'al dente'. Drain thoroughly and reserve.

2 Heat the butter in a large frying pan or wok, add the spring onions and stir-fry for 1 minute. Stir in the garlic and cook for a further 1 minute. Pour the vodka into the pan; it will bubble and steam. Cook until the vodka is reduced by about half, then add the double cream and return to the boil. Simmer gently for 2–3 minutes, or until the sauce has thickened slightly.

3 Stir in the tomatoes, then stir in all but 1 tablespoon of the caviar and season to taste with salt and pepper. Add the penne and toss lightly to coat. Cook for 1 minute, or until heated through. Divide the mixture among 4 warmed pasta bowls and garnish with the reserved caviar. Serve immediately.

INGREDIENTS
Serves 4

400 g / 14 oz penne

25 g / 1 oz butter

4–6 spring onions, trimmed and thinly sliced

1 garlic clove, peeled and finely chopped

125 ml / 4 fl oz vodka

200 ml / 7 fl oz double cream

1–2 ripe plum tomatoes, skinned, deseeded and chopped

75 g / 3 oz caviar

salt and freshly ground black pepper

Food Fact

Authentic sturgeon caviar is very expensive. Red caviar from salmon, or black or red lump-fish roe, can be substituted. Alternatively, 175 g / 6 oz thinly sliced smoked salmon pieces, can also be substituted. Sturgeon caviar has a salty flavour, so always check the taste before adding salt. Smoked salmon and lump-fish roe have a much saltier taste, however, so no additional salt would be necessary.

Rigatoni with Gorgonzola & Walnuts

1 Bring a large pan of lightly salted water to a rolling boil. Add the rigatoni and cook according to the packet instructions, or until 'al dente'. Drain the pasta thoroughly, reserve and keep warm.

2 Melt the butter in a large saucepan or wok over a medium heat. Add the Gorgonzola cheese and stir until just melted. Add the brandy if using and cook for 30 seconds, then pour in the cream and cook for 1–2 minutes, stirring until the sauce is smooth.

3 Stir in the walnut pieces, basil and half the Parmesan cheese, then add the rigatoni. Season to taste with salt and pepper. Return to the heat, stirring frequently, until heated through. Divide the pasta among 4 warmed pasta bowls, sprinkle with the remaining Parmesan cheese and serve immediately with cherry tomatoes and fresh green salad leaves.

INGREDIENTS
Serves 4

400 g/14 oz rigatoni
50 g/2 oz butter
125 g/4 oz crumbled Gorgonzola cheese
2 tbsp brandy, optional
200 ml/7 fl oz whipping or double cream
75 g/3 oz walnut pieces, lightly toasted and coarsely chopped
1 tbsp freshly chopped basil
50 g/2 oz freshly grated Parmesan cheese
salt and freshly ground black pepper

TO SERVE:
cherry tomatoes
fresh green salad leaves

Tasty Tip

This blue cheese sauce is also very good with pappardelle or lasagnette, both very wide egg pasta noodles. Either whipping or double cream may be used here; double cream is higher in fat, so will give a richer, creamier finish to the sauce. If preferred, you could use soured cream, but it must be heated gently as it can curdle at high temperatures.

Pumpkin-filled Pasta with Butter & Sage

1 Mix together the ingredients for the filling in a bowl, seasoning to taste with freshly grated nutmeg, salt and pepper. If the mixture seems too wet, add a few more breadcrumbs to bind.

2 Cut the pasta dough into quarters. Work with one quarter at a time, covering the remaining quarters with a damp tea towel. Roll out a quarter very thinly into a strip 10 cm/ 4 inches wide. Drop spoonfuls of the filling along the strip 6.5 cm/2½ inches apart, in 2 rows about 5 cm/2 inches apart. Moisten the outside edges and the spaces between the filling with water.

3 Roll out another strip of pasta and lay it over the filled strip. Press down gently along both edges and between the filled sections. Using a fluted pastry wheel, cut along both long sides, down the centre and between the fillings to form cushions. Transfer the cushions to a lightly floured baking sheet. Continue making cushions and allow to dry for 30 minutes.

4 Bring a large saucepan of slightly salted water to the boil. Add the pasta cushions and return to the boil. Cook, stirring frequently, for 4–5 minutes, or until 'al dente'. Drain carefully.

5 Heat the butter in a pan, stir in the shredded sage leaves and cook for 30 seconds. Add the pasta cushions, stir gently then spoon into serving bowls. Sprinkle with the grated Parmesan cheese and serve immediately.

INGREDIENTS
Serves 6-8

1 quantity fresh pasta dough, see page 70
125 g/4 oz butter
2 tbsp freshly shredded sage leaves
50 g/2 oz freshly grated Parmesan cheese, to serve

FOR THE FILLING:

250 g/9 oz freshly cooked pumpkin or sweet potato flesh, mashed and cooled
75–125 g/3–4 oz dried breadcrumbs
125 g/4 oz freshly grated Parmesan cheese
1 medium egg yolk
½ tsp soft brown sugar
2 tbsp freshly chopped parsley
freshly grated nutmeg
salt and freshly ground black pepper

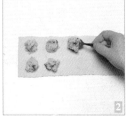

Cold Sesame Noodles

1 Bring a large pan of lightly salted water to a rolling boil. Add the noodles or spaghetti and cook according to the packet instructions, or until 'al dente'. Drain, rinse and drain again, then toss in the sesame oil and reserve.

2 Heat the groundnut oil in a wok or large frying pan over a high heat. Add the green pepper, daikon and mangetout or green beans and stir-fry for 1 minute. Stir in the garlic and cook for 30 seconds.

3 Add the soy sauce to the pan with the vinegar, chilli sauce, sugar, peanut butter and 50 ml/2 fl oz of hot water. Simmer, stirring constantly, until the peanut butter is smooth, adding a little more water if necessary and adjusting the seasoning to taste.

4 Add the spring onions and the reserved noodles or spaghetti to the peanut sauce and cook, stirring, for 2–3 minutes, or until heated through. Tip the mixture into a large serving bowl and allow to cool to room temperature, stirring occasionally. Garnish with the toasted sesame seeds and cucumber julienne strips before serving.

Food Fact

Daikon, also known as mooli or white radish, resembles a parsnip in shape. It has a very fresh, peppery flavour and is often used in salads either peeled or grated. Because it has a high water content, it should be sprinkled with salt and allowed to drain in a sieve over a bowl for about 30 minutes after preparing. Rinse well under cold running water and pat dry on absorbent kitchen paper before stir-frying.

INGREDIENTS
Serves 4–8

450 g/1 lb buckwheat (soba) noodles or wholewheat spaghetti
salt
1 tbsp sesame oil
1 tbsp groundnut oil
1 green pepper, deseeded and thinly sliced
125 g/4 oz daikon (mooli), cut into julienne strips
125 g/4 oz mangetout or green beans, trimmed and sliced
2 garlic cloves, peeled and finely chopped
2 tbsp soy sauce, or to taste
1 tbsp cider vinegar
2 tbsp sweet chilli sauce, or to taste
2 tsp sugar
75 g/3 oz peanut butter
6–8 spring onions, trimmed and diagonally sliced

GARNISH:
toasted sesame seeds
julienne strips of cucumber

Singapore Noodles

1 Bring a large pan of lightly salted water to a rolling boil. Add the noodles and cook according to the packet instructions, or until 'al dente'. Drain thoroughly and toss with 1 tablespoon of the oil.

2 Heat the remaining oil in a wok or large frying pan over high heat. Add the mushrooms, ginger, chilli and red pepper and stir-fry for 2 minutes. Add the garlic, courgettes, spring onions and garden peas and stir lightly.

3 Push the vegetables to one side and add the curry paste, tomato ketchup and about 125 ml/4 fl oz hot water. Season to taste with salt or a few drops of soy sauce and allow to boil vigorously, stirring, until the paste is smooth.

4 Stir the reserved egg noodles and the beansprouts into the vegetable mixture and stir-fry until coated with the paste and thoroughly heated through. Season with more soy sauce if necessary, then turn into a large warmed serving bowl or spoon on to individual plates. Garnish with sesame seeds and coriander leaves. Serve immediately.

INGREDIENTS
Serves 4

225 g/8 oz thin round egg noodles
3 tbsp groundnut or vegetable oil
125 g/4 oz field mushrooms, wiped and thinly sliced
2.5 cm/1 inch piece root ginger, peeled and finely chopped
1 red chilli, deseeded and thinly sliced
1 red pepper, deseeded and thinly sliced
2 garlic cloves, peeled and crushed
1 medium courgette, cut in half lengthwise and diagonally sliced
4-6 spring onions, trimmed and thinly sliced
50 g/2 oz frozen garden peas, thawed
1 tbsp curry paste
2 tbsp tomato ketchup
salt or soy sauce
125 g/4 oz beansprouts, rinsed and drained

TO GARNISH:
sesame seeds
fresh coriander leaves

Helpful Hint

There is a huge range of curry pastes available, varying from very mild to extremely hot. Obviously, the choice here depends very much on your personal preference, but try to select one with oriental rather than Indian overtones – Thai green or red curry paste would be a good choice.

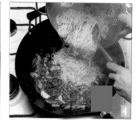

Tortellini, Cherry Tomato & Mozzarella Skewers

1 Preheat the grill and line a grill pan with tinfoil, just before cooking. Bring a large pan of lightly salted water to a rolling boil. Add the tortellini and cook according to the packet instructions, or until 'al dente'. Drain, rinse under cold running water, drain again and toss with 2 tablespoons of the olive oil and reserve.

2 Pour the remaining olive oil into a small bowl. Add the crushed garlic and thyme or basil, then blend well. Season to taste with salt and black pepper and reserve.

3 To assemble the skewers, thread the tortellini alternately with the cherry tomatoes and cubes of mozzarella. Arrange the skewers on the grill pan and brush generously on all sides with the olive oil mixture.

4 Cook the skewers under the preheated grill for about 5 minutes, or until they begin to turn golden, turning them halfway through cooking. Arrange 2 skewers on each plate and garnish with a few basil leaves. Serve immediately with dressed salad leaves.

INGREDIENTS
Serves 6

250 g/9 oz mixed green and plain cheese or vegetable-filled fresh tortellini

150 ml/¼ pint extra virgin olive oil

2 garlic cloves, peeled and crushed

pinch dried thyme or basil

salt and freshly ground black pepper

225 g/8 oz cherry tomatoes

450 g/1 lb mozzarella, cut into 2.5 cm/1 inch cubes

basil leaves, to garnish

dressed salad leaves, to serve

Helpful Hint

These skewers make an ideal starter for a barbecue. Alternatively, a small quantity of the prepared ingredients can be threaded on to smaller skewers and served as canapés. If using wooden skewers for this recipe, soak them in cold water for at least 30 minutes before cooking to prevent them scorching under the grill. The tips of the skewers may be protected with small pieces of foil.

Tortellini & Summer Vegetable Salad

1 Bring a large pan of lightly salted water to a rolling boil. Add the tortellini and cook according to the packet instructions, or until 'al dente'.

2 Using a large slotted spoon, transfer the tortellini to a colander to drain. Rinse under cold running water and drain again. Transfer to a large bowl and toss with 2 tablespoons of the olive oil.

3 Return the pasta water to the boil and drop in the green beans and broccoli florets; blanch them for 2 minutes, or until just beginning to soften. Drain, rinse under cold running water and drain again thoroughly. Add the vegetables to the reserved tortellini.

4 Add the pepper, onion, artichoke hearts, capers and olives to the bowl; stir lightly.

5 Whisk together the vinegar, mustard and brown sugar in a bowl and season to taste with salt and pepper. Slowly whisk in the remaining olive oil to form a thick, creamy dressing. Pour over the tortellini and vegetables, add the chopped basil or parsley and stir until lightly coated. Transfer to a shallow serving dish or salad bowl. Garnish with the hard-boiled egg quarters and serve.

INGREDIENTS
Serves 6

350 g / 12 oz mixed green and plain cheese-filled fresh tortellini
150 ml / ¼ pint extra virgin olive oil
225 g / 8 oz fine green beans, trimmed
175 g / 6 oz broccoli florets
1 yellow or red pepper, deseeded and thinly sliced
1 red onion, peeled and sliced
175 g jar marinated artichoke hearts, drained and halved
2 tbsp capers
75 g / 3 oz dry-cured pitted black olives
3 tbsp raspberry or balsamic vinegar
1 tbsp Dijon mustard
1 tsp soft brown sugar
salt and freshly ground black pepper
2 tbsp freshly chopped basil or flat-leaf parsley
2 quartered hard-boiled eggs, to garnish

Food Fact

Black olives are picked when fully ripe and a brownish pink colour and then fermented and oxidised until they become black. Dry-cured black olives can be bought from Italian food shops or the delicatessen counter of some large supermarkets, but if you are unable to get them, use ordinary small black olives instead.

Fettuccine with Calves' Liver & Calvados

1 Season the flour with the salt, black pepper and paprika, then toss the liver in the flour until well coated.

2 Melt half the butter and 1 tablespoon of the olive oil in a large frying pan and fry the liver in batches for 1 minute, or until just browned but still slightly pink inside. Remove using a slotted spoon and place in a warmed dish.

3 Add the remaining butter to the pan, stir in 1 tablespoon of the seasoned flour and cook for 1 minute. Pour in the Calvados and cider and cook over a high heat for 30 seconds. Stir the cream into the sauce and simmer for 1 minute to thicken slightly, then season to taste. Return the liver to the pan and heat through.

4 Bring a large pan of lightly salted water to a rolling boil. Add the fettuccine and cook according to the packet instructions, about 3–4 minutes, or until 'al dente'.

5 Drain the fettuccine thoroughly, return to the pan and toss in the remaining olive oil. Divide among 4 warmed plates and spoon the liver and sauce over the pasta. Garnish with thyme sprigs and serve immediately.

INGREDIENTS
Serves 4

450 g / 1 lb calves' liver, trimmed
   and thinly sliced
50 g / 2 oz plain flour
salt and freshly ground black
   pepper
1 tsp paprika
50 g / 2 oz butter
1½ tbsp olive oil
2 tbsp Calvados
150 ml / ¼ pint cider
150 ml / ¼ pint whipping cream
350 g / 12 oz fresh fettuccine
fresh thyme sprigs,
   to garnish

Helpful Hint

Calvados is made from apples and adds a fruity taste
to this dish, although you can, of course, use ordinary brandy
instead. Calves' liver is very tender, with a delicate flavour. It
should be cooked over a high heat until the outside is brown
and crusty and the centre still slightly pink. Take care not to

Tagliatelle with Stuffed Pork Escalopes

1 Preheat the oven to 180°C/350°F/Gas Mark 4, 10 minutes before cooking. Mix the broccoli with the mozzarella cheese, garlic and beaten eggs. Season to taste with salt and pepper and reserve.

2 Using a meat mallet or rolling pin, pound the escalopes on a sheet of greaseproof paper until 5 mm/¼ inch thick. Divide the broccoli mixture between the escalopes and roll each one up from the shortest side. Place the pork rolls in a lightly oiled oven-proof dish, drizzle over the olive oil and bake in the preheated oven for 40–50 minutes, or until cooked.

3 Meanwhile, melt the butter in a heavy-based pan, stir in the flour and cook for 2 minutes. Remove from the heat and whisk in the milk and stock. Season to taste, stir in the mustard then cook until smooth and thickened. Keep warm.

4 Bring a large pan of lightly salted water to a rolling boil. Add the taglietelle and cook according to the packet instructions, about 3–4 minutes, or until 'al dente'. Drain thoroughly and tip into a warmed serving dish. Slice each pork roll into 3, place on top of the pasta and pour the sauce over. Garnish with sage leaves and serve immediately.

INGREDIENTS
Serves 4

150 g/5 oz broccoli florets, finely chopped and blanched
125 g/4 oz mozzarella cheese, grated
1 garlic clove, peeled and crushed
2 large eggs, beaten
salt and freshly ground black pepper
4 thin pork escalopes, weighing about 100 g/3½ oz each
1 tbsp olive oil
25 g/1 oz butter
2 tbsp flour
150 ml/¼ pint milk
150 ml/¼ pint chicken stock
1 tbsp Dijon mustard
225 g/8 oz fresh tagliatelle
sage leaves, to garnish

Helpful Hint

Pounding the pork escalopes makes them thinner, but tenderises the meat. Brush with a little oil to prevent them sticking to the mallet or rolling pin, or pound (with the blunt side of the mallet) between two sheets of oiled greaseproof paper or clingfilm. Take care not to tear the fibres.

Spicy Chicken with Open Ravioli & Tomato Sauce

1 Heat the olive oil in a frying pan, add the onion and cook gently for 2–3 minutes then add the cumin, paprika pepper and cinnamon and cook for a further 1 minute. Add the chicken, season to taste with salt and pepper and cook for 3–4 minutes, or until tender. Add the peanut butter and stir until well mixed and reserve.

2 Melt the butter in the frying pan, add the shallot and cook for 2 minutes. Add the tomatoes and garlic and season to taste. Simmer gently for 20 minutes, or until thickened, then keep the sauce warm.

3 Cut each sheet of lasagne into 6 squares. Bring a large pan of lightly salted water to a rolling boil. Add the lasagne squares and cook according to the packet instructions, about 3–4 minutes, or until 'al dente'. Drain the lasagne pieces thoroughly, reserve and keep warm.

4 Layer the pasta squares with the spicy filling on individual warmed plates. Pour over a little of the hot tomato sauce and sprinkle with chopped coriander. Serve immediately.

INGREDIENTS
Serves 2–3

2 tbsp olive oil
1 onion, peeled and finely chopped
1 tsp ground cumin
1 tsp hot paprika pepper
1 tsp ground cinnamon
175 g/6 oz boneless and skinless chicken breasts, chopped
salt and freshly ground black pepper
1 tbsp smooth peanut butter
50 g/2 oz butter
1 shallot, peeled and finely chopped
2 garlic cloves, peeled and crushed
400 g can chopped tomatoes
125 g/4 oz fresh egg lasagne
2 tbsp freshly chopped coriander

Helpful Hint

Remember that fresh pasta should be exactly that; buy no more than two days ahead and preferably on the day that you plan to cook it. Because it contains fresh eggs it should always be stored in the refrigerator, kept in its packet or wrapped in non-stick baking parchment, then in clingfilm.

Farfalle & Chicken in White Wine Sauce

1 Place the chicken breasts between two sheets of greaseproof paper and, using a meat mallet or wooden rolling pin, pound as thinly as possible. Season with salt and pepper and reserve.

2 Mash the feta cheese with a fork and blend with the egg and half the tarragon. Divide the mixture between the chicken breasts and roll up each one. Secure with cocktail sticks.

3 Heat half the butter and all the olive oil in a frying pan, add the onion and cook for 2–3 minutes. Remove, using a slotted spoon, and reserve. Add the chicken parcels to the pan and cook for 3–4 minutes, or until browned.

4 Pour in the wine and the stock and stir in the remaining tarragon. Cover and simmer gently for 10–15 minutes, or until the chicken is cooked.

5 Meanwhile, bring a large pan of lightly salted water to a rolling boil. Add the farfalle and cook according to the packet instructions, about 3–4 minutes, or until 'al dente'. Drain, toss in the remaining butter and tip into a warmed serving dish.

6 Slice each chicken roll into 4 and place on the pasta. Whisk the sauce until smooth, then stir in the soured cream and the reserved onions. Heat the sauce gently, then pour over the chicken. Sprinkle with the parsley and serve immediately.

INGREDIENTS
Serves 4

4 boneless and skinless chicken breasts, about 450 g / 1 lb in total weight
salt and freshly ground black pepper
125 g / 4 oz feta cheese
1 small egg, beaten
2 tbsp freshly chopped tarragon
50 g / 2 oz butter
1 tbsp olive oil
1 onion, peeled and sliced into rings
150 ml / ¼ pint white wine
150 ml / ¼ pint chicken stock
350 g / 12 oz fresh farfalle
3–4 tbsp soured cream
2 tbsp freshly chopped parsley

Food Fact

Feta is a Greek cheese, traditionally made from ewe's milk, but now more often from cow's milk. It is preserved in brine, which gives it a salty flavour; always drain feta before using.

Gnocchi Roulade
with Mozzarella & Spinach

1 Preheat the oven to 240°C/ 475°F/Gas Mark 9, 15 minutes before cooking. Oil and line a large Swiss roll tin (23 cm/9 inch x 33 cm/13 inch) with non-stick baking parchment.

2 Pour the milk into a heavy-based pan and whisk in the semolina. Bring to the boil then simmer, stirring continuously with a wooden spoon, for 3–4 minutes, or until very thick. Remove from heat and stir in the butter and Cheddar cheese until melted. Whisk in the egg yolks and season to taste with salt and pepper. Pour into the lined tin. Cover and allow to cool for 1 hour.

3 Cook the baby spinach in batches in a large pan with 1 teaspoon of water for 3–4 minutes, or until wilted. Drain thoroughly, season to taste with salt, pepper and nutmeg, then allow to cool.

4 Spread the spinach over the cooled semolina mixture and sprinkle over 75 g/3 oz of the mozzarella and half the Parmesan cheese. Bake in the preheated oven for 20 minutes, or until golden.

5 Allow to cool, then roll up like a Swiss roll. Sprinkle with the remaining mozzarella and Parmesan cheese, then bake for another 15–20 minutes, or until golden. Serve immediately with freshly made tomato sauce.

INGREDIENTS
Serves 8

600 ml/1 pint milk
125 g/4 oz fine semolina or polenta
25 g/1 oz butter
75 g/3 oz Cheddar cheese, grated
2 medium egg yolks
salt and freshly ground black pepper
700 g/1½ lb baby spinach leaves
½ tsp freshly grated nutmeg
1 garlic clove, peeled and crushed
2 tbsp olive oil
150 g/5 oz mozzarella cheese, grated
2 tbsp freshly grated Parmesan cheese
freshly made tomato sauce, to serve

Helpful Hint

It is important to use the correct size of tin for this dish, so that the gnocchi mixture is thin enough to roll up. Do not be tempted to put it in the refrigerator to cool or it will become too hard and crack when rolled.

Penne with Mixed Peppers & Garlic

1 Preheat the grill and line the grill rack with tinfoil. Cut the peppers in half, deseed and place cut side down on the grill rack. Cook under the grill until the skins become blistered and black all over. Place the peppers in a polythene bag and allow to cool, then discard the skin and slice thinly.

2 Heat the oil in a heavy-based pan. Add the onion, celery, garlic and bacon and cook for 4–5 minutes, or until the onion has softened. Add the peppers and cook for 1 minute. Pour in the stock and season to taste with salt and pepper. Cover and simmer for 20 minutes.

3 Meanwhile, bring a large pan of lightly salted water to a rolling boil. Add the penne and cook according to the packet instructions, about 3–4 minutes, or until 'al dente'. Drain thoroughly and return to the pan.

4 Pour the pepper sauce over the pasta and toss lightly. Tip into a warmed serving dish and sprinkle with the chopped parsley and grated pecorino cheese. Serve immediately with a green salad and warm granary bread.

INGREDIENTS
Serves 4

450 g/1 lb green, red and yellow peppers
2 tbsp olive oil
1 large onion, peeled and sliced
1 celery stick, trimmed and finely chopped
2 garlic cloves, peeled and crushed
4 rashers smoked streaky bacon, finely chopped
300 ml/½ pint chicken stock
salt and freshly ground black pepper
350 g/12 oz fresh penne
2 tbsp freshly chopped parsley
2 tbsp pecorino cheese, finely grated

TO SERVE:
green salad
warm granary bread

Helpful Hint

Grilling brings out all the delicious flavour of peppers. Do make sure that they are blackened and blistered so that the skins simply slip off. You could also roast the peppers in the oven for this recipe, if preferred. Place them in a roasting tin, brush with a little olive oil and cook at 200°C/400°F/Gas Mark 6 for 25 minutes, or until the skins are slightly charred.

Spaghetti with Smoked Salmon & Tiger Prawns

1 Cook the baby spinach leaves in a large pan with 1 teaspoon of water for 3–4 minutes, or until wilted. Drain thoroughly, season to taste with salt, pepper and nutmeg and keep warm. Remove the shells from all but 4 of the tiger prawns and reserve.

2 Bring a large pan of lightly salted water to a rolling boil. Add the pasta and cook according to the packet instructions, about 3–4 minutes, or until 'al dente'. Drain thoroughly and return to the pan. Stir in the butter and the peeled prawns, cover and keep warm.

3 Beat the eggs with the dill, season well, then stir into the spaghettini and prawns. Return the pan to the heat briefly, just long enough to lightly scramble the eggs, then remove from the heat. Carefully mix in the smoked salmon strips and the cooked spinach. Toss gently to mix. Tip into a warmed serving dish and garnish with the reserved prawns and dill sprigs. Serve immediately with grated Parmesan cheese.

INGREDIENTS
Serves 4

225 g/8 oz baby spinach leaves
salt and freshly ground black pepper
pinch freshly grated nutmeg
225 g/8 oz cooked tiger prawns in their shells, cooked
450 g/1 lb fresh angel hair spaghetti
50 g/2 oz butter
3 medium eggs
1 tbsp freshly chopped dill, plus extra to garnish
125 g/4 oz smoked salmon, cut into strips
dill sprigs, to garnish
2 tbsp grated Parmesan cheese, to serve

Helpful Hint

Make sure that you use cooked and not raw king prawns for this dish. If you buy them raw, remove the heads and shells then briefly sauté in a little olive oil until just pink and opaque. This will take only 3–4 minutes; take care not to overcook them or they will toughen.

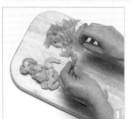

Pasta Ring with Chicken & Sun-dried Tomatoes

1 Preheat the oven to 190°C/ 375°F/Gas Mark 5, 10 minutes before cooking. Lightly brush a 20.5 cm/8 inch ring mould with a little melted butter and dust with the breadcrumbs.

2 Melt 50 g/2 oz of the butter in a heavy-based pan. Add the flour and cook for 1 minute. Whisk in the milk and cook, stirring, until thickened. Add the chopped onion, season to taste with salt and pepper and reserve.

3 Bring a large pan of lightly salted water to a rolling boil. Add the tagliatelle and cook according to the packet instructions, about 3–4 minutes, or until 'al dente'. Drain thoroughly and stir into the white sauce. Pour the

pasta mixture into the prepared mould and bake in the preheated oven for 25–30 minutes.

4 Melt the remaining butter in a frying pan, add the chicken and cook for 4–5 minutes, or until cooked. Pour in the wine and cook over a high heat for 30 seconds. Blend the cornflour with 1 teaspoon of water and stir into the pan. Add 1 tablespoon chopped tarragon and the tomatoes. Season well, then cook for a few minutes, until thickened.

5 Allow the pasta to cool for 5 minutes, then unmould on to a large serving plate. Fill the centre with the chicken sauce. Garnish with the remaining tarragon and serve immediately.

INGREDIENTS
Serves 6

125 g/4 oz butter, plus extra for brushing
2 tbsp natural white breadcrumbs
40 g/1½ oz flour
450 ml/¾ pint milk
1 small onion, peeled and very finely chopped
salt and freshly ground black pepper
225 g/8 oz fresh tagliatelle
450 g/1 lb chicken breast fillets, skinned and cut into strips
200 ml/7 fl oz white wine
1 tsp cornflour
2 tbsp freshly chopped tarragon
2 tbsp chopped sun-dried tomatoes

Helpful Hint

To ensure that the pasta turns out easily, brush the ring mould with melted butter, then put in the freezer for 3–4 minutes to harden. Brush again with butter before dusting with the breadcrumbs, making sure it is well-coated.

Salmon & Mushroom Linguine

1 Preheat the oven to 190°C/ 375°F/Gas Mark 5, 10 minutes before cooking. Place the salmon in a shallow pan and cover with water. Season well with salt and pepper and bring to the boil, then lower the heat and simmer for 6–8 minutes, or until cooked. Drain and keep warm.

2 Melt 50 g/2 oz of the butter in a heavy-based pan, stir in the flour, cook for 1 minute then whisk in the chicken stock. Simmer gently until thickened. Stir in the cream and season to taste. Keep the sauce warm.

3 Melt the remaining butter, in a pan, add the sliced mushrooms and cook for 2–3 minutes.

Stir the mushrooms into the white sauce.

4 Bring a large pan of lightly salted water to a rolling boil. Add the linguine and cook according to the packet instructions, or until 'al dente'.

5 Drain the pasta thoroughly and return to the pan. Stir in half the sauce, then spoon into a lightly oiled a 1.4 litre/2½ pint shallow ovenproof dish. Flake the salmon, add to the remaining sauce then pour over the pasta. Sprinkle with the cheese and breadcrumbs, then bake in the preheated for 15–20 minutes, or until golden. Garnish with the parsley and serve immediately.

INGREDIENTS
Serves 4

450 g/1 lb salmon fillets, skinned
salt and freshly ground black
  pepper
75 g/3 oz butter
40 g/1½ oz flour
300 ml/½ pint chicken stock
150 ml/¼ pint whipping cream
225 g/8 oz mushrooms, wiped
  and sliced
350 g/12 oz linguine
50 g/2 oz Cheddar cheese, grated
50 g/2 oz fresh white
  breadcrumbs
2 tbsp freshly chopped parsley,
to garnish

Helpful Hint

When cooking the salmon, the poaching liquid should be just simmering and not boiling rapidly. Add extra flavour if you like by putting in a bay leaf and a sprig of fresh thyme or a thinly pared strip of lemon rind. The salmon should be slightly undercooked in this recipe, as it will then be baked in the oven.

Spaghetti with Hot Chilli Mussels

1 Scrub the mussels and remove any beards. Discard any that do not close when tapped. Place in a large pan with the white wine and half the crushed garlic. Cover and cook over a high heat for 5–6 minutes, shaking the pan from time to time. When the mussels have opened, drain, reserving the juices and straining them through a muslin-lined sieve. Discard any mussels that have not opened and keep the rest warm.

2 Heat the oil in a heavy-based pan, add the remaining garlic with the chillies and cook for 30 seconds. Stir in the chopped tomatoes and 75 ml/ 3 fl oz of the reserved cooking liquor and simmer for 15–20 minutes. Season to taste with salt and pepper.

3 Meanwhile, bring a large pan of lightly salted water to a rolling boil. Add the spaghetti and cook according to the packet instructions, about 3–4 minutes, or until 'al dente'.

4 Drain the spaghetti thoroughly and return to the pan. Add the mussels and tomato sauce to the pasta, toss lightly to cover, then tip into a warmed serving dish or spoon on to individual plates. Garnish with chopped parsley and serve immediately with warm crusty bread.

INGREDIENTS
Serves 4

900 g/2 lb fresh live mussels
300 ml/½ pint white wine
3–4 garlic cloves, peeled and crushed
2 tbsp olive oil
1–2 bird's-eye chillies, deseeded and chopped
2 x 400 g cans chopped tomatoes
salt and freshly ground black pepper
350 g/12 oz fresh spaghetti
2 tbsp freshly chopped parsley, to garnish
warm crusty bread, to serve

Food Fact

Mussels are bivalves (which means they have two shells hinged together) with blue-black coloured shells. They attach themselves to rocks on the sea-bed and take up to two years to mature. They are usually sold in netted bags, either by weight or volume. If you buy by volume, you will need 1.1 litres/2 pints/1 quart for this recipe.

Conchiglioni with Crab au Gratin

1 Preheat the oven to 200°C/ 400°F/Gas Mark 6, 15 minutes before cooking. Bring a large pan of lightly salted water to a rolling boil. Add the pasta shells and cook according to the packet instructions, or until 'al dente'. Drain thoroughly and allow to dry completely.

2 Melt half the butter in a heavy-based pan, add the shallots and chilli and cook for 2 minutes, then stir in the crabmeat. Stuff the cooled shells with the crab mixture and reserve.

3 Melt the remaining butter in a small pan and stir in the flour. Cook for 1 minute, then whisk in the wine and milk and cook, stirring, until thickened. Stir in the crème fraîche and grated cheese and season the sauce to taste with salt and pepper.

4 Place the crab filled shells in a lightly oiled, large shallow baking dish or tray and spoon a little of the sauce over. Toss the breadcrumbs in the melted butter or oil, then sprinkle over the pasta shells. Bake in the preheated oven for 10 minutes. Serve immediately with a cheese or tomato sauce and a tossed green salad or cooked baby vegetables.

INGREDIENTS
Serves 4

175 g/6 oz large pasta shells
50 g/2 oz butter
1 shallot, peeled and finely chopped
1 bird's-eye chilli, deseeded and finely chopped
2 x 200 g cans crabmeat, drained
3 tbsp plain flour
50 ml/2 fl oz white wine
50 ml/2 fl oz milk
3 tbsp crème fraîche
15 g/½ oz Cheddar cheese, grated
salt and freshly ground black pepper
1 tbsp oil or melted butter
50 g/2 oz fresh white breadcrumbs

TO SERVE:
cheese or tomato sauce
tossed green salad or freshly cooked baby vegetables

Helpful Hint

Canned crabmeat is preserved in brine, so drain well and do not add too much salt when seasoning. Crab is in season between April and December and is least expensive during these months, so consider buying fresh white crabmeat for this recipe; you will need a medium-sized crab which weighs about 350 g/12 oz.

Pappardelle with Spicy Lamb & Peppers

1 Preheat the grill just before cooking. Dry fry the minced lamb in a frying pan until browned. Heat the olive oil in a heavy-based pan, add the onion, garlic and all the chopped peppers and cook gently for 3–4 minutes, or until softened. Add the browned lamb mince to the pan and cook stirring, until the onions have softened, then drain off any remaining oil.

2 Stir the chilli powder and cumin into the pan and cook gently for 2 mintues, stirring frequently. Add the tomato paste, pour in the wine and season to taste with salt and pepper. Reduce the heat and simmer for 10–15 minutes, or until the sauce has reduced.

3 Meanwhile, bring a large pan of lightly salted water to a rolling boil. Add the papardelle and cook according to the packet instructions, or until 'al dente'. Drain thoroughly, then return to the pan and stir the meat sauce into the pasta. Keep warm.

4 Meanwhile, place the breadcrumbs on a baking tray, drizzle over the melted butter and place under the preheated grill for 3–4 minutes, or until golden and crispy. Allow to cool, then mix with the grated Cheddar cheese. Tip the pasta mixture into a warmed serving dish, sprinkle with the breadcrumbs and the parsley. Serve immediately.

INGREDIENTS
Serves 4

450 g / 1 lb fresh lamb mince
2 tbsp olive oil
1 onion, peeled and finely chopped
2 garlic cloves, peeled and crushed
1 green pepper, deseeded and chopped
1 yellow pepper, deseeded and chopped
½ tsp hot chilli powder
1 tsp ground cumin
1 tbsp tomato paste
150 ml / ¼ pint red wine
salt and freshly ground black pepper
350 g / 12 oz pappardelle
2 oz fresh white breadcrumbs
25 g / 1 oz butter, melted
25 g / 1 oz Cheddar cheese, grated
1 tbsp freshly chopped parsley

Tasty Tip

Choose very lean lamb mince for this dish. To add extra flavour, add a fresh bay leaf or a sprig of fresh rosemary to the pan when frying the mince and remove at the end of step 2, when the sauce has reduced.

Farfalle with Courgettes & Mushrooms

1 Heat the butter and olive oil in a large pan, add the onion, garlic and bacon lardons and cook for 3–4 minutes, or until the onion has softened. Add the courgettes and cook, stirring, for 3–4 minutes. Add the mushrooms, lower the heat and cook, covered, for 4–5 minutes.

2 Meanwhile, bring a large pan of lightly salted water to a rolling boil. Add the fusilli and cook according to the packet instructions, or until 'al dente'. Drain thoroughly, return to the pan and keep warm.

3 Season the mushroom mixture to taste with salt and pepper, then stir in the crème fraîche and half the chopped parsley. Simmer for 2–3 minutes, or until the sauce is thick and creamy.

4 Pour the sauce over the cooked pasta, toss lightly, then reheat for 2 minutes, or until piping hot. Tip into a warmed serving dish and sprinkle over the chopped parsley. Garnish with pecorino cheese shavings and serve immediately with a mixed salad and crusty bread.

INGREDIENTS
Serves 4

25 g / 1 oz butter
2 tsp olive oil
1 small onion, peeled and finely chopped
2 garlic cloves, peeled and crushed
125 g / 4 oz bacon lardons
450 g / 1 lb courgettes, trimmed and diced
125 g / 4 oz button mushrooms, wiped and roughly chopped
350 g / 12 oz farfalle
salt and freshly ground black pepper
250 ml carton crème fraîche
2 tbsp freshly chopped parsley
shaved pecorino cheese, to garnish

TO SERVE:
mixed salad
crusty bread

Helpful Hint

To shave pecorino or Parmesan cheese, use a sharp knife or a vegetable peeler. If you find this difficult, you could coarsely grate the cheese instead. Avoid tubs of ready-grated pecorino and Parmesan; they tend to be powdery and flavourless and are a poor substitute for fresh cheese.

Cannelloni with Tomato & Red Wine Sauce

1 Preheat the oven to 200°C/ 400°F/Gas Mark 6, 15 minutes before cooking. Heat the oil in a heavy-based pan, add the onion and garlic and cook for 2–3 minutes. Cool slightly, then stir in the ricotta cheese and pine nuts. Season the filling to taste with salt, pepper and the nutmeg.

2 Cut each lasagne sheet in half, put a little of the ricotta filling on each piece and roll up like a cigar to resemble cannelloni tubes. Arrange the cannelloni, seam-side down, in a single layer, in a lightly oiled, 2.3 litre/4 pint shallow ovenproof dish.

3 Melt the butter in a pan, add the shallot and cook for 2 minutes. Pour in the red wine, tomatoes and sugar and season well. Bring to the boil, lower the heat and simmer for about 20 minutes, or until thickened. Add a little more sugar if desired. Transfer to a food processor and blend until a smooth sauce is formed.

4 Pour the warm tomato sauce over the cannelloni and sprinkle with the grated mozzarella cheese. Bake in the preheated oven for about 30 minutes, or until golden and bubbling. Garnish and serve immediately with a green salad.

INGREDIENTS
Serves 6

2 tbsp olive oil
1 onion, peeled and finely chopped
1 garlic clove, peeled and crushed
250 g carton ricotta cheese
50 g/2 oz pine nuts
salt and freshly ground black pepper
pinch freshly grated nutmeg
250 g/9 oz fresh spinach lasagne
25 g/1 oz butter
1 shallot, peeled and finely chopped
150 ml/¼ pint red wine
400 g can chopped tomatoes
½ tsp sugar
50 g/2 oz mozzarella cheese, grated, plus extra to serve
1 tbsp freshly chopped parsley, to garnish
fresh green salad, to serve

Food Fact

Mozzarella is the Italian cheese often used to top pizzas, as it is elastic and stringy when cooked. It is a soft, kneaded, brilliantly white cheese with a delicate, almost spongy texture. Traditionally, it was made from buffalo milk, but now cow's milk is used more often.

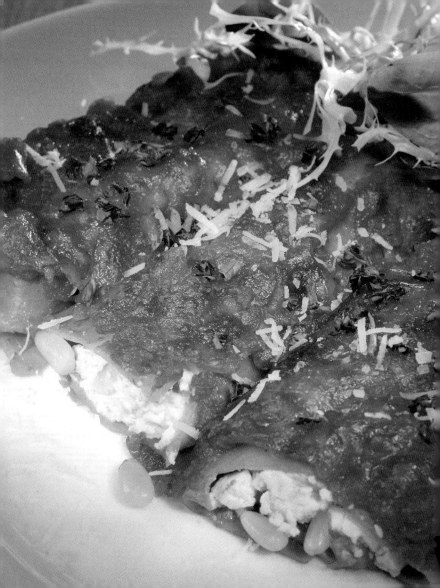

Pasta Triangles with Pesto & Walnut Dressing

1 Preheat the grill to high. Cut the lasagne sheets in half, then into triangles and reserve. Mix the pesto and ricotta cheese together and warm gently in a pan.

2 Toast the walnuts under the preheated grill until golden. Rub off the papery skins. Place the nuts in a food processor with the bread and grind finely.

3 Mix the soured cream with the mascarpone cheese in a bowl. Add the ground walnuts and grated pecorino cheese and season to taste with salt and pepper. Whisk in the olive oil. Pour into a pan and warm gently.

4 Bring a large pan of lightly salted water to a rolling boil. Add the pasta triangles and cook, according to the packet instructions, about 3–4 minutes, or until 'al dente'.

5 Drain the pasta thoroughly and arrange a few triangles on each serving plate. Top each one with a spoonful of the pesto mixture then place another triangle on top. Continue to layer the pasta and pesto mixture, then spoon a little of the walnut sauce on top of each stack. Garnish with dill, basil or parsley and serve immediately with a freshly dressed tomato and cucumber salad.

INGREDIENTS
Serves 6

450 g / 1 lb fresh egg lasagne
4 tbsp ricotta cheese
4 tbsp pesto
125 g / 4 oz walnuts
1 slice white bread, crusts removed
150 ml / ¼ pint soured cream
75 g / 3 oz mascarpone cheese
25 g / 1 oz pecorino cheese, grated
salt and freshly ground black pepper
1 tbsp olive oil
sprig of dill or freshly chopped basil or parsley, to garnish
tomato and cucumber salad, to serve

Tasty Tip

For a simple tomato and cucumber salad, arrange overlapping thin slices of cucumber and beef and plum tomatoes on a large plate. Drizzle over a dressing made with 1 teaspoon Dijon mustard, 4 tablespoons extra virgin olive oil, 1 tablespoon lemon juice and a pinch each of caster sugar, salt and pepper. Leave at room temperature for 15 minutes before serving.

Aubergine & Tomato Layer

1 Preheat the oven to 190°C/ 375°F/Gas Mark 5, 10 minutes before cooking. Brush the aubergine slices with 5 tablespoons of the olive oil and place on a baking sheet. Bake in the preheated oven for 20 minutes, or until tender. Remove from the oven and increase the temperature to 200°C/400°F/ Gas Mark 6.

2 Heat the remaining oil in a heavy-based pan. Add the onion and garlic, cook for 2–3 minutes then add the tomatoes, wine and sugar. Season to taste with salt and pepper, then simmer for 20 minutes.

3 Melt the butter in another pan. Stir in the flour, cook for 2 minutes, then whisk in the milk. Cook for 2–3 minutes, or until thickened. Season to taste.

4 Pour a little white sauce into a lightly oiled, 1.7 litre/3 pint baking dish. Cover with a layer of lasagne, spread with tomato sauce, then add some of the aubergines. Cover thinly with white sauce and sprinkle with a little cheese. Continue to layer in this way, finishing with a layer of lasagne.

5 Beat together the eggs and yogurt. Season, then pour over the lasagne. Sprinkle with the remaining cheese and bake in the preheated oven for 25–30 minutes, or until golden. Garnish with basil leaves and serve.

INGREDIENTS
Serves 4

2 aubergines, about 700 g/1½ lb, trimmed and thinly sliced
6 tbsp olive oil
1 onion, peeled and finely sliced
1 garlic clove, peeled and crushed
400 g can chopped tomatoes
50 ml/2 fl oz red wine
½ tsp sugar
salt and freshly ground black pepper
50 g/2 oz butter
40 g/1½ oz flour
450 ml/¾ pint milk
225 g/8 oz fresh egg lasagne
2 medium eggs, beaten
200 ml/7 fl oz Greek yogurt
125 g/3 oz mozzarella cheese, grated
fresh basil leaves, to garnish

Food Fact

Greek yogurt can be made from either ewe's or cow's milk. Ewes milk is very rich and creamy, with a fat content of around 6 per cent. Cow's milk has less fat, so the yogurt is strained to concentrate it.

Cannelloni with Gorgonzola Sauce

1 Preheat the oven to 190°C/ 375°F/Gas Mark 5, 10 minutes before cooking. Melt the salted butter in a heavy-based pan, add the shallot and bacon and cook for about 4–5 minutes.

2 Add the mushrooms to the pan and cook for 5–6 minutes, or until the mushrooms are very soft. Stir in the flour, cook for 1 minute, then stir in the double cream and cook gently for 2 minutes. Allow to cool.

3 Cut each sheet of lasagne in half. Spoon some filling on to each piece and roll up from the longest side to resemble cannelloni. Arrange the cannelloni in a lightly oiled, shallow 1.4 litre/2½ pint ovenproof dish.

4 Heat the unsalted butter very slowly in a pan and when melted, add the Gorgonzola cheese. Stir until the cheese has melted, then stir in the whipping cream. Bring to the boil slowly, then simmer gently for about 5 minutes, or until thickened.

5 Pour the cream sauce over the cannelloni. Place in the preheated oven and bake for 20 minutes, or until golden and thoroughly heated through. Serve immediately with assorted salad leaves.

INGREDIENTS
Serves 2–3

50 g/2 oz salted butter

1 shallot, peeled and finely chopped

2 rashers streaky bacon, rind removed and chopped

225 g/8 oz mushrooms, wiped and finely chopped

25 g/1 oz plain flour

120 ml/4 fl oz double cream

125 g/4 oz fresh egg lasagne, 6 sheets in total

40 g/1½ oz unsalted butter

150 g/5 oz Gorgonzola cheese, diced

150 ml/¼ pint whipping cream

assorted salad leaves, to serve

Tasty Tip

Gorgonzola cheese is very salty. As it is combined in this recipe with bacon, which is also salty, some of the butter used here is unsalted in order to balance the flavour. Italians use a wide range of mushrooms in their cooking, so for extra taste, you could use chestnut or large open field mushrooms instead of ordinary button mushrooms.

Ratatouille & Pasta Bake

1 Preheat the oven to 190°C/375°F/Gas Mark 5, 10 minutes before cooking. Heat the olive oil in a heavy-based pan, add half the onion and cook gently for 2–3 minutes. Stir in the tomatoes and wine, then simmer for 20 minutes, or until a thick consistency is formed. Add the sugar and season to taste with salt and pepper. Reserve.

2 Meanwhile, melt the butter in another pan, add the remaining onion, the garlic, mushrooms and courgettes and cook for 10 minutes, or until softened.

3 Spread a little tomato sauce in the base of a lightly oiled, 1.4 litre/2 ½ pint baking dish. Top with a layer of lasagne and spoon over half the mushroom and courgette mixture. Repeat the layers, finishing with a layer of lasagne.

4 Beat the eggs and cream together, then pour over the lasagne. Mix the mozzarella and pecorino cheeses together then sprinkle on top of the lasagne. Place in the preheated oven and cook for 20 minutes, or until golden-brown. Serve immediately with a green salad.

INGREDIENTS
Serves 4

1 tbsp olive oil
2 large onions, peeled and finely chopped
400 g can chopped tomatoes
100 ml/3½ fl oz white wine
½ tsp caster sugar
salt and freshly ground black pepper
40 g/1½ oz butter
2 garlic cloves, peeled and crushed
125 g/4 oz mushrooms, wiped and thickly sliced
700 g/1½ lb courgettes, trimmed and thickly sliced
125 g/4 oz fresh spinach lasagne
2 large eggs
2 tbsp double cream
75 g/3 oz mozzarella cheese, grated
25 g/1 oz pecorino cheese, grated
green salad, to serve

Tasty Tip

For speed and simplicity, this recipe is a simplified version of ratatouille. If preferred, it can be made more traditionally by substituting a small chopped aubergine and a deseeded and chopped green or red pepper for some of the courgettes.

Lamb & Pasta Pie

1 Preheat the oven to 190° C/ 375°F/Gas Mark 5, 10 minutes before cooking. Lightly oil a 20.5 cm/8 inch spring-form cake tin. Blend the flour, salt, margarine and white vegetable fat in a food processor and add sufficient cold water to make a smooth, pliable dough. Knead on a lightly floured surface, then roll out two-thirds to line the base and sides of the tin. Brush the pastry with egg white and reserve.

2 Melt the butter in a heavy-based pan, stir in the flour and cook for 2 minutes. Stir in the milk and cook, stirring, until a smooth, thick sauce is formed. Season to taste with salt and pepper and reserve.

3 Bring a large pan of lightly salted water to a rolling boil. Add the macaroni and cook according to the packet instructions, or until 'al dente'.

Drain, then stir into the white sauce with the grated cheese.

4 Heat the oil in a frying pan, add the onion, garlic, celery and lamb mince and cook, stirring, for 5–6 minutes. Stir in the tomato paste and tomatoes and cook for 10 minutes. Cool slightly.

5 Place half the pasta mixture, then all the mince in the pastry-lined tin. Top with a layer of pasta. Roll out the remaining pastry and cut out a lid. Brush the edge with water, place over the filling and pinch the edges together. Use trimmings to decorate the top of the pie.

6 Brush the pie with beaten egg yolk and bake in the preheated oven for 50–60 minutes, covering the top with tin-foil if browning too quickly. Stand for 15 minutes before turning out. Serve immediately.

INGREDIENTS
Serves 8
400 g/14 oz plain white flour
100 g/3½ oz margarine
100 g/3½ oz white vegetable fat
pinch of salt
1 small egg, separated
50 g/2 oz butter
50 g/2 oz flour
450 ml/¼ pint milk
salt and freshly ground black pepper
225 g/8 oz macaroni
50 g/2 oz Cheddar cheese, grated
1 tbsp vegetable oil
1 onion, peeled and chopped
1 garlic clove, peeled and crushed
2 celery sticks, trimmed and chopped
450 g/1 lb lamb mince
1 tbsp tomato paste
400 g can chopped tomatoes

Baked Macaroni
with Mushrooms & Leeks

1 Preheat the oven to 220°C/ 425° F/Gas Mark 7, 15 minutes before cooking. Heat 1 tablespoon of the olive oil in a large frying pan, add the onion and garlic and cook for 2 minutes. Add the leeks, mushrooms and 25 g/1 oz of the butter then cook for 5 minutes. Pour in the white wine, cook for 2 minutes then stir in the crème fraîche or cream. Season to taste with salt and pepper.

2 Meanwhile, bring a large pan of lightly salted water to a rolling boil. Add the macaroni and cook according to the packet instructions, or until 'al dente'.

3 Melt 25 g/1 oz of the butter with the remaining oil in a small frying pan. Add the breadcrumbs and fry until just beginning to turn golden-brown. Drain on absorbent kitchen paper.

4 Drain the pasta thoroughly, toss in the remaining butter then tip into a lightly oiled, 1.4 litre/2½ pint shallow baking dish. Cover the pasta with the leek and mushroom mixture then sprinkle with the fried breadcrumbs. Bake in the preheated oven for 5–10 minutes, or until golden and crisp. Garnish with chopped parsley and serve.

INGREDIENTS
Serves 4

2 tbsp olive oil
1 onion, peeled and finely chopped
1 garlic clove, peeled and crushed
2 small leeks, trimmed and chopped
450 g/1 lb assorted wild mushrooms, trimmed
50 ml/2 fl oz white wine
75 g/3 oz butter
150 ml/¼ pint crème fraîche or whipping cream
salt and freshly ground black pepper
75 g/3 oz fresh white breadcrumbs
350 g/12 oz short cut macaroni
1 tbsp freshly chopped parsley, to garnish

Helpful Hint

Some wild mushrooms are more tender and cook faster than others. Chestnut, porcini (ceps), portabello, enoki and shiitake would all be good used here. If you use chanterelles or oyster mushrooms, sauté them with the leeks for 1 minute only as they are fairly delicate.

Vanilla & Lemon Panna Cotta with Raspberry Sauce

1 Put the cream, vanilla pod and sugar into a saucepan. Bring to the boil, then simmer for 10 minutes until slightly reduced, stirring to prevent scalding. Remove from the heat, stir in the lemon zest and remove the vanilla pod.

2 Soak the gelatine in the milk for 5 minutes, or until softened. Squeeze out any excess milk and add to the hot cream. Stir well until dissolved.

3 Pour the cream mixture into 6 ramekins or mini pudding moulds and leave in the refrigerator for 4 hours, or until set.

4 Meanwhile, put 175 g/ 6 oz of the raspberries in a food processor with the icing sugar and lemon juice. Blend to a purée then pass the mixture through a sieve. Fold in the remaining raspberries with a metal spoon or rubber spatula and chill in the refrigerator until ready to serve.

5 To serve, dip each of the moulds into hot water for a few seconds, then turn out on to 6 individual serving plates. Spoon some of the raspberry sauce over and around the panna cotta, decorate with extra lemon zest and serve.

INGREDIENTS
Serves 6

900 ml / 1½ pints double cream
1 vanilla pod, split
100 g / 3½ oz caster sugar
zest of 1 lemon
3 sheets gelatine
5 tbsp milk
450 g / 1 lb raspberries
3–4 tbsp icing sugar, to taste
1 tbsp lemon juice
extra lemon zest, to decorate

Tasty Tip

Sheet gelatine is readily available from large supermarkets. It is much easier to measure and use than powdered gelatine and also gives a glossier finish to clear jellies.

Ricotta Cheesecake with Strawberry Coulis

1 Preheat oven to 170°C/ 325°F/Gas Mark 3. Line a 20.5 cm/8 inch springform tin with baking parchment. Place the biscuits into a food processor together with the peel. Blend until the biscuits are crushed and the peel is chopped. Add 50 g/ 2 oz of the melted butter and process until mixed. Tip into the tin and spread evenly over the bottom. Press firmly into place and reserve.

2 Blend together the crème fraîche, ricotta cheese, sugar, vanilla seeds and eggs in a food processor. With the motor running, add the remaining melted butter and blend for a few seconds. Pour the mixture on to the base. Transfer to the

preheated oven and cook for about 1 hour, until set and risen round the edges, but slightly wobbly in the centre. Switch off the oven and allow to cool there. chill in the refrigerator for at least 8 hours, or preferably overnight.

3 Wash and drain the strawberries. Hull the fruit and remove any soft spots. Put into the food processor along with 25 g/1 oz of the sugar and orange juice and zest. Blend until smooth. Add the remaining sugar to taste. Pass through a sieve to remove seeds and chill in the refrigerator until needed.

4 Cut the cheesecake into wedges, spoon over some of the strawberry coulis and serve.

INGREDIENTS
Serves 6–8

125 g/4 oz digestive biscuits
100 g/3½ oz candied peel, chopped
65 g/2½ oz butter, melted
150 ml/¼ pint crème fraîche
575 g/4 oz ricotta cheese
100 g/3½ oz caster sugar
1 vanilla pod, seeds only
2 large eggs
225 g/8 oz strawberries
25–50 g/1–2 oz caster sugar, to taste
zest and juice of 1 orange

Tasty Tip

This cheesecake has a soft, creamy texture compared to some baked cheesecakes. This is because of the addition of crème fraîche. If ricotta is unavailable, substitute with full-fat soft cheese.

Cantuccini

1 Preheat oven to 180°C/ 350°F/Gas Mark 4. Line a large baking sheet with non-stick baking parchment. Place the flour, caster sugar, baking powder, vanilla essence, the whole eggs and one of the egg yolks into a food processor and blend until the mixture forms a ball, scraping down the sides once or twice. Turn the mixture out on to a lightly floured surface and knead in the chopped nuts and aniseed.

2 Divide the paste into 3 pieces and roll into logs about 4 cm/1½ inches wide.

Place the logs on to the baking sheet at least 5 cm/2 inches apart. Brush lightly with the other egg yolk beaten with 1 tablespoon of water and bake in the preheated oven for 30–35 minutes.

3 Remove from the oven and reduce the oven temperature to 150°C/300°F/Gas Mark 2. Cut the logs diagonally into 2.5 cm/ 1 inch slices and lay cut-side down on the baking sheet. Return to the oven for a further 30–40 minutes, or until dry and firm. Cool on a wire rack and store in an airtight container. Serve with Vin Santo or coffee.

INGREDIENTS
Makes 24 biscuits

250 g/9 oz plain flour
250 g/9 oz caster sugar
½ tsp baking powder
½ tsp vanilla essence
2 medium eggs
1 medium egg yolk
100 g/3½ oz mixed almonds and
  hazelnuts, toasted and roughly
  chopped
1 tsp whole aniseed
1 medium egg yolk mixed with
  1 tbsp water, to glaze
Vin Santo or coffee, to serve

Food Fact

Cantuccini are simply small biscuits, traditionally served with a sweet dessert wine called Vin Santo. Cantucci are large biscuits that are made in the same way.

Almond & Pistachio Biscotti

1 Preheat oven to 180°C/ 350°F/Gas Mark 4. Line a large baking sheet with non-stick baking parchment. Toast the ground almonds and whole nuts lightly and reserve until cool.

2 Beat together the eggs, egg yolk and icing sugar until thick, then beat in the flour, baking powder and salt. Add the lemon zest, ground almonds and whole nuts and mix to form a slightly sticky dough.

3 Turn the dough on to a lightly floured surface and, using lightly floured hands, form

into a log measuring approximately 30 cm/12 inches long. Place down the centre of the prepared baking sheet and transfer to the preheated oven. Bake for 20 minutes.

4 Remove from the oven and increase the oven temperature to 200°C/400°F/Gas Mark 6. Cut the log diagonally into 2.5 cm/1 inch slices. Return to the baking sheet, cut-side down and bake for a further 10–15 minutes until golden, turning once after 10 minutes. Leave to cool on a wire rack and store in an airtight container.

INGREDIENTS
Makes 12 biscuits

125 g/4 oz ground almonds
50 g/2 oz shelled pistachios
50 g/2 oz blanched almonds
2 medium eggs
1 medium egg yolk
125 g/4 oz icing sugar
225 g/8 oz plain flour
1 tsp baking powder
pinch of salt
zest of ½ lemon

Tasty Tip

These biscuits are also delicious made with a single kind of nut – try hazelnuts or just almonds. When toasting nuts spread them out on a baking sheet then place in a preheated oven at 200°C/400°F/Gas Mark 6. Leave for 5–10 minutes, stirring occasionally. If using a lower temperature, leave for a few more minutes.

Hazelnut, Chocolate & Chestnut Meringue Torte

1 Preheat oven to 130°C/
250°F/Gas Mark ½. Line 3
baking sheets with non-stick
baking parchment and draw a
20.5 cm/8 inch circle on each.

2 Beat 1 egg white until stiff
peaks form. Add 25 g/1 oz
of the sugar and beat until shiny.
Mix the cocoa with the remaining 25 g/1 oz of sugar and add 1
tablespoon at a time, beating well
after each addition, until all the
sugar is added and the mixture is
stiff and glossy. Spread on to 1
of the baking sheets within the
circle drawn on the underside.

3 Put the hazelnuts in a food
processor and blend until
chopped. In a clean bowl, beat
the 2 egg whites until stiff. Add
50 g/2 oz of the sugar and beat.
Add the remaining sugar about
1 tablespoon at a time, beating
after each addition until all the
sugar is added and the mixture is
stiff and glossy.

4 Reserve 2 tablespoons of
the nuts, then fold in the
remainder and divide between
the 2 remaining baking sheets.
Sprinkle one of the hazelnut
meringues with the reserved
hazelnuts and transfer all the
baking sheets to the oven. Bake
in the preheated oven for 1½
hours. Turn the oven off and
leave in the oven until cold.

5 Whip the cream until thick.
Beat the chestnut purée in
another bowl until soft. Add a
spoonful of the cream and fold
together before adding the
remaining cream and melted
chocolate and fold together.

6 Place the plain hazelnut
meringue on a serving
plate. Top with half the cream
and chestnut mixture. Add the
chocolate meringue and top
with the remaining cream. Add
the final meringue. Sprinkle over
the grated chocolate and serve.

INGREDIENTS
Serves 8–10

*FOR THE CHOCOLATE
MERINGUE:*
1 medium egg white
50 g/2 oz caster sugar
2 tbsp cocoa powder

*FOR THE HAZELNUT
MERINGUE:*
75 g/3 oz hazelnuts, toasted
2 medium egg whites
125 g/4 oz caster sugar

FOR THE FILLING:
300 ml/½ pint double cream
*250 g can sweetened chestnut
purée*
*50 g/2 oz plain dark chocolate,
melted*
*25 g/1 oz plain dark chocolate,
grated*

Bomba Siciliana

1 Melt the plain chocolate in bowl set over a saucepan of simmering water until smooth, then cool. Whisk together the custard with the whipping cream and slightly cooled chocolate Spoon the mixture into a shallow, lidded freezer box and freeze. Every 2 hours, remove from the freezer and using an electric whisk or balloon whisk, whisk thoroughly. Repeat 3 times, then leave until frozen solid. Soak the candied peel, cherries and sultanas in the rum and leave until needed.

2 Chill a bombe or 1 litre/ 1¾ pint pudding mould in the freezer for about 30 minutes. Remove the chocolate ice cream from the freezer to soften, then spoon the ice cream into the mould and press down well, smoothing around the edges and leaving a hollow in the centre. Return the ice cream to the freezer for about 1 hour, or until frozen hard.

3 Remove the vanilla ice cream from the freezer to soften. Spoon the softened vanilla ice cream into the hollow, making sure to leave another hollow for the cream. Return to the freezer again and freeze until hard.

4 Whip the cream and sugar until it is just holding its shape then fold in the soaked fruit. Remove the mould from the freezer and spoon in the cream mixture. Return to the freezer for at least another hour.

5 When ready to serve, remove the mould from the freezer and dip into hot water for a few seconds, then turn on to a large serving plate. Dip a knife into hot water and cut into wedges to serve.

INGREDIENTS
Serves 6–8

100 g / 3½ oz plain chocolate, broken into pieces
200 g / 7 oz fresh chilled custard
150 ml / ¼ pint whipping cream
25 g / 1 oz candied peel, finely chopped
25 g / 1 oz glacé cherries, chopped
25 g / 1 oz sultanas
3 tbsp rum
225 g / 8 oz good-quality vanilla ice cream
200 ml / ¼ pint double cream
3 tbsp caster sugar

Tasty Tip

For the best flavour, buy whole candied peel. Cut it into strips using kitchen scissors, then chop crosswise into small pieces.

Summer Fruit Semifreddo

1 Wash and hull or remove stalks from the fruits, as necessary, then put them into a food processor or blender with the icing sugar and lemon juice. Blend to a purée, pour into a jug and chill in the refrigerator, until needed.

2 Remove the seeds from the vanilla pod by opening the pod and scraping with the back of a knife. Add the seeds to the sugar and whisk with the egg yolks until pale and thick.

3 In another bowl, whip the cream until soft peaks form. Do not overwhip. In a third bowl, whip the egg whites with the salt until stiff peaks form.

4 Using a large metal spoon – to avoid knocking any air from the mixture – fold together the fruit purée, egg yolk mixture, the cream and egg whites. Transfer the mixture to a round, shallow, lidded freezer box and put into the freezer until almost frozen. If the mixture freezes solid, thaw in the refrigerator until semi-frozen. Turn out the semi-frozen mixture, cut into wedges and serve decorated with a few fresh redcurrants. If the mixture thaws completely, eat immediately and do not refreeze.

INGREDIENTS
Serves 6–8

225 g/8 oz raspberries
125 g/4 oz blueberries
125 g/4 oz redcurrants
50 g/2 oz icing sugar
juice of 1 lemon
1 vanilla pod, split
50 g/2 oz sugar
4 large eggs, separated
600 ml/1 pint double cream
pinch of salt
fresh redcurrants, to decorate

Tasty Tip

Use the egg and cream mixture as the basis for a host of other flavours, such as praline, chocolate, or autumn berries.

Cassatta

1 Line a 450 g/1 lb loaf tin with clingfilm. Place in the freezer. Melt 100 g/3½ oz of the chocolate into a heatproof bowl set over a saucepan of simmering water, stir until smooth, then cool. Place the custard into a bowl. Stir in the cream and the chocolate and stir until mixed. Spoon into a shallow, lidded freezer box and transfer to the freezer. Every 2 hours remove from the freezer and using an electric whisk, whisk thoroughly. Repeat 3 times, then leave until frozen solid.

2 Remove the chocolate ice cream from the freezer and allow to soften. Remove the loaf tin from the freezer and press the chocolate ice cream into the bottom of the tin, press down well and allow it to come up the sides of the tin. Return to the freezer and leave until solid.

3 Soften the pistachio ice cream, then beat in the pistachios, candied peel and cherries. Spoon into the tin, pressing down well and smoothing the top. Return to the freezer until hard. Soften the strawberry ice cream and spread on to the pistachio ice cream. Smooth the top. Return to the freezer for at least 1 hour, or until completely solid.

4 Meanwhile, melt the remaining chocolate, stir until smooth and cool slightly. Remove the loaf tin from the freezer. Dip into hot water and turn on to a serving dish. Using a teaspoon, drizzle the chocolate over the ice cream in a haphazard pattern. Return the cassatta to the freezer, until the chocolate has set. Dip a knife in hot water and use to slice the cassatta. Serve immediately.

INGREDIENTS
Serves 6–8

300 g/11 oz plain chocolate, broken into pieces
200 g/7 oz fresh chilled custard
150 ml/¼ pint whipping cream
275 g/10 oz good-quality pistachio ice cream
25 g/1 oz shelled pistachios, toasted
50 g/2 oz candied peel, finely chopped
25 g/1 oz glacé cherries, finely chopped
275 g/10 oz good-quality strawberry ice cream

Tasty Tip

To make your own pistachio ice cream, toast 50 g/2 oz of shelled pistachios and when cold, chop finely. Follow the recipe for chocolate ice cream above, omitting the chocolate and folding in the nuts along with the cream. Add a few drops of green food colour, if liked.

Marzipan Cake

1 Grind the blanched almonds in a food processor until fairly fine. Mix with 200 g/7 oz of the icing sugar. Beat the egg whites until stiff then fold into the almond mixture using a metal spoon or rubber spatula to form a stiffish dough. It will still be quite sticky but will firm up as it rests. Leave for 30 minutes.

2 Dust a work surface very generously with some of the remaining icing sugar so that the marzipan does not stick. Roll out two-thirds of the marzipan into a large sheet to a thickness of about 5 mm/¼ inch. Use to line a sloping-sided baking dish with a base measuring 25.5 cm x 20.5 cm/10 x 8 inches. Trim the edges and put any trimmings with the remainder of the marzipan.

3 Cut the Madeira cake into thin slices and make a layer of sponge to cover the bottom of the marzipan. Sprinkle with the Marsala wine. Beat the ricotta with the sugar and add the lemon zest, candied peel and cherries. Spread this over the sponge. Slice the peaches and put them on top of the ricotta. Whip the cream and spread it over the peaches. Roll out the remaining marzipan and lay it over the cream to seal the whole cake, pressing down gently to remove any air. Press the edges of the marzipan together. Chill in the refrigerator for 2 hours.

4 Turn the cake out on to a serving plate and dust generously with icing sugar. Slice thickly and serve immediately.

INGREDIENTS
Serves 12–14

450 g/1 lb blanched almonds

300 g/11 oz icing sugar (includes sugar for dusting and rolling)

4 medium egg whites

125 g/4 oz Madeira cake

2 tbsp Marsala wine

225 g/8 oz ricotta cheese

50 g/2 oz caster sugar

grated zest of 1 lemon

50 g/2 oz candied peel, finely chopped

25 g/1 oz glacé cherries, finely chopped

425 g can peach halves, drained

200 ml/⅓ pint double cream

Helpful Hint

Homemade marzipan is stickier than commercially prepared versions. Use plenty of icing sugar when rolling it as well as sprinkling the dish liberally with it.

Chestnut Cake

1 Preheat oven to 150°C/ 300°F/Gas Mark 2. Oil and line a 23 cm/9 inch springform tin. Beat together the butter and sugar until light and fluffy. Add the chestnut purée and beat. Gradually add the eggs, beating after each addition. Sift in the flour with the baking powder and cloves. Add the fennel seeds and beat. The mixture should drop easily from a wooden spoon when tapped against the side of the bowl. If not, add a little milk.

2 Beat in the raisins and pine nuts. Spoon the mixture into the prepared tin and smooth the top. Transfer to the centre of the oven and bake in the preheated oven for 55–60 minutes, or until a skewer inserted in the centre of the cake comes out clean. Remove from the oven and leave in the tin.

3 Meanwhile, mix together the icing sugar and lemon juice in a small saucepan until smooth. Heat gently until hot, but not boiling. Using a cocktail stick or skewer, poke holes into the cake all over. Pour the hot syrup evenly over the cake and leave to soak into the cake. Decorate with pared strips of lemon and serve.

INGREDIENTS
Serves 8–10

175 g/6 oz butter, softened
175 g/6 oz caster sugar
250 g can sweetened chestnut
    purée
3 medium eggs, lightly beaten
175 g/6 oz plain flour
1 tsp baking powder
pinch of ground cloves
1 tsp fennel seeds, crushed
75 g/3 oz raisins
50 g/2 oz pine nuts, toasted
125 g/4 oz icing sugar
5 tbsp lemons juice
pared strips of lemon rind, to
    decorate

Tasty Tip

There are 2 methods for toasting pine nuts. Either, tip the nuts into a hot, dry frying pan and stir often until the nuts have browned on both sides. Tip immediately on to a large plate and leave to cool. Or, spread the pine nuts on to a large baking sheet and transfer to a preheated oven 200°C/400°F/Gas Mark 6 and bake for about 3–5 minutes, checking often as they burn very easily. Remove the toasted pine nuts from the oven, tip on to a plate and leave to cool, then use as required.

Sauternes & Olive Oil Cake

1 Preheat oven to 140°C/ 275°F/Gas Mark 1. Oil and line a 25.5 cm/10 inch spring-form tin. Sift the flour on to a large sheet of greaseproof paper and reserve. Using a freestanding electric mixer, if possible, whisk the eggs and sugar together, until pale and stiff. Add the lemon and orange zest.

2 Turn the speed to low and pour the flour from the paper in a slow, steady stream on to the eggs and sugar mixture. Immediately add the wine and olive oil and switch the machine off as the olive oil should not be incorporated completely.

3 Using a rubber spatula, fold the mixture very gently 3 or 4 times so that the ingredients

are just incorporated. Pour the mixture immediately into the prepared tin and bake in the pre-heated oven for 20–25 minutes, without opening the door for at least 15 minutes. Test if cooked by pressing the top lightly with a clean finger – if it springs back, remove from the oven, if not, bake for a little longer.

4 Leave the cake to cool in the tin on a wire rack. Remove the cake from the tin when cool enough to handle.

5 Meanwhile, skin the peaches and cut into segments. Toss with the brown sugar and lemon juice and reserve. When the cake is cold, dust generously with icing sugar, cut into wedges and serve with the peaches.

INGREDIENTS
Serves 8–10

125 g/4 oz plain flour, plus extra for dusting
4 medium eggs
125 g/4 oz caster sugar
grated zest of ½ lemon
grated zest of ½ orange
2 tbsp Sauternes or other sweet dessert wine
3 tbsp very best quality extra-virgin olive oil
4 ripe peaches
1–2 tsp soft brown sugar, or to taste
1 tbsp lemon juice
icing sugar, to dust

Helpful Hint

Be careful in step 3 when folding the mixture together not to overmix or the finished cake will be very heavy.

Frozen Amaretti Soufflé with Strawberries

1 Wrap a collar of greaseproof paper around a 900 ml/1½ pint soufflé dish or 6–8 individual ramekin dishes to extend at least 5 cm/2 inch above the rim and secure with string. Break the Amaretti biscuits into a bowl. Sprinkle over 6 tablespoons of the Amaretto liqueur and leave to soak.

2 Put the lemon zest and juice into a small heatproof bowl and sprinkle over the gelatine. Leave for 5 minutes to sponge, then put the bowl over a saucepan of simmering water, ensuring that the base of the bowl does not touch the water. Stir occasionally until the gelatine has dissolved completely.

3 In a clean bowl, whisk the egg yolks and sugar until pale and thick then stir in the gelatine and the soaked biscuits. In another bowl, lightly whip

450 ml/¾ pint of the cream and using a large metal spoon or rubber spatula fold into the mixture. In a third clean bowl, whisk the egg whites until stiff, then fold into the soufflé mixture. Transfer to the prepared dish, or individual ramekin dishes, and level the top. Freeze for at least 8 hours, or preferably overnight.

4 Put the strawberries into a bowl with the vanilla pod and seeds, sugar and remaining Amaretto liqueur. Leave overnight in the refrigerator, then allow to come to room temperature before serving.

5 Place the soufflé in the refrigerator for about 1 hour. Whip the remaining cream and use to decorate the soufflé then sprinkle a few finely crushed Amaretti biscuits on the top and serve with the strawberries.

INGREDIENTS
Serves 6–8

125 g/4 oz Amaretti biscuits
9 tbsp Amaretto liqueur
grated zest and juice of 1 lemon
1 tbsp powdered gelatine
6 medium eggs, separated
175 g/6 oz soft brown sugar
600 ml/1 pint double cream
450 g/1 lb fresh strawberries, halved if large
1 vanilla pod, split and seeds scraped out
2 tbsp caster sugar
few finely crushed Amaretti biscuits, to decorate

Helpful Hint

When making ice cream it is important to set the freezer to rapid freeze at least 2 hours beforehand. Remember to return the freezer to its normal setting when you have finished.

Baked Stuffed Amaretti Peaches

1 Preheat oven to 180°C/ 350°F/Gas Mark 4. Halve the peaches and remove the stones. Take a very thin slice from the bottom of each peach half so that it will sit flat on the baking sheet. Dip the peach halves in lemon juice and arrange on a baking sheet.

2 Crush the Amaretti biscuits lightly and put into a large bowl. Add the almonds, pine nuts, sugar, lemon zest and butter. Work with the fingertips until the mixture resembles coarse bread-crumbs. Add the egg yolk and mix well until the mixture is just binding.

3 Divide the Amaretti and nut mixture between the peach halves, pressing down lightly. Bake in the preheated oven for 15 minutes, or until the peaches are tender and the filling is golden. Remove from the oven and drizzle with the honey.

4 Place 2 peach halves on each serving plate and spoon over a little crème fraîche or Greek yogurt, then serve.

INGREDIENTS
Serves 4

4 ripe peaches
grated zest and juice of 1 lemon
75 g/3 oz Amaretti biscuits
50 g/2 oz chopped blanched
    almonds, toasted
50 g/2 oz pine nuts, toasted
40 g/1½ oz light muscovado
    sugar
50 g/2 oz butter
1 medium egg yolk
2 tsp clear honey
crème fraîche or Greek yogurt, to
    serve

Tasty Tip

If fresh peaches are unavailable, use nectarines. Alternatively, use drained, tinned peach halves that have been packed in juice, rather than syrup. You can vary the filling according to personal preference – try ground almonds, caster sugar, crumbled trifle sponge cakes and lemon rind, moistened with medium sherry.

Almond & Pine Nut Tart

1 Preheat oven to 200°C/ 400°F/Gas Mark 6. Roll out the pastry and use to line a 23 cm/9 inch fluted flan tin. Chill in the refrigerator for 10 minutes, then line with grease-proof paper and baking beans and bake blind in the preheated oven for 10 minutes. Remove the paper and beans and bake for a further 10–12 minutes until cooked. Leave to cool. Reduce the temperature to 190°C/375°F/Gas Mark 5.

2 Grind the almonds in a food processor until fine. Add the sugar, salt, eggs, vanilla and almond essence and blend. Add the butter, flour and baking powder and blend until smooth.

3 Spread a thick layer of the raspberry jam over the cooled pastry case, then pour in the almond filling. Sprinkle the pine nuts evenly over the top and bake for 30 minutes, until firm and browned.

4 Remove the tart from the oven and leave to cool. Dust generously with icing sugar and serve cut into wedges with whipped cream.

INGREDIENTS
Serves 6

250 g/9 oz ready-made sweet
  shortcrust pastry
75 g/3 oz blanched almonds
75 g/3 oz caster sugar
pinch of salt
2 medium eggs
1 tsp vanilla essence
2–3 drops almond essence
125 g/4 oz unsalted butter,
  softened
2 tbsp flour
½ tsp baking powder
3–4 tbsp raspberry jam
50 g/2 oz pine nuts
icing sugar, to decorate
whipped cream, to serve

Tasty Tip

Blend 175 g/6 oz plain flour and 75 g/3 oz diced cold butter together in a food processor until they resemble coarse bread-crumbs. Add 25 g/1 oz caster sugar and blend briefly to mix. Whisk together 1 medium egg yolk with 2 tablespoons of cold water and add to the food processor. Pulse until the mixture begins to form a ball, adding a little more cold water if necessary. Tip on to a floured surface and knead briefly until smooth. Wrap and refrigerate for at least 30 minutes.

Coffee Ricotta

1 Preheat oven to 220°C/
425°F/Gas Mark 7, 15
minutes before baking. Beat
the ricotta and cream together
until smooth. Stir in the ground
coffee beans, sugar and brandy.
Cover and refrigerate for at least
2 hours (the flavour improves the
longer it stands). Meanwhile, oil
2 baking sheets and line with
non-stick baking parchment.

2 Cream together the butter
and sugar until fluffy.
Gradually beat in the egg, a
little at a time. In a bowl, sift
the flour then fold into the
butter mixture to form a soft
dough. Spoon the mixture

into a piping bag fitted with a 1
cm/½ inch plain nozzle. Pipe 7.5
cm/3 inch lengths of the mixture spaced well apart on to the
baking sheet. Use a sharp knife
to cut the dough off cleanly at
the nozzle.

3 Bake in the preheated oven
for 6–8 minutes, until just
golden at the edges. Cool on
the baking sheet for 5 minutes
before transferring to a wire
rack to cool completely.

4 To serve, spoon the coffee
and ricotta mixture into
small coffee cups. Serve with
the biscuits.

INGREDIENTS
Serves 6

700 g/1½ lb fresh ricotta cheese
125 ml/4 fl oz double cream
25 g/1 oz espresso beans, freshly
  ground
4 tbsp caster sugar
3 tbsp brandy
50 g/2 oz butter, softened
75 g/3 oz caster sugar
1 medium egg, beaten
50 g/2 oz plain flour

Helpful Hint

When making the biscuits, spoon the mixture very
carefully into the piping bag to avoid getting large air
bubbles in the mixture. This will help to pipe the
biscuits smoothly on to the baking sheet.

Zabaglione with Rum-soaked Raisin Compote

1 Put the raisins in a small bowl with the lemon zest and ground cinnamon. Pour over the Marsala wine to cover and leave to macerate for at least one hour. When the raisins are plump, lift out of the Marsala wine and reserve the raisins and wine, discarding the lemon zest.

2 In a large heatproof bowl, mix together the egg yolks and sugar. Add the white wine and Marsala wine and stir well to combine. Put the bowl over a saucepan of simmering water, ensuring that the bottom of the bowl does not touch the water. Whisk constantly until the mixture doubles in bulk.

3 Remove from the heat and continue whisking for about 5 minutes until the mixture has cooled slightly. Fold in the raisins and then immediately fold in the whipped cream. Spoon into dessert glasses or goblets and serve with crisp biscuits.

INGREDIENTS
Serves 6

2 tbsp raisins
1 strip thinly pared lemon zest
½ tsp ground cinnamon
3 tbsp Marsala wine
3 medium egg yolks
3 tbsp caster sugar
125 ml / 4 fl oz dry white wine
150 ml / ¼ pint double cream,
  lightly whipped
crisp biscuits, to serve

Food Fact

Zabaglione, an Italian concoction of eggs, sugar and wine is virtually identical to Sabayon – a French concoction of eggs, sugar and wine. Make the zabaglione as above and omit the raisins. Serve with poached pears, summer fruits or on its own in stemmed glasses.

Raspberry & Almond Tart

1 Preheat oven to 200°C/ 400°F/Gas Mark 6, 15 minutes before cooking. Blend the flour, salt and butter in a food processor until the mixture resembles breadcrumbs. Add the sugar and lemon zest and blend again for 1 minute. Mix the egg yolk with 2 tablespoons of cold water and add to the mixture. Blend until the mixture starts to come together, adding a little more water if necessary, then tip out on to a lightly floured surface. Knead until smooth, wrap in clingfilm and chill in the refrigerator for 30 minutes.

2 Roll the dough out thinly on a lightly floured surface and use to line a 23 cm/9 inch fluted tart tin. Chill in the refrigerator for 10 minutes. Line the pastry case with greaseproof paper and baking beans. Bake for 10 minutes, then remove the paper and beans and return to the oven for a further 10–12 minutes until cooked. Allow to cool slightly, then reduce the oven temperature to 190°C/ 375°F/Gas Mark 5.

3 Blend together the butter, sugar, ground almonds, and eggs until smooth. Spread the raspberries over the base of the pastry, then cover with the almond mixture. Bake for 15 minutes. Remove from the oven and sprinkle with the slivered or flaked almonds and dust generously with icing sugar. Bake for a further 15–20 minutes, until firm and golden brown. Leave to cool, then serve.

INGREDIENTS
Serves 6–8

FOR THE PASTRY:
225 g/8 oz plain flour
pinch of salt
125 g/4 oz butter, cut into pieces
50 g/2 oz caster sugar
grated zest of ½ lemon
1 medium egg yolk

FOR THE FILLING:
75 g/3 oz butter
75 g/3 oz caster sugar
75 g/3 oz ground almonds
2 medium eggs
225 g/8 oz raspberries, thawed if frozen
2 tbsp slivered or flaked almonds
icing sugar for dusting

Tasty Tip

Omit the raspberries in the above tart. Spread the almond mixture over the base of the pastry case and top with poached or drained, tinned pear halves. Scatter over flaked almonds and bake as above.

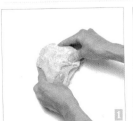

Goats' Cheese & Lemon Tart

1 Preheat oven to 200°C/ 400°F/Gas Mark 6, 15 minutes before cooking. Rub the butter into the plain flour and salt until the mixture resembles breadcrumbs, then stir in the sugar. Beat the egg yolk with 2 tablespoons of cold water and add to the mixture. Mix together until a dough is formed then turn the dough out on to a lightly floured surface and knead until smooth. Chill in the refrigerator for 30 minutes.

2 Roll the dough out thinly on a lightly floured surface and use to line a 4 cm/1½ inch deep 23 cm/9 inch fluted flan tin. Chill in the refrigerator for 10 minutes. Line the pastry case with greaseproof paper and baking beans or tinfoil and bake blind in the preheated oven for 10 minutes. Remove the paper

and beans or tinfoil. Return to the oven for a further 12–15 minutes until cooked. Leave to cool slightly, then reduce the oven temperature to 150°C/300°F/Gas Mark 2.

3 Beat the goats' cheese until smooth. Whisk in the eggs, sugar, lemon rind and juice. Add the cream and mix well.

4 Carefully pour the cheese mixture into the pastry case and return to the oven. Bake in the oven for 35–40 minutes, or until just set. If it begins to brown or swell, open the oven door for 2 minutes, then reduce the temperature to 120°C/250°F/Gas Mark ½ and leave the tart to cool in the oven. Chill in the refrigerator until cold. Decorate and serve with fresh raspberries.

INGREDIENTS
Serves 8–10

FOR THE PASTRY:
125 g/4 oz butter, cut into small pieces
225 g/8 oz plain flour
pinch of salt
50 g/2 oz caster sugar
1 medium egg yolk

FOR THE FILLING:
350 g/12 oz mild fresh goats' cheese, eg Chavroux
3 medium eggs, beaten
150 g/5 oz caster sugar
grated rind and juice of 3 lemons
450 ml/¾ pint double cream
fresh raspberries, to decorate and serve

Tasty Tip
The goat's cheese adds a certain unusual piquancy to this tart. Substitute full-fat soft cheese or ricotta, if preferred.

Tiramisu

1 Lightly oil and line a 900 g/2 lb loaf tin with a piece of clingfilm. Put the mascarpone cheese and icing sugar into a large bowl and using a rubber spatula, beat until smooth. Stir in 2 tablespoons of chilled coffee and mix thoroughly.

2 Whip the cream with 1 tablespoon of the coffee liqueur until just thickened. Stir a spoonful of the whipped cream into the mascarpone mixture, then fold in the rest. Spoon half of the the mascarpone mixture into the prepared loaf tin and smooth the top.

3 Put the remaining coffee and coffee liqueur into a shallow dish just bigger than the biscuits. Using half of the biscuits, dip one side of each biscuit into the coffee mixture, then arrange on top of the mascarpone mixture in a single layer. Spoon the rest of the mascarpone mixture over the biscuits and smooth the top.

4 Dip the remaining biscuits in the coffee mixture and arrange on top of the mascarpone mixture. Drizzle with any remaining coffee mixture. Cover with clingfilm and chill in the refrigerator for 4 hours.

5 Carefully turn the tiramisu out on to a large serving plate and sprinkle with the grated chocolate or chocolate curls. Dust with cocoa powder, cut into slices and serve with a few summer berries.

INGREDIENTS
Serves 4

225 g/8 oz mascarpone cheese
25 g/1 oz icing sugar, sifted
150 ml/¼ pint strong brewed coffee, chilled
300 ml/½ pint double cream
3 tbsp coffee liqueur
125 g/4 oz Savoiardi or sponge finger biscuits
50 g/2 oz plain dark chocolate, grated or made into small curls
cocoa powder, for dusting
assorted summer berries, to serve

Food Fact

This now classic Italian dessert appears in all kinds of forms in most Italian cookery books. The name literally means 'pick me up'.

Cannoli with Ricotta Cheese

1 Beat together the butter and 25 g/1 oz of the sugar until light and fluffy. Add the white wine and salt and mix together well. Fold in the flour and knead to form a soft dough. Reserve for 2 hours.

2 Lightly flour a work surface and roll the dough out to a thickness of about ½ cm/¼ inch. Cut into 12.5 cm/5 inch squares. Wrap the pastry around the cannoli or cream horn moulds using the beaten egg to seal. Make 3–4 at a time.

3 Heat the vegetable oil to 180°C/350°F in a deep-fat fryer and fry the cannoli for 1–2 minutes, or until puffed and golden. Drain well on absorbent kitchen paper and leave to cool. Remove the moulds when the cannoli are cool enough to handle. Repeat until all the cannoli are cooked.

4 Beat the ricotta cheese with 125 g/4 oz of sugar, orange water and vanilla essence until creamy. Add the cherries, angelica, candied peel and chopped chocolate. Fill each cannoli using a piping bag with a large plain nozzle or a small spoon. Dust with icing sugar and serve cool, but not cold.

INGREDIENTS
Makes 24

FOR THE PASTRY:
25 g/1 oz butter
25 g/1 oz caster sugar
3 tbsp dry white wine
pinch of salt
150 g/5 oz plain flour
1 medium egg, lightly beaten
vegetable oil, for deep frying

FOR THE FILLING:
450 g/1 lb ricotta cheese
125 g/4 oz caster sugar
2 tbsp orange water
1 tsp vanilla essence
50 g/2 oz glacé cherries, chopped
50 g/2 oz angelica, chopped
125 g/4 oz candied peel, chopped
75 g/3 oz plain dark chocolate, finely chopped
icing sugar, for dusting

Helpful Hint

Cannoli moulds are difficult to come by outside Italy.
Substitute cream horn moulds for lengths of 2.5 cm/1 inch thick bamboo or cane (washed thoroughly).

Index